# BLESS THIS FOOD

# BLESS THIS FOOD

## *Four Seasons of Menus, Recipes, and Table Graces*

JULIA M. PITKIN,
KAREN B. GRANT,
AND GEORGE GRANT

A CUMBERLAND HOUSE *Hearthside* BOOK

CUMBERLAND HOUSE PUBLISHING
NASHVILLE, TENNESSEE

Copyright © 1996, Julia M. Pitkin, Karen B. Grant, and George Grant

Published by Cumberland House Publishing, Inc.
2200 Abbott Martin Road, Suite 102
Nashville, Tennessee 37215

All Rights Reserved.
Written permission must be secured from the publisher
to use or reproduce any part of this work, except for
brief quotations in critical reviews or articles.

Typography by D&T/Bailey Typesetting, Inc., Nashville, Tennessee.
Design by Harriette Bateman.
Art by Tonya Presley.

Distributed to the trade by Andrews and McMeel
4520 Main Street, Kansas City, Missouri 64111-7701.

**Library of Congress Cataloging-in Publication Data**

Pitkin, Julia M.
    Bless this food : four seasons of menus, recipes, and table graces / Julia M. Pitkin, Karen
B. Grant, and Geroge Grant.
      p.    cm.
    "A Cumberland House hearthside book."
    Includes index.
    ISBN 1-888952-05-9  (hc : alk. paper)
    1. Cookery, International.  2. Holiday cookery.  3. Menus.  4. Grace at meals.  I.
Grant, Karen B., 1955– .  II. Grant, George, 1954– .  III. Title.
TX725.A1P58  1996
642'.4—dc20
                                                       96-42173
                                                          CIP

Printed in the United States of America

1 2 3 4 5 6 7 — 00 99 98 97 96

To our children

Tonya, Jennifer, Alexander, Jackson, Grant,
Joel, Joanna, and Jesse

# Contents

*Preface 9*

*Introduction 11*

## Spring Menus

## Summer Menus

## Fall Menus

## Winter Menus

# Preface

Of the more than two dozen cookbooks I have created or edited in the last ten years, *Bless This Food* is the one I most wanted to do. I strongly believe that there is an unbreakable link between the sacred and everyday life, a connection that our secularized culture all too frequently misses. So it seemed important for me to create a cookbook that points out how our lives are touched and sustained by God in the midst of ordinary daily events like preparing meals, gathering with friends and families, sharing laughter and serious conversation, and remembering those who have blessed our lives. I am not by nature one who glibly talks about my faith in public, but I felt this would be one way in which I could give witness to my belief that God has provided for all our needs and that He is delighted when we enjoy His gifts.

How easily we miss the connection between loving God and loving our families and friends, to say nothing of the world and the people in it. And how easy it is to forget that being with one another at the table is a mirror of the relationship we are to enjoy with God and His people. As a mother, I like to think that the pleasure I experience when my family is gathered together around a good meal is at least in some small way similar to the joy God experiences when we pause to thank him for his many blessings, including our food. Thus *Bless This Food*.

So I set out to create a cookbook for the occasions our family enjoys celebrating. I specifically wanted it to be a menu cookbook, and I wanted it to contain information about why people celebrate these occa-sions, as well as prayers, poems, hymns, and perhaps other inspirational thoughts that might be appropriate. By bringing these items together in one book, I thought, it would be more likely that we—and perhaps you—might remember to thank God for our blessings and to celebrate the events in a properly respectful and reverent way.

As I began to make a list of the occasions my family celebrates, I realized there probably were not enough of them to fill an entire book. Soon my publisher and I approached Karen and George Grant with the idea. A historian, theologian, writer, and educator, George is as close to being a Renaissance Man as these busy times are likely to produce; Karen's talents as a cook and creative homemaker are widely known. If any couple could widen our horizons, we knew that George and Karen were our most likely candidates. If anyone would understand what we wanted to happen in *Bless This Food*, it would be them.

Since then, Karen and I have researched the backgrounds of the occasions we already celebrate and have even added a few new ones we would like to include in our lives. Our list is mostly made up of occasions that we personally find most interesting for our families. Since we think we are pretty much like other people in our interests and tastes, we hope you, too, will find them interesting. After much thought and discussion—and more than one prayer for guidance—we began to shape our ideas into a manuscript.

Once we settled on a list of occasions, George and Karen found prayers, hymns, poems, and inspirational thoughts that were appropriate for each meal. Karen wrote the introductions for each menu, and I created the menus and selected the recipes. The result is a menu cookbook that contains a wide range of occasions to celebrate. Some of the recipes are from our own collections, some are our own creations, and a few are longtime family favorites.

One of the ideas we settled on early was that of creating menus for Blessings in Deed. It is one thing to thank God for our food; it is another to bless some-one else with a meal lovingly prepared for them. So *Bless This Food* isn't just about preparing and eating wonderful meals by ourselves; it also is about bless-ing others with what God has provided us. We encourage you and your family to take time to pre-pare and give at least one of the Blessings in Deed to someone you know who would be grateful for your thoughtfulness.

See, this blessing thing is contagious!

# Introduction

66 "The way to a man's heart is his stomach," said the inimitable Samuel Johnson. "Similarly, the way to a man's theology is the setting of his table at the various seasonal celebrations."[1] Indeed, there is little more revealing of our ultimate concerns than what we eat and how we eat it.

Generally, we moderns tend to think of faith as a rather other-worldly concern, while we think of food as a rather this-worldly matter. It is difficult for us to see how the two could ever meet. In reality, though, food and faith are inextricably linked. And while that is true to one degree or another in every culture the world over, it is especially evident in the Judeo-Christian tradition of the West.

Interestingly, the word *faith* is used less than three hundred times in the Bible, while the verb *to eat* is used more than eight hundred times. You can hardly read a single page of the Scriptures without running into a discussion of bread and wine, milk and honey, leeks and onions, glistening oil and plump figs, sweet grapes and delectable pomegranates, roast lamb and savory stew. Throughout there are images of feasts and celebrations.

Even the themes of justice and virtue are often defined in terms of food, while the themes of hungering and thirsting are inevitably defined in terms of faith. Community and hospitality are evidences of a faithful covenant, and righteousness and holiness are evidences of a healthy appetite. In both the Old and New Testaments, worship does not revolve around an esoteric discussion of philosophy or ascetic ritual enactments, but around a family meal.

As if to underscore this, all of the resurrection appearances of Christ occurred at meals—with the single exception of the garden tomb. On the road to Emmaus, in the Upper Room, and at the edge of the Sea of Galilee, Jesus ate and drank with His disciples. Indeed, He did not say, "Behold, I stand at the door and knock. If anyone opens the door, I will enter in and discuss theology with him." No, Jesus said, "I will come in and sup with him."[2]

Food is the stuff of life. For a Christian, faith declares that Jesus came to give us life. Indeed, He came to give us "abundant life."[3] So it is not surprising for Him—and all the other biblical teachers, writers, prophets, and apostles—to utilize food as a primary image in the language of theology.

A few years ago I saw a small plaque in a kitchen supply store that read, "A good theology will invariably produce a good meal." At first I chuckled and quickly dismissed it as just another bit of a gourmet's hyperbole. But the more I thought about it, the more I began to realize that the epigram actually conveys a substantive and healthy worldview—one that uniquely expresses the Judeo-Christian tradition.

Like a fine feast, a good theology is more than the sum of its parts. While it is composed of certain essential beliefs, each of those essentials must also be carefully related to all the others. It sees all too clearly the crucial connection between the profound and the mundane, and it places as much significance on the bits and pieces as it does on the sums, and vice versa.

While a good theology is good for the soul, it also is good for the world. Its spiritual vision gives vitality to all it touches—from herb gardens and table settings to nation states and cultures—simply because the integrity of what it sees ultimately depends as much on a balanced perspective of everyday life as on a solid comprehension of our highest aspirations. A good meal, a joyous family celebration, or a seasonal feast effectively portrays that truth in a tangible way.

A good theology, with its comprehensive worldview, inevitably affects the world for good. It cheers the heart like a sumptuous dish. So also, a bad theology, with its fragmented worldview, can only leave a bitter taste in the mouth. In our day, that basic fact has been borne out again and again.

When the subject of worldview comes up, we generally think of philosophy—not cooking. In fact, a worldview is as practical as potatoes. You have a worldview. I have a worldview. Everyone does. It is our perspective—our frame of reference. It is the means by which we interpret the circumstances around us.

In his book, *Future Shock*, Alvin Toffler said, "Every person carries in his head a mental model of the world, a subjective representation of external reality."[4] This mental model is, he says, like a giant filing cabinet. It contains a slot for every item of information coming to us. It organizes our knowledge and gives us a grid from which to think. None of us are completely open-minded or genuinely objective. "When we think," said economic philosopher E. F. Schumacher, "we can only do so because our mind is already filled with all sorts of ideas with which to think."[5] These more or less fixed notions make up our mental model of the world, our frame of reference, what we assume to be true—in other words, our worldview.

In his marvelous book, *How to Read Slowly*, James Sire writes, "A worldview is a map of reality; and like any map, it may fit what is actually there, or it may be grossly misleading. The map is not the world itself, of course, only an image of it, more or less accurate in some place, distorted in others. All our thinking presupposes it. Most of our experience fits into it."[6]

A worldview is simply a way of viewing the world, and the Judeo-Christian view of the world and everything in it is fraught with a sort of cook's paradox—an appreciation for the potential and the risks of creation. It must be engaged in the world; it must be unengaged in worldliness. It must somehow correlate spiritual concerns with temporal ones; it must coordinate heartfelt faith and down-to-earth practice.

That is a difficult ideal to visualize, much less to implement in our lives. And without some tangible models set before us, it is bound to be an unrealized goal.

But that is just what a healthy awareness of the connection between food and faith does. By placing emphasis on the whole of life—our relationships, traditions, simple joys, family celebrations, tastes, pleasures, and expressions of thanksgiving—the high ideals of a fundamentally biblical worldview are happily established in the very warp and woof of our culture.

Western civilization is rich with such models. In *Bless This Food* we have attempted to introduce that richness with a representative selection of foods and festivals, traditions and celebrations, blessings and supplications.

Our aim was simple: to illustrate the inviolate link between what we are and what we do, between what we think and how we act, and between what we believe and what we eat. Samuel Johnson apparently believed that link is ultimately inescapable. Looking over these recipes, epigrams, addresses, poems, and prayers, it is obvious he was right. Isn't it amazing how easily we overlook the obvious?

"Taste and see that the Lord, He is good."[7]

---

[1]Howard Tannenbaum, *English Masters*, (London: Cassell, 1979), 89.
[2]Revelation:3:20.
[3]John 10:10.
[4]Alvin Toffler, *Future Shock*, (New York: Bantam, 1971), 158
[5]E. F. Schumacher, *Small Is Beautiful*, (New York: HarperCollins, 1975), 52.
[6]James Sire, *How to Read Slowly*, (Wheaton, IL: Harold Shaw, 1978), 14-15.
[7]Psalm 34:8.

# BLESS THIS FOOD

# Spring Menus

# A Fancy Chicken Supper

*A moment of silence for every chicken who gave its life only to end up a dry,*
*tasteless sacrifice on the altar of an unmotivated chef at a banquet factory.*
*Chicken may have gotten a bad reputation because of some less-than-honorable associations,*
*but it's not the chickens' fault. You may feature it at your most elegant affair,*
*but pay a little attention to how you prepare it. Familiarity must not breed*
*contempt with this versatile fowl who will serve you well when treated with respect,*
*as in the following recipe.*
*The blessing we've chosen for your fine dinner is a familiar one, as well.*
*Some thoughts are so profound, they deserve frequent repetition*
*before we can begin to plumb their depths.*

STUFFED MUSHROOMS

BIBB LETTUCE SALAD

ROAST CHICKEN

MARINATED VEGETABLES

RICE PILAF

WHITE CHOCOLATE BREAD PUDDING

*Our Father which art in heaven,*
*Hallowed be Thy name.*
*Thy kingdom come.*
*Thy will be done in earth,*
*As it is in heaven.*
*Give us this day our daily bread.*
*And forgive us our debts,*
*As we forgive our debtors.*
*And lead us not into temptation,*
*But deliver us from evil.*
*For Thine is the kingdom,*
*and the power, and the glory forever.*
*Amen.*

MATTHEW 6:9-13

## Stuffed Mushrooms

2 pounds large mushrooms
1 tablespoon olive oil
2 cloves garlic, crushed
½ cup fresh basil leaves (or 1 tablespoon dried)
3 tablespoons ricotta cheese
2 tablespoons breadcrumbs
2 tablespoons grated Parmesan cheese
Pinch ground red pepper
1 tablespoon chopped pine nuts

Clean the mushrooms, remove the stems, and chop. Set the caps aside.

In a large skillet heat the olive oil and sauté mushroom stems and garlic for 2 to 3 minutes. Add the basil and cook about 1 minute. Remove the pan from the heat. Add the ricotta cheese, breadcrumbs, Parmesan cheese, red pepper, and pine nuts. Fill the mushroom caps. Bake at 400° for 12 to 15 minutes or until lightly browned.

MAKES 10 SERVINGS.

## Bibb Lettuce Salad

3 heads Bibb lettuce
1 tablespoon balsamic vinegar
½ teaspoon salt
½ teaspoon green peppercorn mustard
Freshly ground black pepper to taste
3 tablespoons safflower oil
2 tablespoons olive oil

Wash and the dry lettuce leaves. Place them in a bowl and refrigerate, covered with paper towels.

In a small bowl combine the vinegar, salt, mustard, and pepper. Whisk in the oils.

To serve, drizzle a few tablespoons of the vinaigrette over the lettuce.

MAKES 6 SERVINGS.

## Roast Chicken

1 4-pound chicken
1 garlic clove, peeled
1 teaspoon chopped fresh rosemary
1 teaspoon chopped fresh thyme
1 teaspoon chopped fresh oregano
    (or marjoram)
¼ teaspoon freshly ground pepper
½ teaspoon salt
1 tablespoon olive oil

Rinse the chicken inside and out with cold water. Remove the pockets of fat just inside the chest cavity. Pat dry.

Hold the tines of a fork against a plate and rub the garlic clove against them to make a juicy purée. Blend in the remaining ingredients to make a paste. Rub the herb paste all over the chicken. Place the chicken in a roasting pan. Roast, breast side up, at 375° for 20 minutes. Turn and roast another 20 minutes. Turn again and roast for another 35 minutes. Remove the chicken from the oven, cover loosely with aluminum foil, and let rest for 15 minutes prior to carving.

MAKES 6 SERVINGS.

## Rice Pilaf

¼ cup butter
1 cup long grain rice
1 cup pearl barley
8 green onions, chopped
2 10-ounce cans consommé
2½ cups water
1 4-ounce can mushrooms with liquid

In a large saucepan melt the butter and brown the rice and barley until golden. Add the onions, consommé, water, and mushrooms with liquid. Cover and simmer for 30 minutes or until the liquid is absorbed. Toss and serve.

MAKES 10 SERVINGS.

## Marinated Vegetables

4 small red potatoes
3 cups small broccoli florets
3 cups small cauliflower florets
3 cups halved cherry tomatoes
3 cups sliced mushrooms
3 cups cubed zucchini
1⅓ cups white wine vinegar
1 cup water
½ cup minced shallots
¼ cup Dijon mustard
3 tablespoons olive oil
2 teaspoons dried basil
2 teaspoons dried oregano
2 teaspoons crushed dried rosemary
1 teaspoon salt
½ teaspoon crushed red pepper

*I*n a stockpot steam the potatoes, covered, for 15 minutes or until tender. Cool. Cut each potato into 4 wedges, and cut each wedge in half crosswise.

In a large serving dish combine the potatoes, broccoli, cauliflower, tomatoes, mushrooms, and zucchini. Set the mixture aside.

In a jar with a tight-fitting lid combine the remaining ingredients. Cover and shake vigorously. Pour the mixture over the vegetables, and toss gently to coat. Cover and marinate in the refrigerator for 8 hours, stirring occasionally.

MAKES 3 SERVINGS.

## White Chocolate Bread Pudding

1 cup whipping cream
8 ounces high-quality white chocolate (such as Lindt or Baker's), finely chopped

3 cups whipping cream
1 cup milk (do not use low-fat or nonfat)
½ cup sugar
10 ounces high-quality white chocolate (such as Lindt or Baker's), finely chopped
8 large egg yolks
2 large eggs
1 1-pound loaf day-old French bread, crust trimmed, cut into 1-inch pieces
Chocolate shavings (optional)
Fresh berries (optional)

*I*n a small heavy saucepan bring 1 cup of cream to a boil. Remove the pan from the heat. Add the white chocolate and whisk until melted and the sauce is smooth.

Butter a 9 x 13-inch glass baking dish. In a medium heavy saucepan combine 3 cups of cream, milk, and sugar over medium heat. Bring to a simmer, stirring until the sugar dissolves. Remove the pan from the heat. Add the white chocolate and whisk until melted and smooth. In a large bowl whisk the yolks and eggs. Gradually whisk in the warm cream mixture. Add the bread and stir until coated. Let stand for about 5 minutes, until the bread is very soft.

Transfer the bread mixture to the prepared dish. Cover with foil. Bake at 350° for 45 minutes. Remove the foil and bake for about 15 minutes, until the pudding is golden brown and set. Cool slightly on a rack.

Rewarm the sauce over low heat, stirring frequently. Garnish the bread pudding with chocolate shavings and berries, if desired. Serve warm with sauce.

MAKES 12 SERVINGS.

# Dinner with the Boss

*You would like to make this evening memorable for all the right reasons! We've done our best to ensure success by providing the elements for a successful evening. The food will be a sure hit, and it toes the line between overly simple and ostentatious. Even the blessing is a great conversation starter. Ever traveled to Scotland? Like to travel?*
*What's your favorite place . . . ?*

---

GREEN SALAD WITH CHINESE NOODLES

CHEESE BISCUITS

ROAST PORK LOIN WITH ORANGE GLAZE

SUGAR SNAP PEAS WITH MUSHROOMS

CHOCOLATE MOUSSE CHEESECAKE

---

### CHIEF OF CHIEFS

*Chief of chiefs beyond my ken,*
*O Chief of chiefs, Amen.*

*God be with me lying down,*
*And God be with me rising,*
*In the sunlight flying down*
*God with me, supervising,*
*No joy nor any light without him,*
*Nor any light without him.*

*Christ be with me sleeping hours,*
*And Christ be with me waking,*
*through all watches aiding powers,*
*Christ with me undertaking,*
*No day nor any night without him,*
*Nor any night without him.*

*God be with me to protect,*
*The Spirit there to strengthen,*
*Lord be with me to direct*
*As span of life doth lengthen,*
*No time, no year, no hope, no fear,*
*No age, no space, no work, no place,*
*No depth nor any height without him,*
*Nor any height without him.*

*Ever, evermore, Amen,*
*O Chief of chiefs, Amen.*

ANCIENT SCOTTISH PRAYER

# Green Salad with Chinese Noodles

3 tablespoons butter, melted
1 teaspoon Worcestershire sauce
1 teaspoon curry powder
1 teaspoon garlic salt
1 3-ounce can chow mein noodles
2 to 3 tablespoons Italian dressing
½ cup mayonnaise
Variety of greens, torn in pieces
Ripe olives, sliced (optional)
Cauliflower florets (optional)

In a baking sheet with sides combine the butter, Worcestershire sauce, curry powder, and garlic salt. Add the noodles and toss to coat. Bake at 200° for 15 minutes, stirring 3 times.

In a small bowl mix the Italian dressing and mayonnaise. In a salad bowl toss the greens with the dressing and add the seasoned noodles. Add the olives and cauliflower, if desired. Serve immediately.

MAKES 8 SERVINGS.

# Cheese Biscuits

½ pound margarine
2 cups shredded sharp Cheddar cheese
Red pepper to taste
1 egg
1 long thinly sliced loaf commercial bread,
    (will cut easier if frozen first)

In a small bowl combine the first 4 ingredients and beat with an electric mixer until fluffy. Stack bread with 3 slices per stack. Remove crusts. Cut stacks into quarters. Spread cheese mixture generously between slices, then very thinly on the top and sides. Bake at 350° for 12 to 15 minutes. Serve warm.

Note: These freeze beautifully and require no thawing before baking. (To freeze, place biscuits on flat tray, and place uncovered in freezer until firm, then store in plastic bag.)
MAKES 2½ DOZEN.

# Roast Pork Loin with Orange Glaze

1 whole pork tenderloin
Olive oil
Freshly ground pepper to taste
1 orange
¾ cup honey
½ cup packed brown sugar

Rub the tenderloin with olive oil. Sprinkle lightly with pepper. Place the pork on a rack in a roasting pan. Bake at 325°, allowing 25 minutes per pound.

Peel the orange and grate the peel. Juice the orange. Combine grated peel, juice, honey, and brown sugar. Mix well.

Remove the pork from the oven 25 minutes before it is done, punch holes in the roast, and coat with orange glaze. Return to the oven and bake until done.

Heat the remaining glaze. Cut the loin into ¼-inch slices and brush the slices with glaze, or serve the glaze on the side.
MAKES 4 SERVINGS.

# Sugar Snap Peas with Mushrooms

¾ pound sugar-snap peas
½ pound mushrooms (wild or cultivated)
1 tablespoon butter
1 tablespoon oil
½ teaspoon salt
½ teaspoon pepper
1 lemon

String the sugar snap peas. Cook them in boiling, salted water for about 5 minutes, until tender. Drain. Slice the mushrooms.

In a large frying pan heat the butter and oil over medium-high heat. Add the mushrooms and cook, stirring occasionally, for 10 to 12 minutes, until they are soft and the liquid has evaporated. Add the peas, salt, and pepper, and heat through, 2 or 3 minutes. Squeeze 2 teaspoons juice from the lemon. Add the juice right before serving.

MAKES 4 SERVINGS.

# Chocolate Mousse Cheesecake

¾ cup graham cracker crumbs
¼ cup unsalted butter, softened
2 tablespoons sugar

3 8-ounce packages cream cheese
2 large eggs
1 cup sugar
8 ounces semisweet chocolate, melted
2 tablespoons heavy cream
7 tablespoons very strong coffee (espresso)
¾ cup sour cream

In a food processor combine the cracker crumbs, butter, and sugar and pulse until mixed. Press into the bottom of an 8-inch springform mold. Set aside.

In a food processor combine the cream cheese, eggs, and sugar, and mix until smooth. Add the remaining ingredients and blend thoroughly. Pour the batter into the crust. Bake at 350° for 45 minutes without opening the oven door (make sure the oven temperature is accurate). At the end of the baking time, turn off the heat and prop the oven door open slightly. Allow cake to cool in the oven for 1 hour before removing. The cheesecake will be slightly soft in the middle, but will firm up as it cools. Refrigerate.

Remove the cake from the refrigerator at least 15 minutes before serving.

MAKES 8 TO 10 SERVINGS.

# Palm Sunday Lunch

*The Sunday before Easter is a hopeful time. Spring is here at last, and the sun is finally becoming a more reliable companion. Lighter colors prevail, and bright flowering bulbs announce the promise of warm weather. Best of all, hosannas still ring throughout the earth, as they have for thousands of years.*

---

OLIVE-FILLED CHEDDAR BALLS

HOT BROWN

FRUIT SALAD

SAUTÉED SPRING VEGETABLES

LEMON CORNMEAL CAKE WITH RASPBERRY FILLING

---

### ALL GLORY, LAUD AND HONOR

*All glory, laud and honor To thee, Redeemer, King,*
*To whom the lips of children Made sweet hosannas ring:*
*Thou art the King of Israel, Thou David's royal Son,*
*Who in the Lord's name comest, The King and blessed One!*

*The company of angels Are praising Thee on high,*
*And mortal men and all things Created make reply:*
*The people of the Hebrews With palms before Thee went:*
*Our praise and prayer and anthems Before Thee we present.*

*To Thee, before Thy passion, They sang their hymns of praise;*
*To Thee, now high exalted, Our melody we raise:*
*Thou didst accept their praises—Accept the praise we bring,*
*Who in all good delightest, Thou good and gracious King!*

THEODULPH OF ORLEANS, c. 800
TRANSLATED BY JOHN M. NEALE, 1854

[ 22 ]

# Olive-filled Cheddar Balls

2 cups shredded sharp Cheddar cheese
¼ cup butter, softened
1 cup all-purpose flour
1½ teaspoons paprika
Cayenne pepper to taste
1 8½-ounce jar pimento-stuffed olives
1 egg
1 tablespoon cream or milk
¼ cup sesame seeds

In a food processor combine the Cheddar cheese and butter, and process until well blended. Add the flour, paprika, and cayenne, and process until smooth.

Line a baking sheet with parchment or foil.

Drain the olives and pat dry. Wrap about 1 teaspoon of dough around each olive, pinching to seal any cracks. Form into balls and arrange on the prepared baking sheet.

In a small bowl beat the egg and cream until well blended. Brush over the tops of the pastries. Sprinkle with sesame seeds. Bake at 350° for 15 minutes or until just golden. Serve hot or at room temperature.

Note: Unbaked nuggets may be frozen, thawed in the refrigerator for a few hours, and baked just before serving.

MAKES 48 APPETIZERS.

# Hot Brown

¼ cup butter, melted
¼ cup all-purpose flour
2 cups milk
¾ cup shredded Cheddar cheese

¼ teaspoon salt
½ teaspoon Worcestershire sauce
6 slices toast, trimmed
1 pound turkey, thinly sliced
8 slices ham
3 tomatoes, sliced
10 strips bacon, partially cooked
2 ounces Parmesan cheese

In a saucepan melt the butter and blend in the flour. Whisk in the milk and cook, stirring constantly, until thickened. Add the Cheddar cheese, salt, and Worcestershire, stirring until smooth.

Place the toast in the bottom of a 9 x 13-inch baking dish. Arrange the turkey and ham over the toast. Top with the tomato slices, bacon, and cheese sauce. Sprinkle with Parmesan cheese. Bake at 425° for 20 minutes or until bubbly.

MAKES 6 SERVINGS.

# Fruit Salad

2 quarts fresh strawberries, sliced
2 fresh pineapples, peeled, cored, and cut into chunks
½ cup orange marmalade
¼ cup orange juice
2 tablespoons lemon juice
½ cup fresh blueberries (or frozen blueberries, thawed)

In a large serving bowl combine the strawberries and pineapple. Set aside.

In a small bowl combine the orange marmalade, orange juice, and lemon juice. Pour the dressing over the fruit, and toss gently. Stir in the blueberries just before serving.

MAKES 8 SERVINGS.

## Sautéed Spring Vegetables

1½ pound fresh peas
1½ pound asparagus, cut obliquely into 1-inch
    pieces
2 tablespoons olive oil
1 tablespoon unsalted butter
1 small red onion, sliced into ⅛-inch strips
1 large red bell pepper, sliced into strips
¾ teaspoon salt
½ teaspoon freshly ground pepper
1 cup chicken stock

*B*ring a large pot of salted water to a boil. Separately boil the fresh peas and asparagus for about 1 minute or until crisp-tender. Plunge into cold water to stop the cooking process, and drain.

In a large skillet heat the olive oil and butter over medium heat. Add the onion and bell pepper and sauté for about 3 minutes or until slightly wilted. Add the peas, asparagus, salt, and pepper, and cook for 1 to 2 minutes. Increase the heat to high and add the chicken stock. Cook for about 3 minutes or until reduced by half. Serve immediately.

MAKES 8 SERVINGS.

## Lemon Cornmeal Cake with Raspberry Filling

2 cups frozen unsweetened raspberries,
    thawed
2 tablespoons sugar
1 tablespoon cornstarch

¾ cup unsalted butter, room temperature
¾ cup sugar
3 large eggs
1¼ cups cake flour
2 teaspoons baking powder
¼ teaspoon salt
½ cup yellow cornmeal
6 teaspoons grated lemon peel
2 teaspoons lemon extract

2 cups chilled whipping cream
2 tablespoons sugar
1 teaspoon lemon extract
3 teaspoons grated lemon peel

¾ cup sliced almonds, toasted

*I*n a food processor purée the berries. Strain into a heavy medium saucepan. Add 2 tablespoons of sugar and the cornstarch. Stir over medium heat for about 3 minutes or until the mixture boils and thickens. Cool. Cover and chill for 2 hours or until cold.

Lightly butter a 9-inch-diameter cake pan with 2-inch-high sides. Line the bottom with parchment paper. Butter the parchment. Dust the pan with flour, and shake out the excess. In a large bowl beat the butter and ¾ cup of sugar with an electric mixer until well blended. Add the eggs 1 at a time, beating well after each addition. In a medium bowl sift together the flour, baking powder and salt. Stir in the cornmeal. Add the dry ingredients to the butter mixture and beat just until blended. Mix in 6 teaspoons of lemon peel and 2 teaspoons of lemon extract.

Transfer the batter to the prepared pan. Bake at 350° for about 35 minutes or until the cake is golden and a toothpick inserted in the center comes out with a few moist crumbs attached. Transfer the cake to a rack to cool. Using a knife, cut around the pan sides to loosen the cake. Turn the cake out. Peel off the parchment.

In a large bowl beat the cream, 2 tablespoons of sugar, and 1 teaspoon of lemon extract until soft peaks form. Beat in 1½ teaspoons of lemon peel. Set aside ⅔ cup of frosting for decoration.

Using a serrated knife, cut the cake horizontally into 3 layers. Using the bottom of a 9-inch-diameter tart pan as an aid, transfer 1 layer to a platter. Spread half of the filling over the layer. Spread 1 cup of frosting over the filling. Top with the second cake layer. Spread the remaining filling over. Spread 1 cup of frosting over the filling. Top with the third cake layer. Spread the sides and top of the cake with the remaining frosting. Press the nuts onto the sides of the cake. Spoon the reserved ⅔ cup of frosting into a pastry bag fitted with the medium star tip. Pipe around the top edge of the cake. Sprinkle the top of the cake with 1½ teaspoons of lemon peel.

MAKES 8 SERVINGS.

# A Passover Seder

*Passover commemorates God's deliverance of the Hebrew people from slavery in Egypt.*
*By placing the blood of a lamb on their doorposts, the Israelites escaped the final plague—the*
*death of the first-born—as they observed the first Passover meal. The theme of deliverance*
*and substitutionary death of a lamb is a common one in Scripture.*

HAROSETH

CHOPPED CHICKEN LIVER

CHICKEN SOUP WITH MINIATURE LEEK-CHIVE MATZO BALLS

HERBED ROAST CHICKEN

MINTED SPINACH SOUFFLÉ

POTATO LATKES

SWEET-AND-SOUR BEET SALAD

PASSOVER SPONGECAKE WITH CITRUS GLAZE

DRIED FRUIT COMPOTE

"This month shall be your beginning of months; it shall be the first
month of the year to you. ..On the tenth day of this month every man
shall take for himself a lamb, according to the house of his father, a lamb
for a household...You shall keep it until the fourteenth day of the same
month. Then the whole assembly of the congregation of Israel shall kill it
at twilight. And they shall take some of the blood and put it on the two
doorposts and on the lintel of the houses where they eat it. ...And thus
you shall eat it: with a belt on your waist, your sandals on your feet,
and your staff in your hand. So you shall eat it in haste. It is the Lord's
Passover."

*EXODUS 12:2–11*

# Haroseth

½ pound walnut meats
¼ pound dried apricots
¼ pound dried pitted prunes
¼ pound pitted dates
3 whole apples, peeled, cored, and quartered
1 large unpeeled seedless orange, quartered
½ cup sweet Passover wine
2 tablespoons kosher-for-Passover brandy
½ teaspoon ground cinnamon
⅛ teaspoon ground cloves
⅛ teaspoon grated nutmeg
1 tablespoon lime juice
2 tablespoons matzo meal (or as needed)

In a food processor combine the walnuts, apricots, prunes, dates apples, and orange, and chop very fine (but not to a paste).

Add the wine, brandy, cinnamon, cloves, nutmeg, and lime juice. If necessary add enough matzo meal to make a mortarlike consistency.

MAKES 6 CUPS.

# Chopped Chicken Liver

1 pound chicken livers, trimmed
3 tablespoons chicken fat
1 large onion, minced
Salt and freshly ground pepper to taste
2 large hard-boiled eggs, quartered
Freshly grated nutmeg to taste
Chopped toasted nuts for garnish

In a bowl of salted water soak the chicken livers for 20 minutes. Drain and pat dry.

Broil the livers on a rack in a broiler pan about 4 inches from the heat, turning once, for 7 to 8 minutes or until browned.

In a skillet heat the fat over moderate heat. Add the onion and salt and pepper to taste, and cook, stirring occasionally, until golden.

In a food processor blend the livers, onion, and eggs until combined well, and add the nutmeg and adjust seasonings to taste. Transfer to a serving bowl and garnish with nuts. Chill, covered, until ready to serve.

MAKES ABOUT 2 CUPS.

## Chicken Soup with Miniature Leek-Chive Matzo Balls

6 tablespoons unsalted pareve margarine
½ cup packed finely chopped leek (white and
    pale green parts only)
½ cup finely chopped fresh chives

4 eggs
2 tablespoons ginger ale
1½ teaspoons coarse kosher salt
Freshly ground pepper to taste
¼ teaspoon ground ginger
1 cup unsalted matzo meal

12 cups chicken broth
Chopped fresh chives

In a heavy small skillet melt the margarine over medium heat. Add the leek and sauté for 5 minutes. Remove from the heat. Add ½ cup of chives.

In a medium bowl beat the eggs, ginger ale, salt, pepper and ginger. Mix in the matzo meal and leek mixture. Cover and chill for at least 2 hours or until firm.

Line a large baking sheet with plastic wrap. Using moistened palms, roll rounded teaspoons of matzo into balls. Place on the prepared baking sheet. Refrigerate for 30 minutes.

Bring a large pot of salted water to a boil. Drop in the matzo balls, cover, and cook for about 40 minutes or until tender and evenly colored throughout. Using a slotted spoon, transfer the matzo balls to a bowl.

In a large pot bring the chicken broth to a simmer. Add the matzo balls and cook for about 10 minutes or until warmed through.

Place 4 matzo balls in each bowl. Ladle the broth over the matzo balls. Garnish with chives and serve.

MAKES 12 SERVINGS.

## Herbed Roast Chicken

1 6½-pound roasting chicken
Salt and freshly ground pepper to taste
½ cup minced shallots
3 tablespoons vegetable oil
2 tablespoons minced fresh tarragon leaves (or
    1 teaspoon dried)
¼ cup snipped fresh chives (or minced fresh
    parsley)
1½ teaspoons grated lemon peel
½ carrot, sliced
½ celery stalk, sliced
1 onion, sliced
2 garlic cloves, sliced
1 bay leaf
1 teaspoon crumbled dried thyme

Season the chicken with salt and pepper. Loosen the breast skin by slipping the fingers between the skin and the flesh, being careful not to pierce the skin.

In a small skillet cook the shallot in 2 tablespoons of the oil over moderate heat, stirring constantly, until softened. Stir in the fresh herbs, lemon peel, and salt and pepper to taste. Spoon the mixture under the breast skin, smoothing to cover the breast meat. Combine the remaining ingredients (except the remaining oil), fill the body cavity with the mixture, and truss the chicken.

Place the chicken on a rack in a roasting pan and brush with the remaining 1 tablespoon oil. Sprinkle the chicken with salt and pepper. Bake at 450° in the middle of the oven for 30 minutes. Reduce the heat to 350° and bake, basting frequently, for 1½ to 2 hours more or until the juices run clear when the fleshy part of a thigh is pricked with a skewer. Let the chicken stand, covered loosely, for 15 minutes before carving.

MAKES 6 SERVINGS.

# Minted Spinach Soufflé

2 tablespoons vegetable oil
½ cup minced onion
1 cup cooked chopped spinach
1 cup chicken stock or canned chicken broth
4 teaspoons potato starch
4 large eggs, separated
2 tablespoons minced fresh mint leaves, or to
    taste
Salt and freshly ground pepper to taste

In a saucepan heat the oil and sauté the onion over moderate heat, stirring constantly, until softened. Add the spinach and cook, stirring constantly, for 2 minutes. In a small bowl combine the stock and starch. Add the stock mixture to the saucepan and cook, stirring constantly, until thickened. Transfer to a large bowl and let cool for 5 minutes.

Stir in the egg yolks, one at a time, and season with the mint, salt, and pepper.

In a large bowl beat the egg whites until they hold stiff peaks. Fold the egg whites into the spinach mixture. Spoon into an oiled 1½-quart soufflé dish and place in the middle of a 400° oven. Immediately reduce the heat to 375° and bake for 30 to 35 minutes or until puffed and golden.

MAKES 6 SERVINGS.

# Potato Latkes

2½ pounds Idaho baking potatoes, unpeeled
1 large yellow onion, quartered
2 eggs, lightly beaten
¼ cup matzo meal
4 to 5 teaspoons chopped fresh parsley
1 teaspoon salt
¼ teaspoon freshly ground black pepper
2 to 3 cups olive oil

Scrub the potatoes and set aside.

In a food processor pulse the onion a few times until diced into crunchy bits. Scrape the onion bits into a small bowl.

Cut the potatoes lengthwise to fit in the food processor feed tube. Process using the medium-coarse shredding disk.

When the potatoes are shredded, place them in a colander over a large bowl. Dump in the onion bits and mix everything using your hands, squeezing the potato moisture out as you work. Let the mixture drip for a few minutes.

Pour out the potato liquid from the bowl, but leave the starch that clings to the bowl. Dump in the shredded potato and onion mix. Add the eggs, matzo meal, parsley, salt, and pepper, and stir well. Let stand for about 10 minutes.

In a large cast-iron skillet, heat ¼ inch of olive oil over high heat until very hot. Using a ¼-cup measure or long-handled serving spoon, start spooning the batter into the skillet. Flatten each with a metal spatula to a diameter of 4 to 5 inches. Reduce the heat to medium and cook the latkes until golden brown on one side. Turn and brown the other side. When crispy on the outside and moist inside, about 5 minutes per side, drain on paper towels.

MAKES 6 SERVINGS.

# Sweet-and-Sour Beet Salad

2 pounds beets (5 or 6 large), trimmed, leaving
    2 inches of stem attached
1 bay leaf
4 whole cloves
Salt and freshly ground pepper to taste
1 large shallot, minced
1 tablespoon sugar
2 to 3 tablespoons white vinegar
3 tablespoons vegetable oil
2 tablespoons minced fresh dill
1 to 2 teaspoons grated fresh horseradish
    (optional)
Endive leaves for garnish

In a saucepan combine the beets with enough water to cover them by 2 inches, the bay leaf, cloves, and salt and pepper to taste. Bring to a boil, cover, and simmer for 35 to 40 minutes or until tender. Drain, discard the bay leaf, and let cool.

Peel and slice the beets. In a large bowl combine the beets and shallot. In a small bowl whisk together the remaining ingredients. Pour over the beets and toss well. Cover and refrigerate for 2 hours or overnight.

Serve with the endive.
MAKES 6 SERVINGS.

# Passover Spongecake with Citrus Glaze

10 large eggs, separated
1¼ cups sugar
¼ cup fresh orange juice
2 tablespoons fresh lemon juice
1 tablespoon grated orange peel
1½ teaspoons grated lemon peel
⅓ cup potato starch
⅓ cup matzo cake meal
1 teaspoon ground cinnamon
¼ teaspoon salt
⅓ cup finely ground blanched almonds

⅔ cup sugar
⅓ cup water
1 tablespoon grated orange peel
2 teaspoons grated lemon peel
1 tablespoon fresh orange juice
1 tablespoon fresh lemon juice

⅓ cup sliced blanched almonds, toasted

In a large bowl beat the egg yolks with an electric mixer until smooth. Gradually add 1 cup of the sugar and beat until the mixture ribbons when the beater is lifted. Beat in the juices and peels. In a medium bowl sift the starch, matzo cake meal, cinnamon, and salt. Gradually add the starch mixture to the yolk mixture and beat until combined well. Stir in the ground almonds.

In a very large bowl beat the egg whites with a pinch of salt until they hold soft peaks. Beat in the remaining ¼ cup of sugar, a little at a time, until the egg whites hold stiff peaks. Stir one-fourth of the whites into the yolk mixture, and then fold in the remaining whites gently but thoroughly.

Pour into an ungreased 10-inch tube pan and smooth the top. Bake for 1 hour and 30 minutes or until a cake tester inserted halfway between the center and edge comes out clean. Remove the pan from the oven and suspend it upside down on the neck of a bottle. Let it cool completely.

In a small heavy saucepan bring the sugar and water to a boil over moderately high heat, stirring constantly, until translucent. Add the peels and simmer for 3 to 5 minutes or until the syrup forms a thread when pressed between 2 fingers. Stir in the juices, and let the glaze cool for 5 minutes.

Run a thin knife around the inside of the pan and invert the cake onto a rack. Brush the glaze over the cake and garnish with the sliced almonds.
MAKES 12 SERVINGS.

# Dried Fruit Compote

1½ pounds mixed dried fruits
1½ cups dry white wine
1½ cups water
4 whole cloves
¾ cup fresh orange juice
2 tablespoons fresh lemon juice
3 tablespoons honey
1 tablespoon grated orange peel
1 tablespoon grated lemon peel
½ teaspoon ground cinnamon
¼ teaspoon ground ginger

In a large stainless steel or enameled saucepan combine the fruits, wine, and water and bring to a boil. Simmer for 15 to 20 minutes or until the fruit is tender. Transfer the fruit with a slotted spoon to a serving bowl.

Add the remaining ingredients to the cooking liquid, and boil the mixture over moderately high heat until reduced to 1 cup. Let it cool and strain over the fruit. Serve cold or at room temperature.

MAKES 6 SERVINGS.

# An Easter Brunch

*If you began the day in church and went on to at least watch an Easter egg hunt, you are, indeed, very blessed. Savor the vibrant tableau before you: the bright colors, the best clothing, and the chubby legs hurrying to find the gooey prize. All in celebration of the brightest of events: the Resurrection! This is indeed a day to provide special fare and to celebrate together.*

HONEY COFFEE

BROILED GRAPEFRUIT

CRÊPES MAGNOLIA

EDWARDIAN BUNS

RASPBERRY-LEMON MARBLED POUND CAKE

*Most glorious Lord of Lyfe! That, on this day,*
*Didst make Thy triumph over death and sin;*
*And, haveing harrowd hell, didst bring away*
*Captivity thence captive, us to win:*
*This joyous day, deare Lord, with joy begin;*
*And grant that we, for whom Thou diddest dye,*
*Being with Thy deare blood clene washt from sin,*
*May live for ever in felicity!*
*And that Thy love we weighing worthily,*
*May likewise love Thee for the same againe;*
*And for Thy sake, that all lyke deare didst buy,*
*With love may one another entertayne!*
*So let us love, deare Love, lyke as we ought,*
*Love is the lesson which the Lord us taught.*

EDMUND SPENSER (1552-1599)

# Honey Coffee

4½ cups coffee
4½ cups milk
6 tablespoons honey

*I*n a blender combine all of the ingredients (half at a time, if necessary) and blend for 10 to 15 seconds.

MAKES 6 SERVINGS.

# Broiled Grapefruit

⅔ cup sugar
3 tablespoons chopped crystallized ginger
¾ teaspoon vanilla extract
6 large pink grapefruits

*I*n a food processor combine the sugar, ginger, and vanilla, and grate fine.

Halve each grapefruit crosswise and run a knife around each section to loosen it from the membranes. Arrange the grapefruits, cut-sides up, in an ovenproof baking dish or baking pan just large enough to hold them in one layer. Sprinkle with the sugar mixture. Broil the grapefruits about 1½ inches from the heat for 10 to 15 minutes or until the sugar melts and the tops begin to brown.

Serve the grapefruits at room temperature.
MAKES 6 SERVINGS.

# Crêpes Magnolia

1½ cups milk
1¼ cups all-purpose flour
2 tablespoon sugar
3 eggs
2 tablespoons melted butter
Salt to taste

9 eggs
¼ cup milk
½ teaspoon salt
¼ teaspoon pepper
6 slices crisp bacon, crumbled
1 cup shredded Gruyère cheese
3 green onions, finely chopped

*I*n a large bowl combine 1½ cups of milk, the flour, sugar, 3 eggs, butter and salt. Beat until well mixed. Heat a lightly greased crêpe pan. Remove the pan from the heat. Spoon in 2 tablespoon of batter at a time, tilting to spread the batter. Return to the heat, and brown one side only. Makes 12 crêpes.

Spray 12 muffin cups with cooking spray. Fit the crêpes into the cups. In a large bowl beat 9 eggs with ¼ cup of milk, ½ teaspoon of salt and ¼ teaspoon of pepper. Sprinkle crumbled bacon in the bottom of the crêpe cups. Ladle the egg mix over the meat. Sprinkle with Gruyère. Bake at 375° for 30 minutes.

Carefully remove the crêpes with a spoon. Top with sour cream and chopped herbs.
MAKES 6 SERVINGS.

# Edwardian Buns

5 to 6 cups all-purpose flour
1 cup sugar
2 packages active dry yeast
1 teaspoon salt
¾ cup water
½ cup butter
2 eggs
½ cup cooked mashed potatoes
⅛ teaspoon grated nutmeg
Melted butter

*I*n a large mixing bowl combine 1 cup of flour, the sugar, yeast, and salt. Stir well. In a small saucepan heat the water and butter (temperature should reach 115° to 120°). Gradually add the hot mixture to the flour mixture, beating at low speed with an electric mixer until combined. Beat 2 minutes more at medium speed. Beat in the eggs, potato, nutmeg, and ¾ cup of flour, and continue beating for 2 minutes. Gradually stir in enough of the remaining flour to make a soft dough.

Turn the dough out onto a well-floured surface and knead for about 10 minutes or until smooth and elastic. Shape into a ball and place in a well-buttered bowl, turning the dough to cover with butter. Cover, and allow to rise in a warm, draft-free place for 1½ hours.

Punch down, and let rise once more until double in bulk. Divide the dough into 12 equal parts. Roll each into a ball and place on a buttered baking sheet. Press the balls lightly with fingertips to shape them into buns. Cover and allow to rise until double in bulk.

Brush the buns with melted butter. Bake at 375° for 15 to 20 minutes or until golden. Remove immediately.

MAKES 12 BUNS.

# Raspberry-Lemon Marbled Pound Cake

1 cup oil
2½ cups sugar
1 cup buttermilk
4 egg whites
1 large egg
1 teaspoon vanilla extract
1 teaspoon butter flavoring
½ teaspoon lemon extract
3 cups all-purpose flour
¼ teaspoon salt
¼ teaspoon baking soda
¼ cup seedless raspberry jam
2 drops red food coloring

*I*n a large bowl beat the oil and sugar at medium speed with a mixer for 2 minutes. In a separate bowl combine the buttermilk, egg whites, egg, vanilla, butter flavoring, and lemon extract, stirring until blended. In a separate bowl combine the flour, salt, and soda. Add the dry ingredients to the oil mixture alternately with the buttermilk mixture, beginning and ending with the flour mixture. Beat at low speed after each addition until just until blended.

Grease and flour a 9 x 5-inch loaf pan. Divide the batter into thirds. Spread one portion into the prepared pan. Stir the raspberry jam and food coloring into the second portion and spread gently over the first layer. Spoon the remaining batter over the top. Stir very gently with a knife. Bake at 325° for 1 hour and 35 minutes or until a wooden pick inserted in the center comes out clean.

Cool in the pan on a wire rack for 10 to 15 minutes. Remove the cake from the pan and cool completely on a wire rack.

MAKES 6 SERVINGS.

# An Easter Dinner

*Easter is so different from the spring observance that is poplarized today. It's not a solemn celebration; rather, it is the most joyous occasion of all. The resurrection does find expression in themes of nature—birth, beauty, bright new hope—and those themes are employed in its celebration. But being the crux of a Christian's faith, Easter is not limited to a pastel pastime. Rejoice and be glad, and celebrate faith.*

---

CRUSTY POPPY SEED ROLLS

LEG OF LAMB

GINGERED CARROTS

SUGAR SNAPS WITH ASPARAGUS AND TOMATOES

COMPANY SCALLOPED POTATOES

PINEAPPLE COCONUT LAYER CAKE

---

*AT THE LAMB'S HIGH FEAST*

*At the lamb's high feast we sing
Praise to our victorious King,
Who hath washed us in the tide
Flowing from His pierced side;
Praise we Him, whose love divine
Gives His sacred Blood for wine,
Gives His Body for the feast,
Christ the victim, Christ the priest.*

*Where the Paschal Blood is poured,
Death's dark angel sheathes his sword;
Israel's hosts triumphant go
Through the wave that drowns the foe.
Praise we Christ, whose Blood was shed,
Paschal victim, Paschal bread;
With sincerity and love
Eat we manna from above.*

*Mighty Victim from the sky,
Hell's fierce powers beneath Thee lie;
Thou hast conquered in the fight,
Thou hast brought us life and light;
Now no more can death enthrall;
Thou hast opened paradise,
And in Thee Thy saints shall rise.*

*Paschal triumph, Paschal joy,
Sin alone can this destroy;
From sin's power do Thou set free
Souls new-born, O Lord, in Thee.
Hymns of glory, songs of praise,
Father, unto Thee we raise:
Risen Lord, all praise to thee
with the Spirit ever be.*

LATIN HYMN
TRANSLATED BY ROBERT CAMPBELL
(1814–1868)

# Crusty Poppy Seed Rolls

3 cups (or more) all-purpose flour
1 package fast-rising dry yeast
1½ teaspoons salt
1 cup (or more) hot water (120 to 130°)
Yellow cornmeal
1 egg white, beaten with 2 teaspoons water
Poppy seeds

*I*n a food processor blend 3 cups of flour, the yeast, and salt. With the machine running, slowly pour 1 cup of hot water through the feed tube. Process until a ball forms. If the mixture is too moist to form a ball, add additional flour by tablespoons, incorporating each completely before adding the next. If too dry, add hot water by teaspoons, incorporating each before adding the next. Knead the dough in the processor 45 seconds.

Grease a large bowl. Add the dough, turning to coat the entire surface. Cover the bowl with a clean cloth. Let the dough rise in warm draft-free place for about 35 minutes or until doubled.

Grease a large baking sheet and sprinkle with cornmeal. Punch the dough down. Knead on a lightly floured surface for 2 to 3 minutes or until smooth. Let rest 10 minutes.

Divide the dough into 12 pieces. Shape each into a 2½-inch rounded oval. Place on the prepared baking sheet, spacing 2 inches apart. Gently pull the rolls to flatten slightly and taper the ends with hands. Cover loosely. Let the rolls rise in a warm draft-free place for about 40 minutes or until almost doubled.

Position one rack in the lowest third of oven and the second rack in the center. Place a shallow pan of hot water on the lower rack. Brush the rolls gently with the egg glaze and sprinkle with poppy seeds. Bake at 450° in the center of the oven for 20 minutes or until golden brown. Transfer to a rack and cool slightly.

MAKES 12 ROLLS.

# Leg of Lamb

1 6-pound leg of lamb
2 cloves garlic
2 teaspoons salt
2½ teaspoons dried oregano
Pepper to taste
1 cup red wine
¼ cup chopped green onions
2½ tablespoons lemon juice
2 tablespoons butter
2 tablespoons all-purpose flour
Milk (optional)
Mint jelly

*C*ut deep slits in the lamb over the entire surface. Crush the garlic and mix it with the salt, oregano, and pepper. Press the mixture into all the slits in the meat. Place the lamb fat-side up on a rack in a roasting pan. Do not cover. Roast at 325° for 30 to 35 minutes per pound for medium.

In a small bowl combine the wine, onions, and lemon juice. Reserve half the mixture for gravy. Baste the lamb often with the remaining half of the mixture. When the meat is done, remove it to a platter.

In a large skillet melt the butter. Blend in the flour and cook until browned. Add the reserved basting mixture and some of the pan juices. If desired, add milk for cream gravy. Cook, stirring constantly, until thickened. Serve the lamb with mint jelly and the gravy.

Note: Overcooking the lamb gives it the "strong" taste some people dislike.

MAKES ABOUT 6 SERVINGS.

## Gingered Carrots

1½ pounds baby carrots, trimmed
⅓ cup fresh orange juice
¼ cup honey
2 tablespoons unsalted butter
1 tablespoon grated orange peel
1 teaspoon ground ginger
Salt and pepper to taste
2 tablespoons minced crystallized ginger

In a large saucepan combine all the ingredients except the crystallized ginger, and add enough cold water to just cover the carrots. Bring to a boil, cover, and simmer for 6 to 8 minutes or until the carrots are just tender.

Add the crystallized ginger and cook, uncovered, over moderately high heat until the liquid is reduced to ¼ cup. Cook, shaking the pan, until the liquid is almost completely reduced and the carrots are glazed. Arrange decoratively on the platter with the lamb.

MAKES 6 SERVINGS.

## Sugar Snaps with Asparagus and Tomatoes

1 pound sugar snap peas, trimmed
1 pound medium or jumbo asparagus, peeled

3 teaspoons chopped fresh tarragon
⅓ cup tarragon or champagne vinegar
1 cup mild vegetable or oil
Freshly ground black pepper to taste

3 large plum tomatoes, seeded and julienned

In a saucepan bring salted water to a boil, add the peas and blanch for 2 minutes or until tender but firm. Remove the peas from the water and plunge into ice water. Drain.

Bring the water back to a boil, add the asparagus, and blanch until tender but firm.

Remove the asparagus from the water and plunge into ice water. Drain in a colander. Cut each asparagus on the diagonal into 3 pieces.

Cover the vegetables with plastic wrap and refrigerate, not longer than overnight.

In a food processor or blender combine the tarragon, vinegar, oil, and pepper to taste, and blend well. The vinaigrette may be made several days ahead and kept in the refrigerator, and blended again just before serving.

To serve, pour the vinaigrette over the peas and asparagus, and toss gently. Add the tomatoes and arrange on a serving platter.

MAKES 8 SERVINGS.

## Company Scalloped Potatoes

2 tablespoons margarine or butter
½ cup chopped onion
2 cloves garlic, minced
2 tablespoons all-purpose flour
4 teaspoons snipped fresh marjoram or basil, or
    1½ teaspoons dried
1¾ cups milk
4 cups sliced potatoes, unpeeled
¼ teaspoon salt
¼ teaspoon pepper
¼ cup grated Parmesan cheese

In a medium saucepan melt the butter and sauté the onion and garlic until tender but not brown. Stir in the flour and marjoram or basil. Add the milk all at once. Cook, stirring constantly, until thickened and bubbly. Remove the pan from the heat.

Grease a 1½-quart casserole dish. In the prepared dish layer half the potatoes. Sprinkle with salt and pepper. Cover with half the sauce. Sprinkle with half of the Parmesan cheese. Repeat the layers of potatoes and sauce. Cover. Bake at 350° for 1 hour and 15 minutes.

Uncover and sprinkle with the remaining Parmesan cheese. Bake about 30 minutes more or until the potatoes are tender. Let the potatoes stand for 5 minutes before serving.

MAKES 6 SERVINGS.

# Pineapple Coconut Layer Cake

2⅓ cups cake flour
2½ teaspoons baking powder
½ teaspoon salt
1 cup milk
1½ teaspoons vanilla extract
1 cup unsalted butter, softened
1½ cups sugar
5 large eggs, beaten lightly

1 28-ounce can crushed pineapple in
    unsweetened juice
1 tablespoon cornstarch
A rounded ¼ cup sugar

2 large egg whites
1½ cups sugar
½ cup water
1 tablespoon light corn syrup
1 teaspoon vanilla extract
1 7-ounce bag sweetened flaked coconut,
    toasted golden and cooled

*L*ine the bottoms of 2 buttered 9 x 2-inch round cake pans with rounds of wax paper or parchment, and butter the paper. Dust the pans with flour, knocking out the excess.

In a medium bowl sift together the flour, baking powder, and salt. In a glass measuring cup stir together the milk and vanilla. In a large bowl with an electric mixer on medium speed cream the butter for 1 minute. Add the sugar in a steady stream, beating for about 4 minutes or until light and fluffy, scraping the bowl occasionally. Beat in the eggs, one at a time, beating well after each addition, until pale and fluffy. Stir in the flour mixture in 4 batches alternately with the milk, beginning and ending with the flour mixture, and stirring after each addition until the batter is smooth.

Divide the batter between the pans, smoothing the tops. Bake at 350° in the middle of the oven for about 30 minutes or until a tester inserted in the center comes out clean. Cool the cake layers in the pans on racks for 10 minutes.

Run a thin knife around the edge of each pan and invert the cake layers onto racks. Remove the wax paper carefully and cool the cake layers completely.

In a heavy saucepan stir together the pineapple, cornstarch, and ¼ cup of sugar until the cornstarch is dissolved. Bring the mixture to a boil and simmer, stirring constantly, for 3 minutes. Cool the filling completely.

With a long serrated knife halve each cake layer horizontally. Stack the cake layers on a cake plate, spreading the filling between layers.

In a double boiler or in a large metal bowl beat together with a hand-held electric mixer the egg whites, 1½ cups of sugar, water, and corn syrup until combined. Set the mixture over a saucepan of boiling water and beat on high speed for about 7 minutes or until it holds stiff, glossy peaks. Remove the pan from the hot water and beat in the vanilla. Beat the frosting until cooled and spreadable. Spread the top and sides of the cake with frosting, and coat the cake with coconut.

MAKES 10 TO 12 SERVINGS.

# A Wedding Anniversary Dinner

*How about a low-key anniversary celebration? Not minimal in effort or intent, but in terms of level of celebration of this very special occasion. Just the two of you, lights turned low, soft music; when was the last time you set aside an entire evening to really talk about why you're still better together than apart? Trendy magazines sell by persuading you that you're missing something new and exciting out there, while priceless books just keep accruing value year after year because with each reading, more insights come through that this one is special. This one is tried and true. What a gift to celebrate together.*

---

DEEP-FRIED MOZZARELLA

ROSEMARY FOCACCIA

DOGES' SOUP

TOMATO AND BREAD SALAD

CANNELLONI WITH RICOTTA AND SAUSAGE FILLING

ZUCCHINI WITH TWO CHEESES

TIRAMISU

---

## TO MY DEAR AND LOVING HUSBAND

*If ever two were one, then surely we.*
*If ever man were lov'd by wife, then thee;*
*If ever wife was happy in a man,*
*Compare with me ye women if ye can.*
*I prize thy love more than whole mines of gold,*
*Or all the riches that the East doth hold.*
*My love is such that rivers cannot quench,*
*Nor aught but love from thee, give recompense.*
*Thy love is such I can no way repay,*
*The heavens reward thee manifold, I pray.*
*Then while we live, in love lets so persever*
*That, when we live no more, we may live ever.*

ANNE BRADSTREET, (1612-1672)

# Deep-fried Mozzarella

12 slices white bread, crusts trimmed
1 cup milk (or more as needed)
1 pound mozzarella cheese, sliced
Dried oregano
3 eggs, beaten
Salt and freshly ground pepper to taste
¾ cup all-purpose flour
Dried breadcrumbs
Oil
Lettuce

*D*ip one side of each slice of bread quickly in the milk, then lay a slice of mozzarella on the dry side of 6 of the slices. Sprinkle the mozzarella with dried oregano and cover with the other 6 slices of bread, dry side inward, to make sandwiches.

In a shallow dish beat the eggs and season with salt and pepper. Coat the sandwiches in flour, then in the beaten egg, and finally in the breadcrumbs. Make sure the edges of the sandwiches are well sealed.

In a large pan heat enough oil to deep fry until a small piece of bread dropped into it sizzles instantly. Fry the sandwiches one or two at a time until crisp. Drain on paper towels, cut into strips or triangles, and serve hot on a bed of lettuce.

MAKES 6 SERVINGS.

# Rosemary Focaccia

1¼-ounce envelope active dry yeast
1¼ cups warm water (105 to 115°)
3½ cups all-purpose flour
1 teaspoon salt
¼ cup butter, melted
½ cup chopped fresh rosemary
2 tablespoons olive oil
4 cloves garlic, minced

*I*n a 2-cup liquid measuring cup combine the yeast and warm water. Let the mixture stand for 5 minutes.

In a large mixing bowl combine the yeast mixture, 2 cups of all-purpose flour, and ½ teaspoon of salt, stirring well.

Cover, and let rise in a warm draft-free place for 1 hour or until the dough is doubled in bulk.

Coat 3 baking sheets with cooking spray. Punch the dough down, and stir in the remaining flour, butter, and ¼ cup of rosemary. Turn the dough out onto a lightly floured surface and knead 10 minutes. Divide the dough into thirds. Roll each portion into a 9-inch circle on the prepared baking sheets. Brush the dough evenly with olive oil and sprinkle evenly with the remaining ¼ cup of rosemary, ½ teaspoon of salt, and garlic. Prick the dough generously with a fork. Bake at 400° for 20 minutes.

MAKES 12 SERVINGS

# Doges' Soup

¾ cup long grain white rice
½ cup grated fontina or Edam cheese
1 egg, lightly beaten
¼ cup freshly grated Parmesan cheese
1 tablespoon olive oil
1½ quarts clear beef broth
1 large beet, boiled, peeled, and julienned
2 carrots, julienned
1 large leek, julienned
¼ pound celeriac (celery root), peeled and cut
     into match sticks
4 to 6 tablespoons all-purpose flour
Oil

In a large saucepan cook the rice in boiling water for about 10 minutes or until still fairly firm in the middle. Drain. In a medium bowl mix the rice with the fontina until well blended. Add half of the egg, the Parmesan, and olive oil. Mix very thoroughly. Shape the mixture into walnut-sized balls squeezing so that it sticks together. Refrigerate the balls until needed. Discard the remaining egg or set aside for another use.

In a large pot bring the broth to a boil. Add the vegetables and simmer for 10 minutes.

Meanwhile, remove the rice balls from the refrigerator and coat them with flour, handling them carefully so that they do not break up. In a large skillet heat oil for deep frying. Add the rice balls and fry until golden. Drain on paper towels. Place the rice balls in soup plates, and ladle the soup over them. Serve immediately.

MAKES 6 SERVINGS.

# Tomato and Bread Salad

3 stale white bread rolls
4 large flavorful tomatoes, cut into wedges
2 large onions, finely sliced
1 hothouse cucumber, peeled and cut into
     cubes

A handful fresh basil leaves
6 tablespoons olive oil
3 tablespoons white wine vinegar
Salt and freshly ground pepper to taste

In a medium bowl soak the rolls in cold water for about 1 hour. In a serving bowl combine the tomatoes, onions, cucumber, and basil leaves. Mix together by hand. Take the bread out of the water, squeeze it dry with your hands, and mix into the salad. Sprinkle with plenty of olive oil, vinegar, and salt and pepper to taste. Toss well, and let stand at least 2 hours.

Note: It is even better if left overnight in the refrigerator.

MAKES 4 TO 6 SERVINGS.

# Cannelloni with a Ricotta and Sausage Filling

1¾ cups all-purpose flour
Salt to taste
3 eggs
2 to 3 tablespoons water

3 tablespoons olive oil
1 clove garlic, finely chopped
1 small onion, finely chopped
1 small carrot, finely chopped
1 small stalk celery, finely chopped
3 tablespoons tomato paste
1 cup water
Salt and freshly ground pepper to taste

3 large Italian sausages
2 cups ricotta cheese
Salt to taste
1 egg, beaten
⅓ cup freshly grated Parmesan cheese
3 tablespoons butter, cubed

*I*n a food processor combine the flour and salt. Add 3 eggs and the water and process until mixed thoroughly. Roll out the dough, then fold it in half and roll out again. Continue to do this until it is smooth and elastic and the air pops out from under the fold as the rolling pin is pressed down. Cover the dough with a cloth and put it to one side.

In a saucepan heat the olive oil and fry the garlic, onion, carrot, and celery until completely soft. Add the tomato paste and water, mix well, and season with salt and pepper to taste. Simmer for about 20-30 minutes.

In a skillet place the sausages, prick them all over, and cover with cold water. Cook over low heat until the water has evaporated, then sizzle the sausages in their own fat for 5 to 7 minutes. Remove the sausages from the pan and allow them to cool.

Press the ricotta through a sieve into a medium bowl. Add the salt, 1 egg, and the grated Parmesan and mix well. Skin the sausages and crumble the meat into the ricotta mixture. Stir it all together.

On a floured surface roll out the pasta dough to about 1/10-inch thickness and cut into 3-inch squares. Bring a very large pot of salted water to a boil and cook the squares 4 at a time for about 1 minute or until they rise to the surface. Scoop the squares out with a slotted spoon as soon as they are ready and lay them on the work top or on wet dish towels.

Butter a 2-quart casserole dish. Place a spoonful of ricotta filling on each pasta square, roll closed and arrange in rows in the dish. Sprinkle with the grated Parmesan, dot with the cubes of butter, and pour the tomato sauce over all. Bake at 375° for about 30 minutes. Serve hot.

MAKES 6 SERVINGS.

# Zucchini with Two Cheeses

6 large zucchini, sliced
1¼ cups oil for frying
¼ cup olive oil
2 cloves garlic, minced
2½ cups puréed tomatoes
½ cup fresh basil leaves
Dried oregano
Salt and freshly ground pepper to taste
1 pound mozzarella cheese, thinly sliced
1¼ cups freshly grated Parmesan cheese

*I*n a large skillet heat the frying oil until sizzling and fry the zucchini for about 3 minutes for each side or until golden brown. Drain and reserve.

In a saucepan heat the olive oil and cook the garlic for about 4 minutes without browning. Add the puréed tomatoes and mix well. Add half the basil and a large pinch of oregano. Season to taste and partly cover. Simmer for 10 minutes or until reduced and no longer watery.

Spread a thin layer of the tomato sauce in the bottom of a 1½ quart casserole dish. Arrange some slices of fried zucchini on top and cover with a few slices of mozzarella, then a little more tomato sauce. Sprinkle with a few basil leaves and finish with a generous sprinkling of Parmesan cheese. Repeat until all the ingredients are used, ending with tomato sauce and basil.

Bake at 350° for 20 to 30 minutes or until the mozzarella is melted and stringy. Serve immediately.

MAKES 6 SERVINGS.

# Tiramisu

1 pound mascarpone (or rich cream cheese)
8 eggs, separated
½ cup sugar
½ cup very strong espresso coffee
1¼ cups weak coffee
⅓ cup brandy
30 ladyfinger cookies
Ground coffee or cocoa powder for dusting

In a large bowl beat the mascarpone with a wooden spoon until soft and creamy. In a separate bowl beat the egg yolks until fluffy and pale yellow. Add the sugar a little at a time until smooth. Add the egg yolks to the cream cheese. Stir in the strong coffee. In a separate bowl beat the egg whites until stiff. Fold the egg whites into the cheese mixture. Set this mixture aside.

In a shallow bowl combine the weak coffee and brandy. Dip the ladyfingers into it one at a time to moisten them. In a shallow serving bowl arrange some of the cookies in a layer. Cover with some of the cheese mixture, and cover with more moistened cookies. Continue to layer until all of the ingredients have been used, ending with cheese mixture. Sprinkle with the ground coffee or cocoa powder. Chill for at least 1 hour.

MAKES 8 SERVINGS.

# A Christening Luncheon

*The bestowing of a name. Will she like it? Does it seem to fit the rosebud mouth? Whose eyes does he have, and is the sweet expression an auspicious beginning or part of the mischievous persona this one will wield over the household? All eyes rest on the unsuspecting guest of honor, the unequivocal center of attention. What any actor would give for such an audience! The next order of business for this crowd is their tummies touching backbone! Wait till they see the luncheon you're about to deliver!*

---

CRAB DIP AND CRACKERS

COTTAGE DILL ROLLS

CREAM OF ZUCCHINI AND ALMOND SOUP

CHICKEN AND TORTELLINI SALAD

LIME CHIFFON CAKE WITH LIME SORBET

ROSEMARY SHORTBREAD

---

Oh my God,
Thou fairest, greatest, first of all objects,
my heart admires, adores, loves thee,
for my little vessel is as full as it can be,
and I would pour out all that fullness before thee
 in ceaseless flow...
I bless thee for the soul thou hast created,
for adorning it, sanctifying it,
though it is fixed in barren soil;
for the body thou hast given me,
for preserving its strength and vigour,
for providing senses to enjoy delights,
for the ease and freedom of my limbs,
for hands, eyes, ears that do thy bidding;
for thy royal bounty providing my daily
 support,
for a full table and overflowing cup,
for appetite, taste, sweetness,
for social joys of relatives and friends,
for ability to serve others,
for a heart that feels sorrows and necessities,
for a mind to care for my fellow-men,
for opportunities of spreading happiness around,
for loved ones in the joys of heaven,
for my own expectation of seeing thee clearly....
Increase my love, O God, through time and
 eternity.

# Crab Dip and Crackers

1 pound crab meat, flaked
2 8-ounce packages cream cheese, softened
1 8-ounce carton sour cream
1 tablespoon dry mustard
¼ cup mayonnaise
Juice of ½ lemon
Dash Worcestershire sauce
3 shakes garlic salt
1½ cups shredded medium Cheddar cheese
Paprika to taste
Buttery crackers

*I*n a large bowl combine the crab meat, cream cheese, sour cream, dry mustard, mayonnaise, lemon juice, Worcestershire sauce, garlic salt, and 1 cup of Cheddar. Spoon the mixture into a 2-quart casserole dish. Sprinkle with the remaining cheese and paprika. Bake at 325° for 40 minutes.

Serve hot or warm with buttery crackers.
MAKES ABOUT 7 CUPS.

# Cottage Dill Rolls

1 pound small-curd cottage cheese
2½ tablespoons sugar
1 tablespoon finely chopped onion
2 tablespoons butter, softened
1 teaspoon salt
1 teaspoon finely chopped fresh dill
½ teaspoon baking soda
1 egg
1 tablespoon horseradish
1 ½-ounce cake yeast (or ¾ ounce dry)
½ cup water
3½ cups bread flour
2 tablespoons butter, melted
Additional melted butter for brushing tops of
    baked rolls

*I*n a mixer with the paddle attachment or at slow speed with a regular beater mix the cottage cheese, sugar, onion, butter, salt, dill, soda, egg, and horseradish. Add the remaining ingredients and mix with a dough hook until well mixed, or knead by hand for 10 minutes. Add any additional flour needed to prevent sticking.

Shape into rolls. Bake at 350° for 30 minutes or until golden brown. Rolls should sound hollow when tapped. Brush with melted butter when done. Serve immediately.
MAKES 12 LARGE ROLLS.

# Cream of Zucchini and Almond Soup

3 tablespoons butter
1 onion, minced
3 zucchini, peeled and thinly sliced
½ cup slivered almonds
4 cups chicken broth
½ cup ground blanched almonds
¾ cup heavy cream
1 tablespoon brown sugar
1 tablespoon amaretto
¼ teaspoon ground cinnamon
½ teaspoon freshly grated nutmeg
Zucchini peel or toasted almonds for garnish
    (optional)

*I*n a large saucepan melt the butter and sauté the onion until soft. Add the zucchini and slivered almonds, and cook for about 5 minutes, until the zucchini is tendercrisp. Add the chicken broth and simmer for about 25 minutes or until the liquid is reduced by one-third.

Add the ground almonds, and simmer for 10 more minutes. Over low heat stir in the cream, brown sugar, amaretto, cinnamon, and nutmeg. Garnish with zucchini peel or toasted almonds, if desired.
MAKES 6 TO 8 SERVINGS.

## Chicken and Tortellini Salad

2 tablespoons olive oil
2 cloves garlic, minced
6 skinless, boneless chicken breast halves,
    cooked, cut into strips
¾ cup cider vinegar
¼ cup honey
1 tablespoon chopped fresh basil leaves (or 1
    teaspoon dried)
3 tablespoons chopped fresh parsley
2 teaspoons Dijon mustard
¾ cup oil
9 to 10 ounces fresh tortellini
1 medium red bell pepper, seeded and
    chopped
1 medium green bell pepper, seeded and
    chopped
2 ribs celery, sliced
1 medium red onion, chopped
Salt and pepper to taste

*I*n a large skillet heat the olive oil and sauté the garlic over medium heat until golden brown. Add the chicken, and sauté 1 for minute, stirring constantly. Remove the garlic and chicken to a large bowl. Set aside.

In a small bowl combine the vinegar, honey, basil, parsley, and Dijon mustard. Slowly whisk in the vegetable oil, blending until the dressing is creamy. Pour the dressing over the garlic and chicken. Cover and marinate for several hours in the refrigerator.

In a large pot cook the tortellini in boiling water until tender but firm. Drain and rinse quickly in cold water to stop the cooking process. Drain well.

In a serving bowl combine the marinated chicken and dressing, drained tortellini, chopped bell peppers, celery, onion, salt, and pepper, and toss well. Refrigerate until chilled.
MAKES 8 SERVINGS.

## Lime Chiffon Cake

2¼ cups sifted cake flour
1¼ cups sugar
3 teaspoons baking powder
¼ teaspoon salt
4 large egg yolks
½ cup vegetable oil
½ cup water
¼ cup lime juice
1 tablespoon finely grated lime peel
8 large egg whites, at room temperature
½ teaspoon cream of tartar

1 cup confectioners' sugar
2 teaspoons fresh lime juice
1 drop green food coloring
Lime Sorbet (recipe follows)

*I*n a medium bowl stir together the cake flour, sugar, baking powder, and salt. Make a well in the center of the flour mixture. Add the egg yolks, oil, water, ¼ cup of lime juice, and peel. Beat with an electric mixer at medium speed until smooth. Wash the beaters. In a large bowl combine the egg whites and cream of tartar and beat at high speed until very stiff peaks form. Very gently fold the lime batter into the egg whites until well combined. Turn into an ungreased 10-inch tube pan with removable bottom.

Bake at 325° for 65 to 70 minutes or until the cake springs back when lightly touched. Invert the pan over a bottle and cool completely.

Remove the cake from the pan and place on a serving plate.

In a small bowl stir together the confectioners' sugar, 2 teaspoons of fresh lime juice, and the food coloring until smooth. Spread the frosting over the cake, allowing it to run down the sides of the cake.

Serve with Lime Sorbet.
MAKES 8 TO 10 SERVINGS.

# Lime Sorbet

4 cups sugar
7½ cups hot water
4½ cups lime juice (about 30 limes)
6 tablespoons lemon juice
4 drops green food coloring
21 egg whites, lightly beaten

In a large bowl dissolve the sugar in the hot water. Add the remaining ingredients. Pour into 2 large rectangular pans and freeze.

A few hours before serving, spoon the sorbet into a food processor and process just until smooth. Return the sorbet to the pans and freeze until firm.

MAKES 6 CUPS.

# Rosemary Shortbread

1½ cups unsalted butter, softened
⅔ cup sugar
2¾ cups all-purpose flour
¼ teaspoon salt
2 tablespoons minced fresh rosemary (or
        2 teaspoons crushed dried)
Sugar for sprinkling

In a large bowl cream the butter with an electric mixer at medium speed for 2 minutes until pale yellow. Add the sugar and beat until fluffy. Add the flour, salt, and rosemary to the butter mixture, and mix well. Divide the dough in half, place on waxed paper, and pat into squares. Refrigerate until firm, about 2 hours.

Line 2 large baking sheets with parchment paper. On a well-floured surface roll each square of dough to ⅜-inch thickness. Cut into shapes. Place on the prepared baking sheets about ½ inch apart. Sprinkle with sugar. Bake at 375° for 18 to 20 minutes until the edges are golden. Transfer the cookies to a rack to cool.

Note: Store in an airtight container. The flavor improves with time. The cookies will keep for about 1 week.

MAKES ABOUT 4 DOZEN.

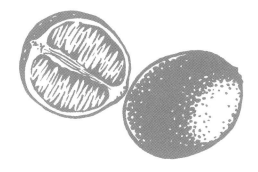

# Cinco De Mayo

*Cinco De Mayo (the Fifth of May) is the day on which Mexicans and Mexican-Americans commemorate the defeat of the French at the Battle of Pueblo in 1862. The successful defense of the city was a decisive halt to Napoleon's attempt to establish a permanent French colony in the region. Celebrated as early as 1863, Cinco De Mayo has come to be a rallying cry for the oppressed. Many Mexican-Americans celebrate it with a party, parade, speeches, and songs. A festive menu is called for.*

GREAT GUACAMOLE

SALSA

CHIMICHANGAS (DEEP-FRIED BURRITOS)

CHILES RELLENOS (STUFFED PEPPERS)

SAVORY CHEESE AND CHILI CHURROS

RED RICE

MEXICAN COOKIES

FLAN

*Blessed be the God and Father of our Lord Jesus Christ, the Father of mercies and God of all comfort, who comforts us in all our affliction, so that we may be able to comfort those who are in any affliction, with the comfort with which we ourselves are comforted by God. For as we share abundantly in Christ's sufferings, so through Christ we share abundantly in comfort too.*

*2 CORINTHIANS 1:3-5*

# Great Guacamole

2 large avocados, halved, pitted and peeled
1 small red onion, finely chopped
¾ cup chopped fresh cilantro
½ red bell pepper, finely chopped
2 tablespoons fresh lime juice
2 tablespoons olive oil
1 jalapeño chili, minced with seeds
Salt and freshly ground pepper to taste
Tortilla chips

*I*n a medium bowl coarsely mash the avocados, onion, cilantro, bell pepper, lime juice, olive oil, and jalapeño with the back of a spoon. Season with salt and pepper to taste. Serve with tortilla chips.
MAKES ABOUT 3 CUPS.

# Salsa

5 tomatoes
2 medium onions
3 jalapeño chilies
2 garlic cloves

1½ avocados, peeled and chopped
¼ cup chopped cilantro
Salt to taste
Tortilla chips

*A*rrange tomatoes, onions, chilies and garlic on a broiler pan. Broil about 4 inches from the heat for 20 to 30 minutes or until the skins are blackened, watching carefully and turning occasionally.

Peel off the skins. Core the tomatoes and stem the jalapeños. In a blender purée the vegetables. Pour the salsa into a serving bowl, and stir in the avocado and cilantro. Season with salt. Serve with tortilla chips.
MAKES ABOUT 5 CUPS.

# Chimichangas (Deep-fried Burritos)

1 pound ground beef
1 medium onion, chopped
½ cup red chile sauce (or enchilada sauce)
12 flour tortillas
Oil
2 cups grated Cheddar cheese
2 cups shredded lettuce
2 cups chopped green onions

*I*n a large skillet brown the meat and drain. Add the onion and chile or enchilada sauce and mix well. Spoon about 3 tablespoons of meat filling in the center of each tortilla. Fold the tortilla, tuck in the ends, and fasten with wooden toothpicks. Only assemble 2 or 3 at a time as they will absorb the liquid from the sauce.

In a large frying pan heat 1 inch of oil over medium heat. Fry the folded tortilla for about 1 to 2 minutes, turning once, until golden. Drain on paper towels and keep warm. Garnish with Cheddar cheese, lettuce, and onion.
MAKES 12 CHIMICHANGAS.

# Chiles Rellenos (Stuffed Peppers)

12 fresh chiles poblanos (or bell peppers)

3 tablespoons shortening
1½ pounds ground pork
1½ pounds lean ground chuck
½ onion, finely chopped
2 cloves garlic, finely chopped
1 tablespoon salt
¼ teaspoon black pepper
1 cup raisins, finely chopped
1 cup pecans, chopped
2 carrots, finely chopped
1 medium tomato, boiled, peeled, and strained
1 teaspoon sugar

6 eggs, separated, room temperature
½ cup all-purpose flour for dusting
Shortening or oil

6 medium fresh tomatoes
½ onion, sliced
1 chicken bouillon cube
3 cloves garlic
Salt and pepper to taste
1 tablespoon oil

*M*ake a slit in each chile to avoid "explosions" during the roasting. Place the chiles on a cookie sheet and set under the broiler 4 to 6 inches from the heat. Watch closely during the broiling. The chiles will blister and burn slightly. Turn the chiles from time to time for even roasting. When the chiles are roasted, place in a plastic bag and seal. Let stand about 20 minutes. The burned skin will flake off very easily, and the flesh will become a little more cooked with the steam in the bag. Make a slit in the side of each chili, carefully removing the seeds and veins. Be careful to leave the top of the chili around the base of the stem intact.

In a large Dutch oven, melt the shortening and brown the pork and ground chuck. Add the onion, garlic, salt, and pepper and cook for 5 minutes. Add the raisins, pecans, carrots, tomato, and sugar. Cover and cook until done. Set aside for stuffing the chiles.

In a mixing bowl beat egg whites with an electric mixer until soft peaks form. Fold in the beaten egg yolks. Set aside.

Stuff the peppers with equal portions of meat stuffing. Dust each chile with flour. Dip in egg batter coating the entire chile. Repeat the procedure with all 12 chiles. Place on a cookie sheet.

In a skillet or Dutch oven, heat enough shortening or oil to deep fry the chiles. Fry until golden brown and place on paper towels to drain.

In a blender combine the tomatoes, onion, chicken bouillon cube, garlic, salt and pepper. Blend until smooth. In a large saucepan combine the oil and tomato mixture and bring to a boil. Reduce the heat, and simmer about 5 minutes.

To serve chiles rellenos, place on plates, and pour a large spoonful of sauce over each chile.

MAKES 12 STUFFED PEPPERS.

## *Savory Cheese and Chili Churros*

1 cup plus 2 tablespoons water
3 tablespoons butter, chopped
Salt to taste
¾ cup all-purpose flour
¼ cup white cornmeal
2 eggs
3 jalapeño peppers, stemmed, seeded and
    minced
2 tablespoons freshly grated Monterey Jack
    cheese
Peanut oil

*I*n a heavy medium saucepan combine the water, butter and salt and cook over medium heat until the butter melts. Remove the pan from the heat. Immediately mix in the flour and cornmeal with a wooden spoon. Cook over medium-high heat for 1 to 2 minutes, stirring constantly, until the mixture pulls away from the sides of the pan to form a ball and begins to form film on the bottom. Transfer the mixture to a food processor. Cool for 5 minutes.

Blend in the eggs 1 at a time. Add the peppers and Monterey Jack cheese and mix until smooth.

In a deep fryer or heavy deep skillet heat oil to 375°. Spoon the dough into a pastry bag fitted with a star tip. Pipe 10-inch strips into the oil in bunches without crowding. Fry for about 3 minutes per side or until golden brown. Drain on paper towels and serve.

MAKES 12 TO 14 CHURROS.

# Red Rice

5 slices bacon
1¾ cups chopped onion
1 6-ounce can tomato paste
1½ cups water
1 tablespoon salt
2 teaspoons sugar
¼ teaspoon pepper
2 cups uncooked rice

In a heavy pot cook the bacon until crisp. Remove the bacon and drain on paper towels Add the onion to the bacon drippings and sauté until soft, stirring occasionally. Add the tomato paste, water, salt, sugar, and pepper. Bring the mixture to a boil. Add the rice, and reduce the heat to low. Cover and cook for 5 to 10 minutes or until the rice is tender but firm. Remove the pot from the heat, add the crumbled bacon, and mix well.

MAKES 6 TO 8 SERVINGS.

# Mexican Cookies

1 cinnamon stick, broken into fine pieces
5 cups all-purpose flour
2 cups sugar
3 teaspoons baking powder
½ teaspoon baking soda
Salt to taste
2 eggs, beaten
1 teaspoon vanilla extract
2 cups shortening, softened
Cinnamon-sugar

In a small skillet roast the broken cinnamon stick. In a large mixing bowl combine the roasted cinnamon, flour, sugar, baking powder, soda, and salt, and mix thoroughly. Add the beaten eggs and vanilla to the flour mixture and blend thoroughly. Add the softened shortening to the flour mixture and mix dough by hand until well blended. The dough should not be sticky.

Lightly grease a cookie sheet. Shape the dough into grape-sized balls. Slash a cross-shaped pattern on top of each cookie, and place on the prepared cookie sheet. Bake at 350° for 12 to 15 minutes or until golden brown. Let cool partially before removing from the cookie sheet. Dip the tip of the cookies into cinnamon sugar while still warm.

MAKES ABOUT 9 DOZEN COOKIES.

# Flan

6 eggs
5 egg yolks
¾ cup sugar
2½ cups milk
2 cups cream of coconut
2 teaspoons vanilla extract (Mexican, if available)
1 cup sliced almonds

In a skillet melt the sugar over medium heat, watching closely so the sugar does not burn. As the sugar bubbles, lift the pan off the heat, tilting to move the caramel around the pan. When the sugar has caramelized, quickly pour the caramel syrup into 8 individual flan molds (or a 10-inch cake pan), tilting to coat evenly. If the caramel hardens, return the pan to the heat to melt.

In a large bowl beat the eggs and egg yolks lightly with a whisk. Add all remaining ingredients except the almonds, whisking together until blended. Pour the custard over the caramel in the molds. Sprinkle evenly with almonds. Cover all the molds with aluminum foil. Place the molds in a large pan filled with hot water. Bake at 325° for 1 hour or until a knife inserted in the custard comes out clean. Remove the flan from the water bath and refrigerate. When ready to serve, invert the molds onto serving dishes.

MAKES 8 SERVINGS.

# Springtime Picnic in the Garden

*Every year it's a miracle. We think the frosts will never cease, and the last cold weather always sneaks in when we've decided we have had enough of it. We greet the forsythia, dogwoods, redbuds, spirea, and all flowering plants as old friends. We know just where to look along the familiar roadsides for the best views. Yes, there is that vista, more magnificent even than we remembered. The warmth of the sun provokes us to stretches and purrs. Everyone's ready for a picnic in the emerging garden. This springtime cuisine will remind your guests of your ability to combine great food, pleasing atmosphere, and authentic hospitality into another memorable event.*

---

FRENCH BREAD

SALMAGUNDI

ENGLISH TEA SANDWICH LOAF

LEMON CREAM SCONES
WITH MOCK DEVONSHIRE CREAM

BLUEBERRY FOOL

---

*THE CHURCH THE GARDEN OF CHRIST*

We are a Garden wall'd around,
Chosen and made peculiar Ground;
A little Spot inclos'd by Grace
Out of the World's wide Wilderness.

Like Trees of Myrrh and Spice we stand,
Planted by God the Father's Hand;
And all his Springs in Sion flow,
To make the young Plantation grow.

Awake, O heavenly Wind, and come,
Blow on this garden of Perfume;
Spirit Divine, descend and breathe
A gracious Gale on Plants beneath.

Make our best Spices flow abroad
To entertain our Saviour-God:
And faith, and Love, and Joy appear,
And every Grace be active here.

Let my Beloved come, and taste
His pleasant Fruits at his own Feast.
I come, my Spouse, I come, he cries,
With love and Pleasure in his Eyes.

Our Lord into his Garden comes,
Well pleas'd to smell our poor Perfumes,
And calls us to a Feast divine,
Sweeter than Honey, Milk, or Wine.

Eat of the Tree of Life, my Friends,
The Blessings that my Father sends;
Your taste shall all my Dainties prove,
And drink abundance of my Love.

Jesus, we will frequent thy Board,
And sing the Bounties of our Lord;
But the rich Food on which we live
Demands more Praise than Tongue can give.

ISAAC WATTS (1674-1748)

# French Bread

2 packages active dry yeast
2½ cups warm water (115°)
2 tablespoons sugar
1 tablespoon salt
7 cups bread flour
Cornmeal
1 egg white, beaten

*I*n a large bowl dissolve the yeast in the water. Stir in the sugar and salt until dissolved. Add 5 cups of flour and mix with a wooden spoon. Add one cup flour and mix until blended. Turn the dough out onto a floured surface and knead for 10 minutes, using as much of the seventh cup of flour as needed to make the dough smooth and elastic and prevent it from sticking.

Lightly grease a large bowl. Place the dough in the prepared bowl and turn the dough to lightly coat with butter. Cover with a damp cloth and let rise for about 1 hour and 30 minutes to 2 hours or until doubled.

Turn the dough onto a lightly floured surface. Punch down and knead for 2 to 3 minutes. Let the dough rest for 15 minutes.

Cut the dough into 4 pieces and roll each one into a rectangle, approximately 12 x 15 inches. Roll up the dough from the long side as you would a jelly roll. Seal the ends. Grease 4 open-ended long bread pans with butter. Lightly sprinkle the greased pans with cornmeal. Place each piece of dough in a pan with the seamed side down. Make 4 diagonal cuts in each piece of dough with a razor blade or sharp knife. Brush the top of each piece with beaten egg white. Let the dough rise until doubled (no need to cover).

Spray the tops of the dough with a fine mist of water. Bake at 450° for 5 minutes. Open the oven and spray again. Bake another 10 minutes, then reduce the oven temperature to 350° and bake 25 minutes. When done, remove the bread from the pans and let cool on wire racks.

Note: This bread freezes very well. To freeze, wrap tightly in aluminum foil. To reheat, remove from the foil and bake at 350° for 20 minutes.

MAKES 4 BAGUETTE LOAVES.

# Salmagundi

¼ cup fresh lemon juice
Salt and freshly ground black pepper to taste
⅓ cup walnut oil
2 tablespoons canola or vegetable oil
¼ cup applejack (apple brandy)
¼ cup water
½ cup golden raisins
1 small head looseleaf lettuce, washed and dried
2 heads Bibb lettuce, washed and dried
¾ pound green beans, cooked crisp-tender and drained
1 cup pearl onions, blanched 3 minutes and peeled
2 tart apples, peeled, cored, and finely chopped
1 cup seedless green grapes
1 tablespoon capers, drained
6 boneless chicken breasts, poached and cut into long, thin strips
½ sweet red bell pepper, seeded, deribbed, and diced
6 quail eggs, hard-boiled, peeled, and halved
1 tablespoon chopped fresh chives

*I*n a small bowl, whisk together the lemon juice, salt, and pepper. Gradually whisk in the oils until well blended. Set aside.

In a saucepan, combine the applejack and water. Bring to a simmer, add the raisins, and set aside to cool.

Tear the lettuce into bite-size pieces, pack in a portable container, and chill. Pack in the cooler for transporting.

In a large portable bowl with a lid toss together the green beans, onions, apples, grapes, and capers with enough of the vinaigrette to coat lightly. Place the remaining vinaigrette in a container with a tight lid, and pack in the cooler.

Drain the raisins, and sprinkle over the salad. Arrange the chicken strips over the salad and sprinkle with the bell pepper. Place the quail eggs over the top and sprinkle with the chives. Cover, and pack in the cooler. When ready to serve, place lettuce leaves on each plate, and top with the salad. Drizzle with the reserved vinaigrette.

MAKES 6 SERVINGS.

## English Tea Sandwich Loaf

1 large loaf whole wheat bread, unsliced
Butter
4 ounces ham
2 tablespoons pickle relish
7 tablespoons mayonnaise
1 cup grated sharp Cheddar cheese
10 ounces red pimientos, drained (reserve 4
    strips for garnish)
4 ounces cooked and cooled shredded chicken
1 tablespoon curry powder
1 8-ounce package cream cheese, softened
Sliced black and green olives for garnish

Trim the crusts from the bread, then cut the loaf lengthwise into 4 slices. Spread 3 slices with butter, leaving the top piece plain.

In a food processor combine the ham, pickle relish, and 2 tablespoons of mayonnaise and blend well. Spread the ham mixture over the bottom layer. In a small bowl blend the Cheddar cheese, pimiento, and 2 tablespoons of mayonnaise. Spread the cheese mixture over the second layer. In a separate bowl blend the chicken, curry powder, and 2 tablespoons of mayonnaise. Spread the chicken mixture over the third layer. Stack the layers, and place the remaining bread on top to complete the loaf.

In a medium bowl blend the cream cheese and 1 tablespoon of mayonnaise with an electric mixer until smooth. Frost the entire loaf as though it were a cake. Fill a pastry bag fitted with the star tube with the remaining cream cheese mixture and decorate the top and base of the loaf. Garnish with olives and pimento strips.

MAKES 12 SLICES.

## Lemon Cream Scones with Mock Devonshire Cream

2 cups all-purpose flour
1 teaspoon salt
¼ cup sugar
1 tablespoon baking powder
3 tablespoons butter
2 egg yolks, beaten well
1 tablespoon finely chopped lemon balm
½ teaspoon freshly grated lemon peel
⅓ cup heavy cream
1 egg white, beaten
Preserves
Mock Devonshire Cream (recipe follows)

In a large bowl stir together the flour, salt, sugar, and baking powder. Cut in the butter with a pastry blender. In a separate bowl combine the beaten egg yolks, lemon balm, lemon peel, and cream. Add the egg mixture to the flour mixture and mix until a soft dough forms. Turn out onto a floured pastry board and knead about 20 times. Roll out about ½-inch thick and cut with a 2-inch round cutter. Place on an ungreased cookie sheet. Brush the tops with beaten egg white. Bake at 450° for 10 minutes or until lightly browned.

Store in an airtight container. Serve with any flavor preserves and Mock Devonshire Cream.

MAKES 12 SCONES.

## Mock Devonshire Cream

½ cup heavy cream
2 tablespoons confectioners' sugar
½ cup sour cream

*I*n a chilled bowl beat the cream until medium-stiff peaks form, adding sugar during the last few minutes of beating. Fold in the sour cream, and blend well.

MAKES 1½ CUPS.

## Blueberry Fool

½ pint fresh blueberries, washed and picked over
1 teaspoon lemon juice
1 tablespoon sugar or to taste
2 tablespoons water
¾ cup heavy cream
2 tablespoons confectioners' sugar
1 teaspoon vanilla extract

*I*n a small saucepan combine the blueberries, lemon juice, sugar, and water. Cook over medium heat, stirring frequently, for 5 minutes or until the blueberries begin to pop and the juices boil and thicken. Remove the pan from the heat and transfer the blueberry sauce to a small bowl. Place the bowl in a larger bowl of ice water and stir the mixture occasionally until cold.

In a separate bowl combine the cream, confectioners' sugar, and vanilla and beat until stiff peaks form. Fold in ⅓ cup of the blueberry sauce. Divide among 4 dessert dishes and spoon the remaining sauce over the tops.

MAKES 4 SERVINGS.

# Mother's Day Brunch

*Once I met a woman who actually hated Mother's Day. She had children who loved her dearly, but she felt that every day should bring forth gratitude and love, not just one big, artificial observance where everyone is compelled to honor mothers and thn go back to their same old ways. Perhaps the same could be said for every holiday. Every day we should remember Christmas. Every day we should be grateful for the food before us. Every day we ought to remember not to take our spouse for granted. And every day we should thank God for our independence. But, you see, that is the nature of holidays. Because we are forgetful and busy and fickle, but really do mean well, we have set aside holidays to specially honor certain themes. So enjoy Mother's Day. It's not about perfect mothers and perfect presents,but about all the wonder that motherly love can be and usually is: selfless, overwhelming, somewhat possessive, and vastly comforting. If you aren't a mother, and even if you don't have a mother, honor someone today who has contributed to your lfe in a mothering way—a mentor or someone who has loved you or taken care of you.*

---

CHICKEN PECAN QUICHE

POACHED PEARS WITH RASPBERRY SAUCE

NUTMEG MUFFINS

CINNAMON SWIRL CAKE

---

*Lord of the home, your only Son*
*Received a mother's tender love,*
*And from an earthly father won*
*His vision of your home above.*

*Teach us to keep our homes so fair*
*That, were our Lord a child once more,*
*He might be glad our hearth to share,*
*And find a welcome at our door.*

# Chicken Pecan Quiche

2 cups finely chopped cooked chicken
1 cup grated Monterey Jack cheese
¼ cup scallions
1 tablespoon chopped parsley
½ cup plus 1 tablespoon all-purpose flour
1 unbaked 9-inch pie shell
3 eggs, beaten
1¼ cups half and half
½ teaspoon brown mustard
½ cup chopped pecans

In a large bowl combine the chicken, cheese, scallions, parsley, and flour. Sprinkle into the pie shell.

In a medium bowl combine the eggs, half and half, and mustard. Pour over the chicken mixture and top with the pecans. Bake at 325° for 60 minutes.

MAKES 6 SERVINGS.

# Poached Pears with Raspberry Sauce

6 medium ripe pears
Lemon juice
½ cup sugar
1 teaspoon grated lemon peel
3 whole cloves
1 cinnamon stick
4 cups water
1 10-ounce package frozen raspberries in syrup (or plain frozen raspberries with sugar to taste)

Peel the pears. Remove the core from the bottom and leave the stems attached. Brush the pears with lemon juice.

In a large kettle combine the sugar, lemon peel, cloves, cinnamon stick, and water, and bring the mixture to a boil. Add the pears in an upright position. Reduce the heat, cover, and simmer for 20 to 25 minutes or until the pears are tender. Chill the pears in the poaching liquid.

Meanwhile, force the raspberries through a sieve to remove the seeds. Chill.

To serve, place the pears upright in individual dessert dishes. Spoon sauce over each pear.

MAKES 6 SERVINGS.

# Nutmeg Muffins

2 cups all-purpose flour
¾ cup sugar
1 tablespoon double-acting baking powder
1½ tablespoons freshly grated nutmeg
½ teaspoon salt
1 large egg at room temperature
¾ cup heavy cream
¾ cup milk
5 tablespoons unsalted butter, melted and cooled

Butter a 12-cup muffin pan. In a large bowl stir together the flour, sugar, baking powder, nutmeg, and salt. In a small bowl whisk together the egg, cream, milk, and butter until well blended. Stir the cream mixture into the flour mixture until the batter is just combined. Divide the batter among the buttered muffin cups. Bake at 400° for 15 to 20 minutes or until the muffins are pale golden and a toothpick inserted in the center comes out clean. Turn the muffins out onto a rack.

MAKES 12 MUFFINS.

# Cinnamon Swirl Cake

3 cups unbleached flour
1½ cups sugar
2 teaspoons baking powder
1 teaspoon baking soda
1 teaspoon salt
1 cup buttermilk
¾ cup butter or margarine, softened
2 tablespoons orange juice
1 tablespoon grated orange peel
3 eggs
¼ cup raisins

½ cup firmly packed brown sugar
⅓ cup all-purpose flour
2 teaspoons ground cinnamon
¼ cup butter or margarine

1 cup confectioners' sugar
1 to 2 tablespoons orange juice

Grease and flour a 12-cup fluted tube pan. In a large mixing bowl, combine 3 cups of flour, 1½ cups of sugar, the baking powder, soda, salt, buttermilk, ¾ cup of butter, 2 tablespoons of orange juice, and the orange peel, and beat with an electric mixer at medium speed for 2 minutes. Add the eggs, one at a time, beating well after each addition. Stir in the raisins. Pour ⅓ of the batter into the prepared pan.

In a small mixing bowl blend the brown sugar, ⅓ cup of flour, cinnamon, and ¼ cup of butter until crumbly. Sprinkle half of the mixture over the batter in the pan.

Pour another ⅓ of the batter into the pan. Sprinkle with the remaining filling mixture, and top with the remaining batter. Bake at 350° for 50 to 60 minutes or until a toothpick inserted in the center comes out clean. Cool upright in the pan 15 minutes. Turn onto a serving plate and cool completely.

In a small bowl blend the confectioners' sugar with 1 to 2 tablespoons of orange juice to make a smooth glaze. Spoon over the cake.

MAKES 12 SERVINGS.

# Memorial Day Picnic

*A day for traditions. In honor of those who risked or gave their lives so we could enjoy simple pleasures such as those we will experience today, we have chosen an all-American menu for you to share with friends and family. Perhaps even in faraway lands today, men and women serving our country are turning thoughts toward home. This holiday is a good reminder to keep them all in our frequent prayers.*

---

ROSEMARY TOASTED WALNUTS

TUNA PASTA SALAD

MELON WEDGES WITH BERRY SAUCE

ROAST BEEF SANDWICHES

BLUEBERRY CARROT CAKE

---

*Almighty God, in whose hands lies the destiny of men and nations, Let not the hopes of men perish, nor the sacrifices of men be in vain.*

*O holy and life-giving Spirit, enable us by thy grace to root out from our common life the bitterness of ancient wrongs and the thirst to avenge the betrayals of long ago. Save us from the tyranny of history and set us free in a new obedience to serve each other in the present hour.*

*Accepting the redemption wrought for us, we believe that all our sins of yesterday are covered by thy mercy; grant us therefore grace and courage to give and to receive the forgiveness which alone can heal today's wounds. Draw us, O Lord, towards loving kindness and guide us into the way of peace.*

*ANONYMOUS*

# Rosemary Toasted Walnuts

2 tablespoons unsalted butter
2 tablespoons walnut oil or olive oil
1 pound walnut halves (about 4 cups)
⅓ cup chopped fresh rosemary or 2
     tablespoons dried, crumbled
1 tablespoon coarse (kosher) salt
1 teaspoon paprika
⅛ teaspoon cayenne

In a large roasting pan combine the butter and oil, and heat in a 325° oven for about 3 minutes or until the butter has melted. Add the nuts, and stir to coat well. Spread in a single layer.

Sprinkle the rosemary, salt, paprika, and cayenne over the nuts. Bake at 325° for 15 to 20 minutes, shaking and stirring several times, until golden brown and fragrant. Drain on paper towels. Serve warm or at room temperature. Store in an airtight container.

MAKES 4 CUPS.

# Tuna Pasta Salad

1 12½-ounce can tuna in water, drained and
     flaked
2 16-ounce cans mixed vegetables, drained
1 10-ounce carton frozen peas, thawed and
     drained
6 stalks celery, finely chopped
1 medium onion, finely chopped
1 green bell pepper, finely chopped
6 eggs, hard-boiled and chopped
2 cups small elbow macaroni, cooked
1½ to 2 cups mayonnaise
1 tablespoon white vinegar
2 teaspoons prepared mustard
Salt, pepper, and paprika to taste

In a large bowl combine all the ingredients. Toss until well mixed.

MAKES 10 TO 12 SERVINGS.

# Melon Wedges with Berry Sauce

1 cup halved fresh strawberries
1 cup fresh blueberries
½ cup orange juice
¼ cup sugar
1 honeydew melon or cantaloupe, halved and
     seeded

In a medium bowl combine the strawberries, blueberries, orange juice, and sugar, and mix well. Chill 1 to 2 hours.

Peel the melon, and cut into 8 wedges. Spoon the chilled mixture over wedges.

MAKES 8 SERVINGS.

# Roast Beef Sandwiches

1 18-inch loaf pumpernickel bread,
     approximately 3½ inches in diameter
1 bunch scallions, chopped
1 8-ounce package cream cheese, room
     temperature
3 pounds cooked beef brisket or thinly sliced
     rare roast beef
4 tomatoes, sliced
1 pound bacon, fried crisp
Mayonnaise

Slice the bread in half lengthwise, hollowing out some of the top and bottom pieces. In a medium bowl combine the scallions and cream cheese, and blend well. Spread the mixture about ¼-inch thick on the bottom half of the loaf, covering to the edge of the bread. Layer the meat and tomato slices twice, and top with bacon slices. Spread the top half of the loaf generously with mayonnaise, and put the sandwich halves together. Slice the sandwich with a serrated knife diagonally at 2-inch intervals.

MAKES 8 TO 10 SERVINGS.

# Blueberry Carrot Cake

2 cups all-purpose flour
2 teaspoons baking powder
2 teaspoons ground cinnamon
1 teaspoon baking soda
1 teaspoon salt
1 cup sugar
½ cup firmly packed light brown sugar
1 cup corn oil
¼ cup walnut oil
4 eggs
4 medium carrots, peeled and coarsely grated
2 cups fresh blueberries, rinsed and picked over
1 cup coarsely chopped walnuts

*B*utter and flour a 10-cup bundt or ring pan. In a medium bowl combine the flour, baking powder, cinnamon, baking soda, and salt. Set aside. In a large bowl combine the sugar and brown sugar. Whisk in the corn oil and walnut oil. Beat in the eggs one at a time, whisking until smooth. Stir in the carrots, blueberries, and walnuts. Add the dry ingredients and mix just until combined (do not overmix). The batter will be thick. Spoon into the prepared pan. Bake at 350° for about 1 hour or until the cake begins to pull away from the sides of the pan and a toothpick inserted in the center comes out clean.

Cool in the pan on a rack for 15 minutes. Invert onto a plate and cool completely before serving.

MAKES 8 SERVINGS.

# Father's Day Supper

*It is a very precious thing to have a man in your life who takes fathering seriously. We should never pass up the opportunity to make this man feel appreciated, even if he fusses about it! The old saying is that the way to a man's heart is through his stomach, and that should be reaffirmed today with the feast in his honor!*

---

MANDARIN TOSSED SALAD

BEEF IN SHIRTSLEEVES

DICED POTATOES

MARINATED SQUASH MEDLEY

BANANA-PINEAPPLE CAKE

---

For a father who looked into my infant eyes and smiled while carrying me in his arms, I thank thee. For a man who toiled long hours so that I could be careless and worry-free, I thank thee. For a daddy who swatted my behind when I sassed my mama, I thank thee. For a poor little boy who grew up devoted to giving his family more than he ever had, I thank thee. For the faults in his character that you used to mold me into the adult you wanted me to be, I thank thee. For giving me a dad who instilled in me the magic of finding humor in impossible situations, I thank thee. For memories and Christmas trees and family vacations, I thank thee. I thank thee for my father, who did his very best all along the way.

# Mandarin Tossed Salad

½ cup oil
¼ cup tarragon wine vinegar
¼ cup sugar
½ teaspoon salt
¼ teaspoon pepper
½ teaspoon hot sauce

1 head leaf lettuce, torn
1 cup sliced celery
6 green onions, chopped
3 tablespoons chopped fresh parsley
2 11-ounce cans mandarin oranges, drained
½ cup slivered almonds, toasted

In a jar with a tight-fitting lid combine the oil, vinegar, sugar, salt, pepper, and hot sauce. Cover tightly, and shake vigorously. Chill.

In a large bowl combine the lettuce, celery, green onions, parsley, mandarin oranges, and almonds. Cover with the dressing.

MAKES 8 SERVINGS.

# Beef in Shirtsleeves

1 beef tenderloin
Salt, freshly ground pepper, and dried thyme
    to taste
Butter, softened
1 large onion, finely chopped
2 tablespoons butter, melted
2 tablespoons olive oil
½ pound mushrooms, finely chopped
1 cup chopped ham
½ cup walnuts, chopped
1 16-ounce package frozen puff pastry
1 egg yolk, beaten

Season the beef generously with salt, pepper, and thyme. Brush with softened butter and roast for 20 minutes or until the beef is half cooked. Baste with pan juices after about 10 minutes. Cool and remove the cords.

In a skillet heat 2 tablespoons of butter and the oil, and sauté the onion until transparent, stirring constantly. Add the mushrooms and continue to cook for about 5 minutes, stirring constantly, until the liquid has almost evaporated. Add the ham and walnuts, and season with salt and pepper. Cook 1 minute more. Cool. Spread the cooled beef generously with the onion-ham mixture.

Roll the puff pastry into a sheet large enough to encase the meat. If desired, puff pastry may be rolled out to encase individual fillet slices. Wrap the beef in pastry, cutting away the excess. Secure neatly. Roll remaining pastry thinly. Cut "cuffs" and "buttons" from the pastry and adhere to the wrapped meat with egg yolk. Place the beef on a baking sheet. Brush the pastry with water. Cover the cuffs and buttons with aluminum foil to keep from becoming too brown. Bake at 425° for 10 minutes. Brush the pastry slightly with egg yolk. Reduce the heat to 375° and continue baking without foil for 10 to 15 minutes or until the crust is browned.

Note: Ask the butcher to trim off outside membrane and excess fat from beef tenderloin. The piece should be about 12 inches long, 3 inches in diameter, and weigh 3 pounds. Have meat tied with a cord at 3-inch intervals around circumference.

MAKES 6 SERVINGS.

# Diced Potatoes

4 Russet potatoes (about 1¼ pounds)
⅓ cup vegetable or corn oil
2 tablespoons butter
Salt to taste

Peel the potatoes, and cut each into tiny ¼-inch or less cubes, dropping them into cold water to prevent discoloration.

When ready to cook, drain the cubes in a colander. Run very hot water over them for 10 seconds. Drain well and dry on paper towels or a dishcloth.

In a large nonstick skillet heat the oil over high heat. Add the potatoes and cook, shaking the skillet and stirring the potatoes, for about 6 to 8 minutes or until they are lightly browned. Drain well in a colander, and wipe out the skillet. Discard the oil.

In the same skillet heat the butter, and add the potatoes with salt to taste. Cook, shaking and stirring, for 5 to 6 minutes longer or until the cubes are nicely browned and crisp. Drain and serve hot.

MAKES 4 SERVINGS.

# Marinated Squash Medley

¾ cup olive oil
⅓ cup tarragon wine vinegar
2 tablespoons finely chopped shallots
1 clove garlic, minced
½ teaspoon salt
¼ teaspoon pepper
¼ teaspoon dried thyme
3 medium yellow squash, sliced
3 medium zucchini, sliced

In a jar with a tight-fitting lid combine the olive oil, vinegar, shallots, garlic, salt, pepper, and thyme, and shake well.

In a serving bowl combine the squash and zucchini. Pour the dressing over the squash, and toss gently. Cover and chill for 4 hours.

Toss again just before serving.

MAKES 8 SERVINGS.

# Banana–Pineapple Cake

3 cups all-purpose flour
1 teaspoon baking soda
1 teaspoon ground cinnamon
2 cups sugar
1 teaspoon salt

1½ cups oil
1 8-ounce can crushed pineapple, with syrup
1½ teaspoons vanilla extract
3 eggs
2 cups diced bananas

Fresh strawberries

Grease a 10-inch tube pan.

In a large mixing bowl, sift together the flour, baking soda, cinnamon, sugar, and salt. Add the oil, pineapple, vanilla, eggs, and banana, and mix until blended. Do not beat. Pour into pan and bake at 350° for 1 hour and 20 minutes.

The cake will crack a little on top. Place the pan on a rack to cool. Serve with fresh strawberries.

MAKES 12 SERVINGS.

# Juneteenth

*Although January 1, 1863, was the official date that the Emancipation Proclamation codified freedom and equality for all races in the United States, that freedom had yet to be enforced in many communities. In Texas, Louisiana, and parts of surrounding states, it was not until some six months later, when General Gordon Granger landed with federal troops in Galveston with the express purpose of forcing slave owners who still held their slaves to give them their freedom, that the real celebrating could begin. Thus, in that part of the country, June 19, 1865, or "Juneteenth," is celebrated as the effective anniversary of freedom from slavery.*

---

CORNMEAL FRITTERS

FRIED CHICKEN

COLLARD GREENS WITH RED ONIONS AND BACON

MACARONI AND CHEESE

SOUTHERN FRIED OKRA

VINEGAR PIE

---

## THEY'D PRAY

My master used to ask us children, "Do your folks pray at night?" We said "No," 'cause our folks had told us what to say. But the Lord have mercy, there was plenty of that going on. They'd pray, "Lord, deliver us from under bondage."

## GO DOWN, MOSES

When Israel was in Egypt's land:
Let my people go;
Opress'd so hard they could not stand,
Let my people go.

Chorus: Go down, Moses,
Way down in Egypt's land,
Tell old Pharaoh,
Let my people go.

"Thus saith the Lord," bold Moses said,
Let my people go;
"If not I'll smite your first-born dead,"
Let my people go.

No more shall they in bondage toil,
Let my people go;
Let them come out with Egypt's spoil,
Let my people go.

When Israel out of Egypt came,
Let my people go;
And left the proud oppressive land,
Let my people go.

O, 'twas a dark and dismal night,
Let my people go;
When Moses led the Israelites,
Let my people go.
'Twas they that led the armies through,
Let my people go.

## Cornmeal Fritters

4 cups white cornmeal
3 tablespoons sugar
2½ teaspoon salt
1 to 2 cups boiling water
Vegetable oil

In a large mixing bowl combine the cornmeal, sugar, and salt. Gradually add boiling water, stirring with a wooden spoon, until the batter holds together.

In a large cast-iron skillet heat ½-inch of vegetable oil over medium-high heat. Drop the batter by the tablespoon into the hot oil, 2 or 3 at a time. Press into 4-inch circles about 1 inch thick and fry, turning once, for about 4 minutes per side or until golden with a thick crust. Drain on paper towels and serve immediately with butter. Repeat the procedure with the remaining batter.

MAKES 10 FRITTERS.

## Fried Chicken

1 3½-pound chicken
4 cups buttermilk
3 cups all-purpose flour
2 teaspoons paprika
1 teaspoon cayenne pepper
2 teaspoons salt
1 teaspoon freshly ground black pepper
Peanut oil

Wash the chicken and cut into 8 pieces. Place in a nonreactive pan, and add the buttermilk. Cover and refrigerate for at least 2 hours or as long as overnight.

In a large plastic bag combine the flour, paprika, cayenne pepper, salt, and freshly ground black pepper, and shake to mix. In a cast-iron skillet heat ¾-inch of oil over medium-high heat. Shake each piece of chicken in the seasoned flour until well coated. When the oil is very hot but not smoking add the chicken, largest pieces first, skin-side down. (Work in batches if the skillet is small.) Reduce the heat to medium and cook, turning once, for 12 to 15 minutes per side or until the chicken is golden brown and crispy. Drain on paper towels.

MAKES 4 SERVINGS.

## Collard Greens with Red Onions and Bacon

4 pounds collard greens (preferably small leaves)
½ pound sliced bacon, cut crosswise into fourths
3 medium red onions, chopped coarse (about 3 cups)
1¼ cups chicken broth
¼ cup cider vinegar
2 tablespoons firmly packed dark brown sugar (or to taste)
Red pepper flakes

Remove and discard the coarse stems and leaves from the collard greens. Wash and drain the greens well, and chop them coarsely.

In a heavy stockpot cook bacon in 2 batches over moderate heat until crisp and transfer to paper towels to drain. Pour off all but about 3 tablespoons drippings and sauté the onions, stirring occasionally, until browned slightly and tender. Transfer the onions with a slotted spoon to a bowl.

To the pot add the broth, vinegar, brown sugar, red pepper flakes, and about half of the bacon, stirring until sugar is dissolved. Add about half the collards, tossing until wilted slightly. Add the remaining collards, cover, and cook 30 minutes more or until the collards are very tender.

Serve topped with remaining bacon.

MAKES 8 SERVINGS.

# Macaroni and Cheese

1 8-ounce package elbow macaroni
3 cups milk
¾ teaspoon salt
White pepper to taste
¼ cup unsalted butter
¼ cup all-purpose flour
3 cups grated extra-sharp Cheddar cheese

In a 6-quart pan cook the macaroni until tender in 5 quarts of boiling salted water. Drain well.

In a saucepan stir together the milk, salt, and pepper, and heat over moderate heat, stirring constantly, until hot but not boiling. Remove pan from heat.

In a heavy saucepan melt the butter over low heat and gradually add the flour, whisking constantly. Cook for 3 minutes, stirring constantly and being careful not to let it brown.

Add the warm milk to the roux in a stream, stirring constantly, and cook over moderate heat until steaming hot and thickened slightly. Do not let the sauce boil. Reduce the heat to low, and add about two-thirds of the Cheddar cheese, stirring until melted. Remove the pan from the heat.

In a large bowl stir together the macaroni and sauce and transfer to a 3-quart shallow baking dish. Sprinkle with the remaining Cheddar cheese.

Bake at 350° in the middle of the oven for 30 minutes or until the cheese is melted and bubbling.

MAKES 4 TO 6 SERVINGS.

# Southern Fried Okra

1½ cups sliced fresh okra, blanched and cooled
   (or 1 10-ounce box frozen sliced okra)
1 cup cornmeal
½ cup all-purpose flour
½ teaspoon salt
Freshly ground pepper to taste
Vegetable oil

If using frozen okra, allow it to thaw. Place the okra in a colander to drain for 30 minutes before proceeding.

In a shallow bowl mix together the cornmeal, flour, and salt. Add pepper if desired. Roll the okra in cornmeal to coat each piece, then set aside for 1 hour. This will keep the coating from falling off during the frying.

In a large skillet heat ½ inch of oil or more. When the oil is hot add the okra pieces 1 layer deep and cook until brown, about 5 minutes. Roll with a fork to turn and brown on the other side. Remove the cooked okra to a paper towel to drain.

Cover with a paper towel to keep warm while cooking the remaining okra. Remove to a warm oven prior to serving, if needed.

Note: Do not crowd the okra. Leave enough space to keep the slices turning so as not to burn.

MAKES 6 SERVINGS.

# Vinegar Pie

5 eggs
2 tablespoons all-purpose flour
1 cup sugar
3 tablespoons melted butter, cooled
3 tablespoons cider vinegar
1 teaspoon vanilla extract
½ cup raisins
½ teaspoon ground cinnamon
½ teaspoon grated nutmeg
1 cup sour cream
1 9-inch unbaked pie crust
Whipped cream (optional)

In a large mixing bowl beat the eggs with a whisk. Add the flour, sugar, butter, vinegar, vanilla, raisins, cinnamon, nutmeg, and sour cream. Stir just until mixed. Pour the filling into the pie crust.

Bake at 350° for about 1 hour until the top is golden. (There will be tiny bubbles on the surface, but the filling should not wiggle when pan is shaken.) Serve warm or cold. Top with whipped cream if desired.

MAKES 6 SERVINGS.

# A Graduation Day Buffet

*Remember the feelings you had upon graduating from high school or college—relief, excitement, just a little apprehension, impatience? One of the most encouraging things was that everyone, even perfect strangers, really wished you well. This buffet in honor of the graduate is one more way to make that statement of affirmation: Well Done!*

BROILED BACON-WRAPPED SHRIMP

CHEESY CORN MUFFINS

APRICOT CHICKEN

GREEN BEANS IN SPRING SAUCE

PEACH CHEESECAKE BARS

## BE THOU MY VISION

Be Thou my vision, O Lord of my heart,
Be all else but naught to me, save that Thou art;
Be Thou my best thought in the day and the
    night,
Both waking and sleeping, thy presence my
    light.

Riches I heed not, nor man's empty praise:
Be Thou mine inheritance now and always;
Be Thou and Thou only the first in my heart:
O Sovereign of heaven, my treasure Thou art.

High King of heaven, Thou heaven's bright Sun,
O grant me its joys after victory is won;
Great Heart of my own heart, whatever befall,
Still be Thou my vision, O Ruler of all.

FROM THE IRISH, C. 8TH CENTURY
TRANSLATED BY MARY ELIZABETH BYRNE
VERSIFIED BY ELEANOR HENRIETTA HULL

# Broiled Bacon-wrapped Shrimp

2 pounds large shrimp (13 to 15 per pound)
1 cup olive oil
¼ cup white wine vinegar
6 tablespoons chopped fresh dill
4 cloves garlic, minced
10 slices very lean bacon, very thinly sliced

Peel and devein the shrimp, leaving the tails intact. In a mixing bowl combine the olive oil, vinegar, dill, and garlic. Add the shrimp and marinate overnight.

Cut each slice of bacon into thirds and wrap each shrimp with a piece. Secure well with toothpicks. Place the shrimp on a baking sheet and broil for 4 minutes on each side, being careful not to burn the bacon or overcook the shrimp.

MAKES ABOUT 30.

# Cheesy Corn Muffins

1 cup sifted all-purpose flour
¼ cup sugar
3 teaspoons baking powder
¼ teaspoon salt
¾ cup cornmeal
1 cup milk
¼ cup cooking oil
1 egg, well beaten
¾ cup shredded Cheddar cheese
Poppy seeds (optional)

Grease 24 mini-muffin cups. In a medium bowl sift together the flour, sugar, baking powder, and salt. Stir in the cornmeal. Add the milk, oil, egg, and Cheddar cheese and stir just until the dry ingredients are moistened. Spoon into the prepared pans, filling each cup two-thirds full. Sprinkle with poppy seeds if desired. Bake at 425° for 15 minutes.

MAKES 2 DOZEN.

# Apricot Chicken

12 fryer quarters
Salt and pepper to taste
2 tablespoons butter
1½ cups chopped onion
2 cloves garlic, crushed
½ cup ketchup
6 tablespoons soy sauce
¾ cup apricot preserves
1½ cups orange juice
3 teaspoons dry mustard
2 green bell peppers, cut into strips
6 cups hot cooked rice

Season the chicken pieces with salt and pepper and place them in a greased baking pan. Cover and bake at 350° for 30 minutes.

In a saucepan melt the butter and sauté the onions and garlic until tender. Add the ketchup, soy sauce, preserves, orange juice, and dry mustard, and simmer for 15 minutes. Spoon half the sauce over the chicken. Return the chicken to oven and continue baking, uncovered, for 20 minutes. Spoon the remaining sauce over the chicken, and sprinkle with the pepper strips. Bake 20 minutes longer.

Serve the chicken and sauce over rice.

MAKES 12 SERVINGS.

## Green Beans in Spring Sauce

2 tablespoons olive oil
1½ cups chopped onion
4 cloves garlic, minced
4 tomatoes, peeled and chopped
1 teaspoon salt
1 teaspoon Tabasco sauce
1 teaspoon sugar
1½ cups light cream
4 pounds French-style green beans, fresh or
    frozen

In a large saucepan heat the oil, and sauté the onion, garlic, and tomatoes for 3 minutes, stirring frequently. Add the remaining ingredients and bring to a boil. Reduce the heat, cover loosely, and cook just until tender. Serve hot or cold.

MAKES 12 SERVINGS.

## Peach Cheesecake Bars

½ cup all-purpose flour
½ cup sugar
½ teaspoon double-acting baking powder
¼ teaspoon salt
¼ cup cold unsalted butter, cut into bits
1 large egg

1 8-ounces package cream cheese, softened
4 tablespoons sugar
1 teaspoon vanilla extract
1 large egg, room temperature
1 teaspoon fresh lemon juice
1 tablespoon all-purpose flour
⅛ teaspoon salt
2 peaches, thinly sliced

In a medium bowl sift together ½ cup of flour, ½ cup of sugar, the baking powder, and ¼ teaspoon salt. Add the butter, and combine the mixture until it resembles coarse meal. Add 1 egg and blend well. Spread the mixture onto the bottom of a 9 x 13-inch baking pan.

In a separate bowl beat together the cream cheese, 2 tablespoons of sugar, and vanilla with an electric mixer until the mixture is combined well. Add 1 egg, the lemon juice, 1 tablespoon of flour, and salt, and beat until smooth. Spread the mixture evenly over the batter.

Arrange the peaches in one layer on top of the cheese layer, and sprinkle with 1 tablespoon of sugar. Bake at 350° for 18 to 20 minutes or until just golden. Sprinkle the cheesecake with the remaining 1 tablespoon of sugar, let it cool, and cut it into 3 x 1-inch bars.

MAKES 36 BARS.

# Summer Menus

# A Wedding Luncheon

*A wedding luncheon is a wonderful way to participate in the celebratory atmosphere and really help the bride out. This is a super time to honor the wedding party and show your devotion to the bride or groom's family as well. Fill the room with flowers and serene music, and give everyone a calm in the flurry! When we think of love, can we ever surpass the eternal words of the apostle Paul?*

---

CUCUMBER MINT BUTTER SANDWICHES

FRESH VEGETABLES WITH DIJON DIP

LIME MUFFINS

FETA AND OREGANO SOUFFLÉS IN TOMATOES

SHRIMP AND CHICKEN SALAD WITH LEMON-BASIL DRESSING

SUNFLOWER CAKE

---

*Though I speak with the tongues of men and of angels, but have not love, I have become sounding brass or a clanging cymbal. And though I have the gift of prophecy, and understand all mysteries and all knowledge, and though I have all faith, so that I could remove mountains, but have not love, I am nothing. And though I bestow all my goods to feed the poor, and though I give my body to be burned, but have not love, it profits me nothing. Love suffers long and is kind; love does not envy; love does not parade itself, is not puffed up; does not behave rudely, does not seek its own, is not provoked, thinks no evil; does not rejoice in iniquity, but rejoices in the truth; bears all things, believes all things, hopes all things, endures all things. Love never fails. But whether there are prophecies, they will fail; whether there are tongues, they will cease; whether there is knowledge, it will vanish away. For we know in part and we prophesy in part. But when that which is perfect has come, then that which is in part will be done away. When I was a child, I spoke as a child, I understood as a child, I thought as a child; but when I became a man, I put away childish things. For now we see in a mirror, dimly, but then face to face. Now I know in part, but then I shall know just as I also am known. And now abide faith, hope, love, these three; but the greatest of these is love.*

*1 CORINTHIANS 13*

# Cucumber Mint Butter Sandwiches

2 tablespoons sour cream
1 ounce fresh mint leaves, chopped
2 cups unsalted butter
⅛ teaspoon salt
3 to 4 large cucumbers, peeled and sliced thin
60 slices thin white bread

In a food processor blend the sour cream and mint. Add the butter 1 tablespoon at a time. Pulse. Add the salt and blend well. Spread half the slices with a thin layer of the mint butter. Add 5 to 6 cucumber slices to each half, overlapping slightly. Top with the remaining bread. Trim the crusts from the sandwiches, and cut each sandwich in half lengthwise.

MAKES 60 SANDWICHES.

# Fresh Vegetables with Dijon Dip

4 cloves garlic
2 tablespoons chopped onion
½ cup Dijon mustard
6 tablespoons red wine vinegar
2 tablespoons white wine vinegar
½ teaspoon salt
2 tablespoons fresh basil or oregano (or
	1 teaspoon dried)
¼ teaspoon black pepper
4 drops Tabasco sauce
½ cup safflower oil
Fresh basil (or oregano) for garnish
Raw vegetables for dipping

In a food processor finely chop the garlic and onion. Add the mustard and vinegars, and blend well. Blend in the salt, basil, pepper, and Tabasco. With the machine running, add the oil very slowly. Refrigerate until ready to serve. Garnish with fresh herbs and serve with vegetables for dipping.

MAKES 2 CUPS.

# Lime Muffins

3½ cups all-purpose flour
½ cup cornmeal
4 teaspoons baking powder
1 teaspoon baking soda
½ teaspoon salt
1 cup melted butter
2 cups sugar
2 tablespoons grated lime peel
4 eggs
2 cups milk
⅔ cup fresh lime juice

Butter 24 muffin cups. In a medium bowl combine the flour, cornmeal, baking powder, baking soda, and salt. In a bowl combine the butter, ⅔ cup of the sugar, lime peel, eggs, and milk. Add the dry ingredients, and beat just until blended.

Fill the buttered muffin cups almost full. Bake at 350° for about 20 to 25 minutes or until golden and a toothpick inserted in a muffin comes out clean. Remove from the pans and cool about 10 minutes.

Dip the top of each muffin in lime juice, then dip in the remaining sugar. Place sugared-side-up on a rack. As they cool, the sugar will form a crumb topping. Serve as soon as possible.

MAKES 24 MUFFINS.

# *Feta and Oregano Soufflés in Tomatoes*

12 firm-ripe small or plum tomatoes (about 1½ pounds)
1 teaspoon salt
2 tablespoons unsalted butter
¼ cup finely chopped shallot
2 tablespoons all-purpose flour
⅔ cup milk
1½ cups finely crumbled feta
2 large egg yolks
6 tablespoons thinly sliced scallion
2 teaspoons dried oregano, crumbled
4 large egg whites, at room temperature
Generous pinch salt
Generous pinch cream of tartar

*L*ightly oil a large baking pan.

Cut ½ inch from the rounded end of each tomato, and scoop out the seeds and inner pulp, leaving a ¼-inch shell. Sprinkle inside the tomatoes with the salt, invert them onto paper towels, and let them drain for 20 minutes.

In a small heavy saucepan melt the butter, and sauté the shallot over moderately low heat for 3 minutes, stirring constantly. Stir in the flour and cook for 3 minutes, stirring constantly. Whisk in the milk, and simmer the mixture for 5 minutes, stirring constantly. Transfer the mixture to a bowl and let it cool for 5 minutes. Whisk in the feta, egg yolks, scallion, and oregano.

In a large bowl beat the egg whites and a pinch of salt with an electric mixer until frothy. Add the cream of tartar, and beat until the egg whites just hold stiff peaks. Stir one-fourth of the whites into the feta mixture, and gently fold in the remaining whites.

Spoon the soufflé mixture into the tomatoes, mounding it slightly. Arrange the tomatoes in the prepared pan. Bake at 400° for 15 to 20 minutes or until the tops are golden and a skewer inserted in the center comes out clean.

MAKES 12 SERVINGS.

# *Shrimp and Chicken Salad with Lemon-Basil Dressing*

4 cups clean, packed fresh basil leaves
2 eggs
2 egg yolks
1 cup plus 2 tablespoons fresh lemon juice, strained
2 teaspoons salt
1 teaspoon freshly ground black pepper
2 cups olive oil
⅔ cup corn or vegetable oil

8 boneless chicken breasts (about 5 pounds)
4 teaspoons salt
1½ pounds medium shrimp, shelled and deveined (about 40)
2 medium heads radicchio, leaves separated, rinsed, and dried
2 medium heads Boston or Bibb lettuce, leaves separated, rinsed, and dried
Sprigs of fresh basil for garnish
Freshly grated pepper to taste

*I*n a food processor fitted with the metal blade combine the basil, eggs, egg yolks, lemon juice, salt, and pepper. Process 1 minute or until smooth. With the machine running, pour in the olive and corn oils in a steady stream. Adjust the seasonings. Refrigerate, allowing the dressing to return to room temperature before using.

In a stockpot cover the chicken breasts in cold water. Stir in the salt, set the pot over medium heat, and simmer for about 15 minutes, turning the chicken breasts once.

Stir in the shrimp and simmer for about 4 minutes or until they are pink, curled, and just cooked through. With a slotted spoon remove the shrimp. Let the chicken breasts cool in the cooking liquid to room temperature. Drain and remove any fat.

Line a platter with alternating leaves of radicchio and lettuce. Slice the chicken breasts on the diagonal. Arrange the chicken and shrimp on the leaves, and drizzle some of the dressing over them. Garnish with sprigs of basil. Top with freshly grated pepper.

MAKES 12 SERVINGS.

## Sunflower Cake

1¼ cups sugar
Peel of 2 lemons
3 eggs
¾ cup unsalted butter, room temperature
¾ cup sour cream
¼ cup plus 2 tablespoons orange juice
2 tablespoons lemon juice
1¾ cups cake flour
2 teaspoons baking powder
¾ teaspoon baking soda
¾ teaspoon salt

⅔ cup sugar
Peel of 1 lemon
5 egg yolks
½ cup lemon juice
Pinch salt
½ cup butter, melted and hot

3 cups confectioners' sugar
Peel of 2 lemons
Salt to taste
4 to 5 tablespoons sour cream
5 tablespoons unsalted butter
2 tablespoons lemon curd

In a food processor mince 1¼ cups of sugar and the peel of 2 lemons until the peel is very fine. Add the eggs and process for 1 minute. Add the butter and process for 1 minute more. Add the sour cream, orange juice, and 2 tablespoons of lemon juice, and mix well. In a medium bowl sift together the flour, baking powder, baking soda, and salt. Add the dry ingredients to the batter and mix just to combine. Do not overmix.

Butter three 8-inch pans, line with waxed paper, and butter again. Divide the batter among the pans. Bake at 350° on the middle rack for 20 minutes. Cool for 10 minutes on wire racks. Remove the cake from the pans, and cool completely.

Mince ⅔ cup of sugar and the peel of 1 lemon in the food processor until peel is very fine. Add the yolks, ½ cup of lemon juice, and a pinch of salt, and process. With the machine running, pour the hot butter through the feed tube. Pour the mixture into a saucepan, and cook over low heat, stirring constantly, until thickened. Do not boil. Set the lemon curd aside to cool.

In the food processor mince the confectioners' sugar and lemon peel until peel is very fine. Add the remaining ingredients. Refrigerate the icing for 15 minutes. If the icing is too thin, add more confectioners' sugar.

To assemble, spread the bottom and middle layers of cake with the lemon curd. Cover the top and sides of the cake with the lemon icing.

MAKES 12 SERVINGS.

# A Schoolmates' Reunion Brunch

*One of the very best things about friendship is that it can pick up just where it left off—months, or even years ago. Common bonds hold strong through the years, and it's always a pleasure to rediscover that at class reunions. We fuss over grayer hair and other insignificant details, and then, when the day comes, none of those small details matter, and we're surprised by the rush of warmth we feel for these people from our past. As our society becomes more and more mobile, events such as this take on a greater significance in our lives. Three cheers for the host and hostess who take the time and effort to make an event like this possible.*

SPICED CREAM COFFEE

CHOCOLATE FRENCH TOAST

SUGARED BACON

STRAWBERRIES DEVONSHIRE

CAPPUCCINO CAKE

*THE ROADMAKER*

God be shielding thee by each dropping sheer,
God make every pass an opening appear,
God make to thee each road a highway clear,
And may he take thee in the clasp
Of his own two hands' grasp.

## Spiced Cream Coffee

3 teaspoons ground cinnamon
2 teaspoons grated nutmeg
¼ cup sugar
2 cups heavy cream
12 cups coffee
8 teaspoons chocolate syrup

In a large bowl stir 1 teaspoon of the cinnamon and the nutmeg and sugar into the cream, and whip. Divide the coffee into 6-ounce portions. Stir 1 teaspoon of chocolate syrup, and ¼ teaspoon of cinnamon into each cup. Top with whipped spiced cream.

MAKES 8 SERVINGS.

## Chocolate French Toast

4 eggs
½ cup milk
1 tablespoon sugar
¼ teaspoon salt
¼ cup semisweet chocolate morsels
2 tablespoons strawberry or raspberry all-fruit preserves
16 slices oatmeal or white bread
2 tablespoons butter or margarine
1 tablespoon confectioners' sugar
2 tablespoons unsweetened cocoa

In a shallow dish combine the eggs, milk, sugar, and salt. Set aside.

In a small glass measure, microwave the chocolate on high for 40 to 60 seconds or until melted, stirring once. Remove from microwave; stir in preserves. Divide the chocolate mixture and spread over 8 slices of the bread. Top with remaining slices to make 8 sandwiches.

In a large nonstick skillet melt 1 tablespoon of butter over medium heat. Dip 4 of the sandwiches in the egg mixture; turning to coat. Place the sandwiches in the skillet. Cook for 4 to 6 min-

utes or until golden brown, turning once. Remove to an ovenproof platter and keep warm in a 200° oven. Repeat with the remaining butter, egg mixture and sandwiches.

In a cup mix the confectioners' sugar and cocoa. Sprinkle or sift over the French toast before serving.

MAKES 6 SERVINGS.

## Sugared Bacon

1 pound bacon (regular bacon, not thick sliced), room temperature
1¼ cups firmly packed brown sugar
1 tablespoon ground cinnamon (optional)

Cut each slice of bacon in half crosswise. Mix sugar and cinnamon together and thoroughly coat each slice of bacon. Twist the slices, and place on rack in a broiler pan or jelly roll pan. Bake at 350° for 15 to 20 minutes or until crisp and the sugar is bubbly. Watch closely because the sugar burns quickly. Cool on foil. Serve at room temperature.

Note: These may be made ahead and left at room temperature.

MAKES 16 SERVINGS.

## Strawberries Devonshire

1 3-ounce package cream cheese, softened
2 tablespoons sugar
Pinch salt
1 cup heavy cream
Fresh whole strawberries, stems on

In a small bowl combine the cream cheese, sugar, salt, and 2 tablespoons of heavy cream. Beat until fluffy. In a separate bowl whip the remaining cream. Fold into the cream cheese mixture. Place in a serving bowl, surrounded by fresh strawberries.

MAKES 1¾ CUPS.

# *Cappuccino Cake*

¾ cup oil
½ cup honey
¾ cup plus 2 tablespoons sugar
4 large eggs
½ cup whole milk
½ cup sour cream

2 cups all-purpose flour
½ cup cocoa
2 teaspoons baking powder
1 teaspoon baking soda
1 tablespoon instant coffee granules
2 teaspoons ground cinnamon
¼ teaspoon grated nutmeg
¼ teaspoon ground cloves

Confectioners' sugar for topping

Grease a bundt pan. In a large bowl combine the oil, honey, sugar, eggs, milk, and sour cream with an electric mixer until thoroughly blended. In a separate bowl combine the remaining ingredients. Add the dry ingredients to the liquid mixture, beating until just blended. Pour the batter into the prepared pan. Bake at 350° oven for about 1 hour or until a toothpick inserted in the center comes out clean. Allow to cool in the pan, then remove to a cake rack to finish cooking. Sprinkle with sifted confectioners' sugar.

MAKES 12 SERVINGS.

# A Canada Day Buffet

*Formerly Dominion Day, Canada Day marks the anniversary of the unifying of Upper and Lower Canada, New Brunswick, and Nova Scotia as the Dominion of Canada. The day is celebrated much as Americans celebrate their Independence Day, mais avec une qualitée unique!*

BASIL CORNBREAD

POACHED SALMON

SAUTÉED VEGETABLE MEDLEY

SOUR CREAM RAISIN PIE

*A   large and lonely land*
*Under a lonely sky*
*Save for the friendly stars;*
*A land not to be wooed in a day*
*But by a long courting.*

THOMAS SAUNDERS
*(1949)*

*O God, the God of all righteousness, mercy, and love: Give us all grace and strength to conceive and execute whatever may be for thine honour and the welfare of the nation; that we may become at last, through the merits and intercession of our common Redeemer, a great and a happy because a wise and understanding people; to thy honour and glory.*

# Basil Corn Bread

⅔ cup all-purpose flour
⅔ cup yellow cornmeal
2 teaspoons baking powder
½ teaspoon salt
⅛ teaspoon freshly ground pepper
1 large egg
⅔ cup milk
2 tablespoons minced fresh basil or 2 teaspoons dried
¼ cup unsalted butter, melted

Grease an 8-inch square baking dish. In a medium bowl sift together the flour, cornmeal, baking powder, salt, and pepper. In a separate bowl beat the egg lightly. Add the milk, basil, and cooled butter. Stir the liquid mixture all at once into the flour mixture, mixing just until blended. Pour the batter into the prepared pan, and smooth the top with a spatula. Bake at 400° for 15 to 18 minutes or until light golden and beginning to pull away from the sides of the pan.

Cool completely. Cut into 2-inch squares, split horizontally, and butter.

Makes 16 servings.

# Poached Salmon

2 cups water
1 cup dry white wine or vermouth
4 slices fresh gingerroot, flattened
1 tablespoon black peppercorns, bruised
1 bay leaf
1 2½-pound piece salmon fillet
Salt to taste

½ cup sour cream
¼ cup mayonnaise
2 teaspoons Dijon mustard
1½ tablespoons grated peeled fresh gingerroot
1 teaspoon freshly grated orange peel

2 tablespoons fresh orange juice
1½ tablespoons drained green peppercorns
½ teaspoon sugar
1 tablespoon white wine vinegar
Salt to taste

Butter a large baking dish. In a small saucepan bring the water and wine to a boil with the gingerroot, black peppercorns, and bay leaf. Remove the pan from the heat and let the mixture stand for 5 minutes. Remove the bay leaf.

In the prepared baking dish arrange the salmon skin-side down. Sprinkle with salt to taste. Add the wine mixture. Bake at 400° for 20 to 25 minutes, until the salmon just flakes and is cooked through.

In a medium bowl whisk together the sour cream, mayonnaise, mustard, gingerroot, orange peel, orange juice, green peppercorns, sugar, vinegar, and salt to taste. Let the sauce stand at room temperature for 20 minutes for the flavor to develop.

Place the fish on a serving dish, and drizzle with some of the sauce. Serve the remaining sauce on the side.

Makes 6 servings.

# Sautéed Vegetable Medley

3 tablespoons oil
8 medium green bell peppers, cut into strips
4 medium onions, thinly sliced
1 16-ounce bag carrots, julienned
1½ teaspoons salt
1 teaspoon basil
½ teaspoon black pepper

In a large skillet heat the oil. Add the peppers, onions, carrots, salt, basil, and black pepper, and sauté over medium heat until the vegetables are tender but still crisp.

Makes 8 servings.

# Sour Cream Raisin Pie

1 cup sugar
2½ tablespoons all-purpose flour
1 teaspoon cinnamon
¼ teaspoon cloves
½ cup raisins
½ cup walnuts (or pecans)
1½ cups sour cream
3 large eggs, separated
1 baked 9-inch pie shell
6 tablespoons sugar

*I*n the top of a double boiler combine 1 cup of sugar, flour, cinnamon, and cloves, and stir to blend. Add the raisins, nuts, and sour cream, and blend well. Place the pan over boiling water and bring the mixture to a boil. Add a small amount of the sour cream mixture to the egg yolks, then slowly add the egg yolks to the boiling sour cream mixture, stirring constantly. Cook until thickened. Remove the top pan from the boiling water, and allow to cool.

Pour the filling into the pie shell. Beat the egg whites until stiff peaks form, adding 6 tablespoons of the sugar gradually while beating. Spread the meringue over the pie. Bake at 300° until the meringue has browned.

MAKES 8 SERVINGS.

# Back Yard Cookout on the Fourth

*Samuel Adams was one of the firebrands of the Revolution. The founder of the Committees of Correspondence and the Sons of Liberty, he challenged the authority of the English to violate the common law tradition in the colonies and eventually led the armed resistance to the King's tyranny following the Boston Massacre. In this widely circulated verse, he detailed the standards for the American demand for freedom.*

RED CABBAGE SLAW

BARBECUED RIBS

SOUTHERN GRILLED CHICKEN

BARBECUED PINTO BEANS

DEVILED EGGS

AMERICAN POTATO SALAD

CHERRY-BLUEBERRY COBBLER

*A ll temporal power is of God,*
*And the magistratal, His institution, laud,*
*To but advance creaturely happiness aubaud:*
        *Let us then affirm the Source of Liberty.*

*Ever agreeable to the nature and will,*
*Of the Supreme and Guardian of all yet still*
*Employed for our rights and freedom's thrill:*
        *Thus proves the only Source of Liberty.*

*Though our civil joy is surely expressed*
*Through hearth, and home, and church manifest,*
*Yet this too shall be a nation's true test:*
        *To acknowledge the divine Source of Liberty.*

# Red Cabbage Slaw

1 large head red cabbage, shredded
1 pound large carrots, coarsely grated
4 celery stalks, cut into 1½-inch julienne strips
⅓ cup fresh lemon juice
¼ cup cider vinegar
1½ tablespoons Dijon mustard (or to taste)
1 cup oil
1 tablespoon celery seeds
Salt and freshly ground pepper to taste

*I*n a large bowl toss the vegetables. In a blender or food processor blend the lemon juice, vinegar, and mustard. With the motor running, add the oil in a stream and blend until just emulsified. Add the celery seeds, and salt and pepper to taste. Pour over the vegetables and toss well. Cover and refrigerate until chilled.
MAKES 12 SERVINGS.

# Barbecued Ribs

1 bottle KC Masterpiece hickory barbecue
    sauce
½ bottle Old El Paso hot taco sauce
1 tablespoon Worcestershire sauce
1 tablespoon soy sauce
1 teaspoon garlic powder
Heavy sprinkle red pepper flakes
6 slabs (6 to 7 pounds) baby back ribs, cut in
    half

*I*n a large bowl combine the barbecue sauce, taco sauce, Worcestershire sauce, soy sauce, garlic powder, and red pepper flakes.

Foil-line a large baking pan. Place 4 half-slabs in the pan meaty-side up. Baste with sauce. Place the remaining slabs in the pan and baste. Bake at 325° for 30 minutes.

Turn meaty-side down and baste. Bake for 30 minutes. Turn meaty-side up, baste, and bake for 30 more minutes.

Heat the broiler or prepare the grill. Cook until charred, turning only once.
MAKES 6 TO 8 SERVINGS.

# Southern Grilled Chicken

2 tablespoons crunchy peanut butter
5 tablespoons fresh lemon juice
4 tablespoons grated onion
¼ cup best-quality olive oil
½ teaspoon salt
¼ teaspoon freshly ground pepper
2 chickens, cut into pieces

*I*n a small saucepan heat the peanut butter with the lemon juice until melted. Add the onion. Slowly add the olive oil, stirring constantly. Season with salt and pepper.

Broil the chicken on the grill, 15 minutes per side, basting several times with sauce. Any remaining sauce may be heated and served with the chicken.
MAKES 6 SERVINGS.

# Barbecued Pinto Beans

1 tablespoon oil
1 large white onion, finely chopped
1 green bell pepper, finely chopped
3 16-ounce cans pinto beans
1½ cups barbecue sauce
½ cup salsa
2 tablespoons sugar

*I*n a large saucepan heat the oil, and sauté the onion and pepper until soft. Add the remaining ingredients and heat thoroughly. Serve warm.
MAKES 6 TO 8 SERVINGS.

# Deviled Eggs

6 hard-cooked eggs, peeled and halved
    lengthwise
3 tablespoons mayonnaise
1 tablespoon Dijon mustard
⅛ teaspoon salt
Paprika

With a small spoon lift the egg yolks out of the whites. In a small bowl combine the egg yolks, mayonnaise, mustard, and salt, and mix well with a fork until smooth. Adjust the seasonings, if necessary.

Arrange the egg white halves on a serving platter. Mound some of the yolk mixture into each and sprinkle with paprika. Serve immediately, or cover and refrigerate until ready to use.

MAKES 1 DOZEN.

# American Potato Salad

4 pounds boiling potatoes, peeled
½ cup white wine vinegar
½ cup olive oil
Salt and freshly ground black pepper to taste
1 cup thinly sliced purple onions
1 cup coarsely chopped celery
3 medium cucumbers, peeled, seeded, and
    sliced
2 cups mayonnaise (or as needed)
¼ cup Dijon mustard (or to taste)
6 hard-cooked eggs, peeled and quartered
1 cup chopped Italian parsley

In a kettle of cold, salted water bring the potatoes to a boil and cook until tender but still firm.

Drain and thickly slice the potatoes into a large bowl. Sprinkle the hot potatoes with vinegar, olive oil, salt, and pepper.

Add the onions, celery, cucumbers, mayonnaise, and mustard, and toss gently to combine.

Add the eggs and parsley, and toss again. Cool to room temperature, cover, and refrigerate overnight.

Before serving toss again, adjust the seasoning, and add more mayonnaise if needed.

MAKES 8 TO 10 SERVINGS.

# Cherry-Blueberry Cobbler

1 cup all-purpose flour
1 cup whole wheat flour
2 teaspoons baking powder
¼ teaspoon salt
½ cup margarine or butter, softened
1 cup sugar
¾ cup milk
2 cups fresh pitted tart red cherries (or frozen
    cherries, thawed)
1 cup fresh blueberries (or frozen blueberries,
    thawed)
½ to ¾ cup sugar
2 cups cherry juice or as needed
Confectioners' sugar
Vanilla ice cream

Grease a 9 x 13-inch baking pan. In a medium bowl stir together the flours, baking powder, and salt. In a separate bowl beat the margarine and 1 cup of sugar with an electric mixer until fluffy. Add the flour mixture alternately with the milk, and beat until smooth. Spread the batter evenly in the prepared pan.

Drain the fruit, reserving the liquid if using frozen fruit. Add enough cherry juice or water to the fruit liquid to equal 2 cups. Sprinkle batter with cherries and blueberries. Sprinkle with the remaining ½ to ¾ cup sugar, depending on the sweetness of the fruit. Pour 2 cups of the fruit juice mixture over the fruit.

Bake at 350° for 40 to 45 minutes or until a toothpick inserted in the center of the cake comes out clean. Cool. Sprinkle lightly with confectioners' sugar. Serve warm with ice cream.

MAKES 12 SERVINGS.

# Independence Day Buffet

*Have you ever followed a time line of history, tracing the origins and demises of civilizations before ours? Untold volumes have been written about the causes and corruptions that led to those sad endings. Perhaps one thread is common to them all: forgetfulness of what makes a people one, of what ideas and convictions were once, and are still, worth living and dying for. In short, what made the voice of that civilization unique? What is America's voice? Is there a difference between freedom and independence? Let the fireworks begin!*

---

PORK ROAST WITH CHERRY GLAZE

BROCCOLI IN LEMON VINAIGRETTE

RICE WITH FRESH DILL

SUMMER FRUIT SALAD WITH MINT

VANISHING BLUEBERRY PIE

BERRY ICE CREAM

---

*The Silent Warrior folds his hands in rest,*
*His labors done, he sleeps in deep repose,*
*Amid the silent hills he loved the best,*
*Enshrouded in the softly sifting snows.*

*The guest of God. A pilgrim on this earth,*
*He struggled long, to bless the sons of men,*
*In every testing time he proved his worth,*
*The value of his truth with tongue and pen.*

*The warrior sleeps, but still his work goes on.*
*His vital words will give the nation power,*
*On many a battle front, the truth he won,*
*Will serve us well, in some perplexing hour.*

*The warrior sleeps, but such men never die,*
*Their influence goes on both broad and deep,*
*It girds the world and reaches to the sky,*
*So still they labor, though they seem to sleep.*

*The warrior sleeps, we may not call him back,*
*Although we miss him on this earthly way,*
*He gave us richly of the things we lack,*
*We well may ponder them each passing day.*

*The warrior sleeps, his victory is won,*
*The nation wept beside the great man's bier,*
*If we remember all that he has done,*
*His name will brighter grow each passing year.*

*If we can build his simple sense of God,*
*Of right and wrong, into our warp and woof,*
*Then we are reconciled that 'neath the sod,*
*The warrior sleeps, a champion of truth.*

*God give us vision as the years go by,*
*To measure up to this great Puritan,*
*Who wrote his title in the earth and sky,*
*And being great, was just a simple man.*

## Pork Roast with Cherry Glaze

1 8-pound pork roast

1 12-ounce jar cherry preserves
¼ cup red wine vinegar
¼ teaspoon ground cinnamon
¼ teaspoon ground cloves
2 tablespoons corn syrup
¼ teaspoon salt
¼ teaspoon grated nutmeg

Place the roast in a large pan and bake at 350° for 2 hours and 30 minutes.

While the roast is cooking, in a small saucepan combine the glaze ingredients. Bring to a boil and simmer for 5 minutes. Drain the grease from the roast. Pour the glaze over the roast, and cook for 30 minutes or until done.

MAKES 6 TO 8 SERVINGS.

## Broccoli in Lemon Vinaigrette

2 pounds fresh broccoli, trimmed and cut into
      4-inch stalks
1 tablespoon fresh lemon juice
2 tablespoons white-wine vinegar
1 teaspoon Dijon mustard
½ cup oil
¼ teaspoon freshly grated lemon peel
½ teaspoon salt
Pinch freshly ground black pepper
Tabasco sauce to taste
¼ cup thinly sliced red onion
8 thin slices lemon for garnish

In a large saucepan of lightly salted boiling water cook the broccoli for about 3 minutes or until crisp-tender. Drain and refresh the broccoli under cold water. Shake off the excess water and drain on paper towels. Place on a serving dish, cover tightly with plastic wrap, and chill.

In a small bowl whisk together the lemon juice, vinegar, and mustard. Whisk in the oil. Add the lemon peel, salt, and pepper, and season with Tabasco sauce to taste.

Just before serving toss the broccoli with the vinaigrette. Arrange the broccoli and red onion slices on a platter. Garnish with lemon slices.

MAKES 6 SERVINGS.

## Rice with Fresh Dill

3 cups water, salted to taste
1½ cups converted rice (not instant)
3 tablespoons unsalted butter
3 tablespoons chopped fresh dill

In a large pot bring the water to boil, and add the rice. When it returns to a boil, reduce the heat to a slow simmer and cook for 10 minutes, uncovered. Test for doneness, allowing 1 or 2 more minutes if needed. Drain in a colander, and rinse with hot water for a minute. Return the rice to the cooking pot along with the butter, and toss. Add the dill just before serving.

MAKES 6 SERVINGS.

# Summer Fruit Salad with Mint

1 pint blueberries
1 pint raspberries
1 pint strawberries
2 to 3 very ripe peaches
Sugar to taste
Lemon juice to taste
Poppy seeds
Fresh mint leaves, chopped
Large mint leaves for garnish

Wash and drain the blueberries, raspberries, strawberries, and peaches. Hull the strawberries and peel, pit, and slice the peaches. In a serving bowl combine all the fruits. Sweeten the fruit mixture with sugar, sprinkle with lemon juice to keep the peaches from turning brown, and toss to mix well. Sprinkle with the poppy seeds and chopped mint, and garnish with the mint leaves.

MAKES 12 SERVINGS.

# Vanishing Blueberry Pie

1 cup sour cream
2 tablespoons all-purpose flour
¾ cup sugar
1 teaspoon vanilla extract
¼ teaspoon salt
1 large egg, beaten
2½ cups fresh blueberries, washed and drained
1 unbaked 9-inch pie shell
3 tablespoons all-purpose flour
3 tablespoons unsalted butter, room
    temperature
3 tablespoons chopped pecans (or walnuts)

In a large bowl blend together the sour cream, flour, sugar, vanilla, salt, and egg until smooth. Fold in the blueberries. Pour the filling into the pastry shell. Bake at 400° for 25 minutes.

In a small bowl combine the flour, butter, and nuts. Sprinkle the topping over the pie, and bake for 10 additional minutes. Chill before serving.

MAKES 8 SERVINGS.

# Berry Ice Cream

6 tablespoons sugar
1½ teaspoons all-purpose flour
Pinch salt
1 cup half and half
1 large egg, lightly beaten
1 cup milk
1 teaspoon vanilla extract
1 pint fresh strawberries, washed, hulled, and
    crushed

In the top of a double boiler mix the sugar, flour, and salt. Stir in the half and half. Place the pan over boiling water and cook for about 5 minutes, stirring constantly. Cover, and continue cooking over boiling water for 10 minutes. Remove the pan from the heat and spoon a little of the hot mixture into the beaten egg to heat it. Add the warmed egg to the milk and return the double boiler to the heat. Cook for about 5 minutes, stirring constantly, until the mixture coats a spoon. Strain and chill.

When cold, stir in the milk, vanilla, and berries. Pour the mixture into an ice-cream maker and freeze according to the manufacturers' directions.

MAKES ABOUT 1½ PINTS.

# Johnny Appleseed Children's Dinner

*The real story of John Chapman, alias Johnny Appleseed, is so enshrouded in myth as to be virtually unknown. With that concern out of the way, enjoy a retelling of the story of a man who planted fruit trees all across the countryside that would one day be front yards and farmland, made friends with the Indians, blew with the West winds singing "Yankee Doodle Dandy," and loved animals, all of nature, and God. And to this day, how do we define what's American? God, country, mother, apple pie!*

---

DATE-PEANUT MALTED MILK

PIGS-IN-A-BLANKET

MACARONI AND CHEESE CASSEROLE

ONION RINGS

GINGERED FRUIT SALAD

JOHNNY APPLESEED PUDDING

PEANUT BUTTER CHOCOLATE CHUNK BROWNIES

---

*L ord help me live from day to day*
*In such a self-forgetful way,*
*That even when I kneel to pray,*
*My prayer shall be for others.*

CHARLES D. MEIGS (1792)


THE JOHNNY APPLESEED PRAYER

*The Lord is good to me*
*And so I thank the Lord*
*For giving me the things I need*
*Like the sun and the rain*
*And the apple seeds.*
*The Lord is good to me.*

# Date-Peanut Malted Milk

2 cups milk
6 tablespoons malted milk powder
3 pints vanilla ice cream, softened slightly
1½ cups chopped pitted dates
¾ cup unsalted dry-roasted peanuts
2 tablespoons finely chopped dry-roasted
    peanuts

In a blender combine the milk, malt powder, ice cream, dates, and peanuts, and blend until the mixture is combined well. Pour the mixture into 12-ounce glasses, and sprinkle chopped peanuts over each serving.

MAKES 6 SERVINGS.

# Pigs-in-a-Blanket

1 cup all-purpose flour
1 teaspoon baking powder
¼ teaspoon baking soda
¼ teaspoon salt
3 tablespoons toasted wheat germ
¼ cup chilled vegetable shortening
⅓ cup buttermilk
1 large egg yolk
10 hot dogs, halved crosswise

Grease a large baking sheet. In a medium bowl stir together the flour, baking powder, baking soda, salt, and wheat germ. Blend in the shortening with a pastry blender or your fingertips until mixture resembles coarse meal. In a small bowl whisk together the buttermilk and egg yolk. Stir the liquid mixture into the flour mixture, stirring until the mixture just forms a moist dough.

Turn the dough onto a floured surface and knead 4 times. Roll out into a 12-inch square. Cut the dough into 1½-inch-wide strips, and roll a strip around the middle of a hot dog until the dough just overlaps. Cut the pig-in-a-blanket free from the strip. Repeat with the remaining hot dogs and dough. Arrange them as they are made seam-side down on the prepared baking sheet.

Bake at 375° for about 15 minutes or until pale golden.

MAKES 20 PIGS-IN-A-BLANKET.

# Macaroni and Cheese Casserole

2 cups corkscrew macaroni
2 tablespoons margarine or butter
½ cup chopped onion
1 clove garlic, minced
2 tablespoons all-purpose flour
¼ teaspoon cracked black pepper
Dash ground red pepper
2 cups milk
1½ cups shredded American cheese
1 3-ounce package cream cheese, cubed and
    softened
2 teaspoons prepared mustard
1 large tomato, peeled, seeded, and finely
    chopped (about 1 cup)
⅓ cup grated Parmesan cheese
¾ cup soft breadcrumbs
2 tablespoons margarine or butter, melted
¼ teaspoon paprika

Cook the macaroni according to package directions and drain well.

In a large saucepan melt 2 tablespoons margarine and cook the onion and garlic until tender but not brown. Stir in the flour, black pepper, and ground red pepper. Add the milk all at once. Cook, stirring constantly, until slightly thickened and bubbly. Add the shredded American cheese, cream cheese, and mustard, and stir until the cheese melts.

Stir the tomato, Parmesan cheese, and cooked macaroni into the cheese sauce. Transfer to a 1½-quart casserole dish. Toss the breadcrumbs with 2 tablespoons of melted margarine. Sprinkle the breadcrumbs over the macaroni mixture. Bake at 350° for 25 to 30 minutes or until bubbly. Sprinkle with paprika. Let the macaroni and cheese stand for 10 minutes before serving.

MAKES 6 SERVINGS.

## Onion Rings

6 large onions
4 eggs, lightly beaten
4 cups buttermilk
4 cups all-purpose flour
2 teaspoons baking soda
Salt to taste
Oil

Peel the onions and cut into ¼-inch slices. Divide into individual rings and soak in a large bowl of ice water for 1 hour.

In a separate bowl beat together the eggs and buttermilk. Add the flour, baking soda, and salt to taste.

Heat the cooking oil in a deep fryer to 350°. Pat the onion rings dry with paper towels, and dip in the buttermilk batter. Fry the onion rings until golden brown, turning once. Cook only a small amount at a time to maintain temperature.

Drain on paper towels. Season with salt while the onion rings are still hot. Keep warm in a 250° oven.
MAKES 6 TO 8 SERVINGS.

## Gingered Fruit Salad

1 8-ounce package cream cheese, softened
⅓ cup orange juice
2 tablespoons sugar
½ teaspoon ground ginger
3 cups green grapes, halved
3 cups strawberries, hulled and halved
3 Granny Smith apples, cored and chopped
1 11-ounce can mandarin oranges, drained

In a small bowl combine the cream cheese, orange juice, sugar, and ginger, blending well.

In a large bowl combine the grapes, strawberries, apples, and oranges. Pour the dressing over the fruit, and toss gently. Serve immediately.
MAKES 8 SERVINGS.

## Johnny Appleseed Pudding

1 cup sugar
1 egg
2 tablespoons all-purpose flour
¼ teaspoon ground cinnamon
¼ teaspoon grated nutmeg
1 teaspoon baking powder
Pinch salt
3 medium cooking apples, peeled, cored, and chopped
½ cup chopped nuts
Whipped cream

Butter a 9-inch pie plate. In a medium bowl beat the sugar and egg with an electric mixer until frothy. In a separate bowl combine the flour, spices, baking powder, and salt. Stir the dry ingredients into the egg mixture. Fold in the apples and nuts. Pour into the prepared pie pan. Bake at 350° for 20 to 25 minutes or until crusty and brown.

Serve warm with whipped cream.
MAKES 6 TO 8 SERVINGS

# Peanut Butter Chocolate Chunk Brownies

6 tablespoons unsalted butter
½ cup chunky peanut butter (or freshly ground)
1¼ cups firmly packed light brown sugar
2 large eggs
2 teaspoons vanilla extract
¾ cup all-purpose flour
1 teaspoon baking powder
¼ teaspoon salt
4 ounces bittersweet or semisweet chocolate, coarsely chopped

Generously butter and flour an 8-inch square baking pan. In large bowl beat butter with an electric mixer until smooth. Add the peanut butter and beat until well blended, scraping down the sides of the bowl occasionally. Beat in the brown sugar. Add the eggs 1 at a time, beating well after each addition. Beat in the vanilla. In a separate bowl sift together the flour, baking powder, and salt. Add the dry ingredients to the peanut butter mixture, and beat until blended. Stir in the chocolate.

Transfer the batter to the prepared pan, and smooth the top with a spatula. Bake at 350° for about 30 minutes or until a toothpick inserted 2 inches from the edge of the pan comes out with moist crumbs attached. Transfer the pan to a rack, and cool completely.

Cut the brownies into squares.

MAKES 9 SERVINGS.

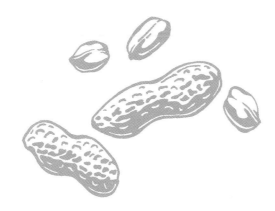

# Postgame Baseball Barbecue

*The sounds stay with us: the crack of the bat, the thud of the glove, the roar of the fans. We could bring to mind smells, too: hot dogs, popcorn, dust, and sweat. But the true baseball fan can outscore us all with the sacrosanct liturgy of the game: the statistic! They can remember the year, the inning, and perhaps even the weather conditions. It's the part of the game that stays with us when the last cleat shuffles out of the last dugout at the end of the season, be it a child's size five or an adult's thirteen. No matter the outcome of the game you've just returned from, we've put together a menu that will rig the results— the cook is going to bat 1000!*

GAZPACHO

CAJUN HAMBURGERS

APPLE SLAW

FRESH CORN AND BLACK-EYED PEA SALAD

GRILLED ONIONS

APPLE PIE WITH PECAN CRUMBLE

*Show us thy mercy, Lord, and grace divine;
Turn thy bright face, that it on us may shine,
That all the men on earth enlightened so,
Their own salvation, and thy ways may know.
O let thy people praise thy blessed name,
And let all tongues and nations do the same,
And let all mortal men rejoice in this,
That God their judge and just his judgment is.
O let thy people praise thy blessed name,
And let all tongues and nations do the same,
Then shall the earth bring forth a rich increase,
And God shall bless us and his holy fear
Possess the hearts of all men everywhere.*

*PSALM 67*

# Gazpacho

2 large tomatoes, peeled, seeded, and coarsely
    chopped
1 large green bell pepper, seeded and finely
    chopped
2 medium cucumbers, peeled, seeded, and
    coarsely chopped
1 clove garlic, peeled and minced
1 Bermuda onion, peeled and thinly sliced
1½ tablespoons chopped fresh basil
1½ tablespoons chopped fresh chervil
1½ tablespoons chopped fresh tarragon
1½ tablespoons chopped fresh chives
1½ tablespoons chopped fresh parsley
½ cup olive oil
3 teaspoons lemon or lime juice
1½ teaspoons salt or to taste
1 14-ounce can beef consommé
1 46-ounce can V-8 Juice
2 cups croutons, fried in olive oil

In a large bowl combine all of the ingredients except the croutons and mix together. Refrigerate for at least 4 hours. Serve in chilled bowls, and top each serving with ¼ cup of croutons.

MAKES 6 TO 8 SERVINGS.

# Cajun Hamburgers

2 pounds ground lean beef
1 green bell pepper, cored, seeded, and minced
½ cup chopped scallions
3 cloves garlic, minced
2 teaspoons ground cumin
2 teaspoons dried oregano
1 teaspoon dried thyme
1 teaspoon paprika
Red pepper flakes to taste
Salt to taste
6 hamburger buns, toasted
Sliced tomatoes
Sour cream

In a large bowl combine the beef, green pepper, scallions, and garlic. Add the cumin, oregano, thyme, paprika, red pepper flakes, and salt to taste, and mix until blended. Shape the meat into 6 patties.

Grill the patties over medium coals to the desired doneness. Place the hamburgers on toasted buns, and top with sliced tomatoes and sour cream.

MAKES 6 HAMBURGERS.

# Apple Slaw

4½ cups thinly sliced cored, unpeeled red
    apples (about 1½ pounds)
3 cups finely shredded green cabbage
1 cup sour cream
3 tablespoons lemon juice
1 tablespoon sugar
¾ teaspoon salt
⅛ teaspoon pepper
1 tablespoon poppy seeds

In a large bowl lightly toss together all of the ingredients until combined. Refrigerate for at least 1 hour before serving.

MAKES 8 SERVINGS.

# Fresh Corn and Black-Eyed Pea Salad

⅓ cup balsamic vinegar
1 tablespoon hot, sweet mustard
¼ cup chopped fresh parsley
½ teaspoon salt
¼ teaspoon freshly ground black pepper
½ teaspoon Creole seasoning
¼ cup extra virgin olive oil
1½ cups fresh scraped cooked corn
½ pound shelled fresh black-eyed peas,
    seasoned, cooked with ham or bacon
1 medium red bell pepper, chopped
1 medium Vidalia or red onion, chopped
3 stalks celery, chopped

*I*n a small bowl blend together the vinegar, mustard, parsley, salt, pepper, and Creole seasoning. Whisk in the oil and set the bowl aside. In a serving bowl combine the corn, peas, bell pepper, onion, and celery. Toss the dressing with the vegetables and refrigerate until ready to serve, but not longer than 12 hours.

MAKES 6 SERVINGS.

# Grilled Onions

6 large onions, thinly sliced
Salt and pepper to taste
¾ cup butter

*P*lace the onion slices on a large piece of heavy duty foil. Season generously with salt and pepper. Place a pat of butter on each serving. Tightly seal the foil and place on the rack over hot coals. Roast for 20 to 25 minutes.

MAKES 6 SERVINGS.

# Apple Pie with Pecan Crumble

1 9-inch pie crust
3 pounds apples, peeled and thinly sliced
2 tablespoons lemon juice
1 tablespoon cornstarch
⅔ cup packed brown sugar
⅓ cup sugar
1¾ teaspoons ground cinnamon
½ teaspoon grated nutmeg
1 cup all-purpose flour
Pinch salt
6 tablespoons butter
⅓ cup chopped pecans

*T*rim and flute the edges of the pie crust. Put in the freezer for 5 minutes to firm.

In a large bowl toss the apples with the lemon juice, cornstarch, ⅓ cup brown sugar, sugar, 1 teaspoon cinnamon and the nutmeg.

In a medium bowl combine the flour, ⅓ cup brown sugar, ¾ teaspoon cinnamon, and pinch of salt. Add the butter and cut until crumbly. Add the pecans.

Fill the pie shell with the apple mixture and sprinkle the crumb mixture over the top. Bake at 375° for 1 hour to 1 hour and 10 minutes or until the crust is golden and the filling bubbles. Cover loosely with foil if the topping browns too quickly.

MAKES 6 SERVINGS.

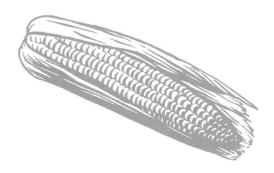

# Welcome to the Neighborhood: A Blessing in Deed

The Selkirk Grace takes its name from Dunbar Douglas, Fourth Earl of Selkirk.
It was probably first delivered as a toast in the Earl's presence at the Heid Inn on
Kirkcudbright High Street in July, 1794. The blessing reminds us in a most simple fashion
that we have reason to pause and show gratitude before each meal for the bounty before us. It
also prods us to share that bounty with and strive to become a blessing to our neighbors and
those within our spheres of influence. Robert Burns, the national bard of Scotland, never met
a stranger. That is a trait worth fostering as we welcome our new neighbors and friends.

---

HONEY-BAKED CHICKEN

BABY CARROTS WITH PINEAPPLE GLAZE

POTATO SALAD

POPPY SEED-HERB DROP BISCUITS

ORANGE POUND CAKE

---

*THE SELKIRK GRACE*

*Some hae meat, and canna eat,*
*And some wad eat that want it;*
*But we hae meat, and we can eat—*
*And sae the Lord be thank it.*

ROBERT BURNS

## Honey-baked Chicken

¼ cup honey
¼ cup soy sauce
¼ cup sesame oil
1 3- to 4-pound chicken, giblets removed,
    rinsed well, and patted dry

*I*n a small bowl whisk together the honey, soy sauce, and sesame oil. Place the chicken in a large plastic bag, and pour the honey mixture over the chicken. Loosely seal the bag and place it in a large dish or bowl in the refrigerator for at least 2 hours. Turn the bag over a few times to evenly coat the chicken.

Remove the chicken from the bag and drain any excess marinade. Place the chicken on a rack in a roasting pan lined with foil. Bake at 400° for 1 hour without opening the oven door. Let the chicken stand for 5 minutes before serving

MAKES 4 SERVINGS.

## Baby Carrots with Pineapple Glaze

3 cups baby carrots (1 pound)
3 medium leeks, sliced ½-inch thick
2 tablespoons water
1 6-ounce can unsweetened pineapple juice
2 teaspoons cornstarch
½ teaspoon grated gingerroot (or ⅛ teaspoon
    ground ginger)
⅛ teaspoon salt
⅛ teaspoon grated nutmeg

*I*n a 2-quart microwave-safe casserole combine the carrots, leeks, and water. Cover and microwave on high power for 9 to 11 minutes or until crisp-tender, stirring once. Drain. Cover to keep warm.

In a 2-cup measure combine the pineapple juice, cornstarch, gingerroot, salt, and nutmeg. Cook uncovered on high for 2½ to 3½ minutes or until thickened and bubbly, stirring every minute until slightly thickened, then stirring every 30 seconds.

Pour the glaze over the carrots and stir to coat.

MAKES 4 SERVINGS.

## New Potato Salad

2 pounds new potatoes, scrubbed and
    quartered
Salt and freshly ground black pepper to taste
2 cups sour cream
⅔ cup chopped purple onion
⅔ cup chopped fresh dill

*I*n a large pot of salted water boil the potatoes for 8 to 10 minutes or until tender but still firm. Drain and place in a salad bowl. Season with salt and pepper to taste. Add the sour cream and toss gently. Add the chopped onion and dill, and toss again. Cool to room temperature. Refrigerate for at least 4 hours.

Just before serving, toss again. Adjust the seasonings to taste, and add more sour cream if needed.

MAKES 4 SERVINGS.

# Poppy Seed-Herb Drop Biscuits

1½ cups all-purpose flour
1 tablespoon baking powder
1 tablespoon poppy seeds
½ teaspoon salt
½ teaspoon dried thyme leaves
⅓ cup butter or margarine, cut into chunks
¾ cup milk

Grease a 9-inch round baking dish. In a large bowl stir together the flour, baking powder, poppy seeds, salt, and thyme leaves. With a pastry blender or 2 knives cut in the butter until the mixture resembles coarse cornmeal. Pour in the milk and stir until the dough is evenly moistened.

Drop the dough in ¼-cup portions about 1 inch apart in the prepared pan. Bake at 450° for 15 to 18 minutes or until the tops of the biscuits are well browned. Serve hot or cold with butter.

MAKES 8 LARGE BISCUITS.

# Orange Pound Cake

1¾ cups sifted cake flour
2 teaspoons baking powder
¼ teaspoon salt
¾ cup sugar
½ cup vegetable oil
½ cup unsweetened orange juice
1 teaspoon grated orange peel
4 egg whites, stiffly beaten

Coat the bottom of an 8½ x 4½-inch loaf pan with cooking spray, dust with flour, and set aside.

In a large bowl combine the flour, baking powder, salt, and sugar. Add the oil and orange juice, and beat with an electric mixer at medium speed until the batter is smooth. Add the orange peel and about one-third of the egg whites, and stir gently. Fold in the remaining egg whites.

Pour the batter into the prepared pan. Bake at 350° for 5 minutes or until a wooden pick inserted in the center comes out clean. Cool in the pan for 10 minutes. Remove the cake from the pan and cool on a wire rack.

MAKES 6 TO 8 SERVINGS.

# A Poolside Buffet

This is the heart of summer: a casual, stress-free style that even applies to our hospitality and entertaining. If you're looking for a great afternoon or evening event that can be very flexible in regard to time and number, here it is! We've even provided a winning menu so you will have one less thing to be concerned with, including several dishes that can be prepared ahead of time so you can enjoy yourself, as well.

HONEYDEW LEMONADE

WILD RICE SALAD

LAYERED GREEN BEAN AND TOMATO SALAD

FISH IN FOIL

SWEET AND SOUR BAKED BEANS

BROWNIE-WALNUT PIE

PEPPERMINT CANDY ICE CREAM

## LEISURE

What is this life if, full of care,
We have no time to stand and stare.

No time to stand beneath the boughs
And stare as long as sheep or cows.

No time to see, when woods we pass,
Where squirrels hide their nuts in grass.

No time to see, in broad daylight,
Streams full of stars, like stars at night.

No time to turn at Beauty's glance,
And watch her feel, how they can dance.

No time to wait till her mouth can
Enrich that smile her eyes began.

A poor life this if, full of care,
We have no time to stand and stare.

W. H. DAVIES

# Honeydew Lemonade

Peel of 2 lemons, removed in strips with a
    vegetable peeler
1 cup fresh lemon juice
¾ cup sugar
1 honeydew melon (about 3½ pounds), seeds
    and peel discarded, cubed
2 cups cold water
2 cups ice cubes
Lemon slices
Mint sprigs

In a small heavy saucepan combine the lemon peel, lemon juice, and sugar. Bring the mixture to a boil, stirring until the sugar is dissolved. Boil for 5 minutes. Pour the syrup through a sieve set over a bowl, and let it cool.

In a food processor purée the honeydew. Force the purée through a fine sieve set over a bowl. In a pitcher combine the syrup, the purée, and the cold water, and stir the mixture well. Just before serving stir in the ice cubes, lemon slices, and mint sprigs.

MAKES ABOUT 8 SERVINGS.

# Wild Rice Salad

1½ cups wild rice
3 cups chicken broth
⅓ cup oil
2 tablespoons raspberry or wine vinegar
2 tablespoons minced shallot (or onion)
2 teaspoons Dijon mustard
¼ teaspoon pepper

Rinse the raw rice and drain well. In a 3-quart saucepan bring the rice and chicken broth to a boil. Reduce the heat, cover, and simmer for 50 minutes or until the rice is tender and most of the liquid has been absorbed, stirring occasionally. Cool.

In a small bowl mix together the oil, vinegar, shallot, mustard, and pepper. Stir the mixture into the cooled rice.

MAKES 8 SERVINGS.

# Layered Green Bean and Tomato Salad

3 tablespoons olive oil
3 tablespoons red wine vinegar
2 tablespoons chopped onion
1 tablespoon snipped fresh basil (or 1 teaspoon
    dried)
1 tablespoon snipped fresh chives
2 teaspoons Dijon mustard
1 teaspoon snipped fresh oregano (or 1/4
    teaspoon dried)
1 teaspoon lemon juice
¼ teaspoon salt
¼ teaspoon pepper
1 pound green beans, cut into 2-inch pieces
2 cups red and/or yellow cherry tomatoes,
    halved
1 large red bell pepper, cut into bite-size pieces
1 large yellow bell pepper, cut into bite-size
    pieces
Fresh chives for garnish (optional)

In a jar with a tight-fitting lid combine the olive oil, vinegar, chopped onion, basil, chives, Dijon mustard, oregano, lemon juice, salt, and pepper. Cover, and shake well. Set the dressing aside.

Place a steamer basket in a saucepan. Add water until it almost touches the bottom of the basket. Bring the water to boiling. Add the fresh green beans, cover, and steam for 18 to 22 minutes or until crisp-tender. Rinse the beans under cold running water, and drain well.

Place the green beans, tomatoes, and sweet pepper pieces in separate bowls. Shake the dressing well and divide it among the 3 bowls containing the vegetables. Cover, and chill the vegetables for 4 to 24 hours, stirring often.

To serve, in a large salad bowl layer the pepper pieces, beans, and tomatoes. If desired, garnish with chives.

MAKES 6 TO 8 SERVINGS.

## Fish in Foil

    8 6-ounce fish fillets (such as red snapper,
        grouper, or pike)
    Salt and freshly ground pepper to taste

    3 medium shallots
    3 medium cloves garlic
    ¾ cup safflower oil
    ¼ cup Dijon mustard
    1 tablespoon plus 2 teaspoons fresh lemon juice
    1 tablespoon dried basil
    4 small tomatoes, thinly sliced
    Salt and freshly ground pepper to taste
    2 tablespoons snipped fresh chives
    Parsley sprigs for garnish

Cut pieces of heavy-duty foil large enough to wrap individual fillets tightly. Rinse the fillets and pat dry. Sprinkle with salt and ground pepper. Set each fillet on foil.

In a food processor mince the shallots and garlic by dropping through the feed tube with the machine running. Add the oil, mustard, lemon juice, and basil, and mix well. Spread over the fillets.

Cover each fillet with overlapping slices of tomato. Sprinkle with salt, pepper, and chives. Wrap the fillets tightly, but do not let the foil touch top of the fish. Place on the grill rack, and grill over medium hot coals, for 10 to 12 minutes, until the fish is firm to the touch. Open a packet to test for doneness. Remove the fish from the foil and transfer to a serving platter. Garnish with parsley sprigs.

MAKES 8 SERVINGS.

## Sweet and Sour Baked Beans

    ¾ cup firmly packed brown sugar
    1 teaspoon dry mustard
    Garlic powder to taste
    ½ teaspoon salt
    ½ cup vinegar
    4 large onions, cut in rings
    2 15-ounce cans cooked dry butter beans,
        drained
    1 16-ounce can baby green lima beans, drained
    1 16-ounce can red kidney beans, drained
    1 16-ounce can baked beans, undrained
    8 bacon slices, fried crisp and crumbled
    4 bacon slices, uncooked

In a small bowl combine the sugar, mustard, garlic powder, salt, and vinegar. In a skillet, pour the vinegar mixture over the onion rings, cover, and simmer for 20 minutes. Add the beans and crumbled bacon, and mix well. Pour into a 3-quart casserole and arrange 4 uncooked strips of bacon on top. Bake at 350° for 1 hour.

MAKES 12 TO 16 SERVINGS.

# Brownie-Walnut Pie

½ cup margarine or butter
3 1-ounce squares unsweetened chocolate, cut up
3 eggs, beaten
1½ cups sugar
½ cup all-purpose flour
1 teaspoon vanilla extract
1 cup chopped walnuts
1 9-inch unbaked pie shell

½ cup margarine
2 1-ounce squares unsweetened chocolate
2 cups sifted confectioners' sugar
1 5-ounce can evaporated milk
1 teaspoon vanilla extract

Peppermint Candy Ice Cream (recipe follows)

*I*n a small heavy saucepan melt ½ cup margarine and 3 squares of chocolate over low heat, stirring frequently. Cool for 20 minutes.

In a large mixing bowl stir together the eggs, sugar, flour, and 1 teaspoon of vanilla. Stir in the cooled chocolate and walnuts. Pour the filling into the pie shell. Bake at 350° for 50 to 55 minutes or until a knife inserted near the center comes out clean. Cool on a wire rack.

In a heavy small saucepan melt ½ margarine or butter and 2 squares unsweetened chocolate over low heat, stirring frequently. Stir in the confectioners' sugar and evaporated milk, and bring to boiling. Reduce the heat and simmer, uncovered, for 8 to 10 minutes, stirring frequently. Remove the pan from the heat. Stir in 1 teaspoon of vanilla. Serve warm with Peppermint Candy Ice Cream.

MAKES 8 SERVINGS.

# Peppermint Candy Ice Cream

2 cups half and half
3½ ounces red-and-white striped peppermint candies, crushed
½ cup superfine sugar

*I*n a large saucepan scald the half and half over medium heat. Remove from the heat and add the candy and sugar. Stir until the candy and sugar are dissolved. Allow the mixture to cool, then chill.

Pour the mixture into an ice-cream maker, and freeze according to the manufacturer's directions.

MAKES APPROXIMATELY 1½ PINTS.

# A Baby Shower Tea

*A life event to celebrate! Anticipation fills the room, and you have brought everyone together to focus on the momentous occasion at hand. Admit it, the room resounds with clucking noises! Advice, family stories, hopes and dreams, and an appropriate place to share (out of hearing of the honoree, of course) that intriguing labor and delivery story one more time. Go ahead, raise your voice a couple of decibels when the gifts are opened. Until men can bear children, this is uniquely feminine territory, and as the menu indicates, we know how to do this right!*

---

SNOW PEAS WITH HONEY MUSTARD AND PECANS

CHICKEN SALAD CREAM PUFFS

AVOCADO PARTY SHRIMP

WHITE CHOCOLATE-DIPPED STRAWBERRIES

BANANA POUND CAKE

PINEAPPLE SHERBET

STRAWBERRY PINEAPPLE ADE

---

## THE CHARACTER OF A HAPPY LIFE

*How happy is he born and taught
That serveth not another's will;
Whose armour is his honest thought,
And simple truth his utmost skill!*

*Whose passions not his masters are;
Whose soul is still prepared for death,
Untied unto the world by care
Of public fame or private breath;*

*Who envies none that chance doth raise,
Nor vice; who never understood
How deepest wounds are given by praise;
Nor rules of state, but rules of good;*

*Who hath his life from rumours freed;
Whose conscience is his strong retreat;*

*Whose state can neither flatterers feed,
Nor ruin make opressors great;*

*Who God doth late and early pray
More of His grace than gifts to lend;
And entertains the harmless day
With a religious book or friend;*

*This man is freed from servile bands
Of hope to rise or fear to fall:
Lord of himself, though not of lands,
And having nothing, yet hath all.*

SIR HENRY WOTTON (1568-1639)

# Snow Peas with Honey Mustard and Pecans

1½ cups pecan halves
¼ cup unsalted butter, melted
½ teaspoon cayenne pepper
¼ teaspoon salt
12 ounces cream cheese
4 teaspoons honey mustard
2 teaspoons packed brown sugar
Salt to taste
Cayenne pepper to taste
50 snow peas, stemmed, strings removed,
    blanched

In a skillet melt the butter. Add the cayenne pepper and salt, and toss the pecan halves in the mixture. Transfer the pecans to a baking sheet. Toast in the oven at 300° for 5 to 10 minutes, until lightly golden (do not overcook—the pecans will darken as they cool). Set aside to cool.

Finely chop the cooled pecans, and place them in a shallow dish. In a medium bowl combine the cream cheese, honey mustard, brown sugar, salt, and cayenne. Spoon the mixture into a pastry bag. Slice each snow pea open along the straight side, and pipe the cream cheese mixture into the pea pods. Dip the stuffing edge of each pea pod into chopped pecans. Arrange the pea pods on a serving platter, cover, and refrigerate until ready to serve.

MAKES 50 APPETIZERS.

# Chicken Salad Cream Puffs

1 cup all-purpose flour
¼ teaspoon salt
⅛ teaspoon ground red pepper
1 cup water
2 tablespoons margarine
2 egg whites
1 egg
Chicken Salad (recipe follows)

In a small bowl combine the flour, salt, and red pepper, and set aside. In a saucepan combine the water and margarine, and bring to a boil. Reduce the heat to low and add the flour mixture, stirring until the mixture is smooth and pulls away from the sides of the pan. Remove the pan from the heat, and cool for 5 minutes.

Spray a baking sheet with cooking spray. Add the egg whites and egg one at a time, beating vigorously with a wooden spoon until smooth. Spoon the mixture into a pastry bag fitted with a ½-inch round tip, and pipe 30 1½-inch mounds onto the prepared baking. Bake at 425° for 10 minutes. Reduce the oven temperature to 350°, and bake and additional 10 minutes. Cool completely on a wire rack.

Cut the tops from the cream puffs, and fill each with Chicken Salad. Serve immediately.

MAKES 30 CREAM PUFFS.

# Chicken Salad

⅓ cup diced celery
¼ cup finely chopped green onions
¼ cup mayonnaise
3 tablespoons chopped fresh parsley
2 tablespoons plain nonfat yogurt
1 tablespoon fresh lemon juice
½ teaspoon salt
½ teaspoon dried basil
¼ teaspoon pepper
1 2-ounce jar diced pimento

1¾ cups chopped cooked chicken breast (about
    ¾ pound)

In a large bowl combine the celery, onions, mayonnaise, parsley, yogurt, lemon juice, salt, basil, pepper, and pimento. Mix well. Add the chicken and mix well. Cover and refrigerate until chilled.

MAKES 3 CUPS.

## Avocado Party Shrimp

10 pounds large shrimp
2 cups sliced celery
2 6-ounce jars whole mushrooms, drained
½ cup chopped green onions

2 large ripe avocados, mashed
1 cup lemon juice
½ cup vegetable oil
2 pods garlic, crushed
1 teaspoon red pepper flakes
¼ cup horseradish
¼ cup Creole mustard
2 tablespoons Worcestershire sauce
½ to 1 cup reserved shrimp stock

Lettuce
Red and green bell pepper slices
1 cup seasoned salad olives and/or ripe olives
Fresh basil leaves for garnish

*I*n a large pot boil the shrimp in salted water. Drain, reserving 1 cup of liquid for the dressing. Cool and peel the shrimp.

In a large bowl combine the shrimp, celery, mushrooms, and onions. In a separate bowl combine the avocados, lemon juice, oil, garlic, red pepper flakes, horseradish, Creole mustard, Worcestershire sauce, and reserved shrimp stock. Toss well with the shrimp mixture. Refrigerate until chilled. Serve on a large platter on a bed of colorful lettuce. Top the shrimp with red and green pepper rings and mounds of olives. Garnish with basil leaves.

MAKES 20 SERVINGS.

## White Chocolate-Dipped Strawberries

16 ounces imported white chocolate (such as Tobler or Lindt), chopped
50 strawberries with stems
8 ounces bittersweet or semisweet chocolate, chopped and melted

*L*ine a baking sheet with waxed paper or foil. In the top of a double boiler over barely simmering water melt the white chocolate, stirring until smooth. Remove the pan from the heat. Hold the strawberries by the stem end, and dip halfway into the chocolate, tilting the pan if necessary. Shake excess chocolate back into the pan. Place the berry on the prepared sheet.

Repeat with the remaining berries. Refrigerate for about 30 minutes until the chocolate sets.

Spoon the melted bittersweet chocolate into a pastry bag fitted with a small tip and pipe over the white chocolate portion of the strawberries in zigzag lines. Refrigerate until the chocolate lines set, about 10 minutes.

MAKES 50 DIPPED STRAWBERRIES.

# Banana Pound Cake

2 cups shortening
1 cup butter, softened
6 cups sugar
10 large eggs
6 ripe bananas, mashed
6 tablespoons milk
4 teaspoons vanilla extract
6 cups all-purpose flour
1 teaspoon salt
2 teaspoons baking powder

Grease and flour two 10-inch tube pans. In a large bowl beat the shortening and butter with an electric mixer at medium speed for about 2 minutes or until creamy. Gradually add the sugar, and beat for 5 to 7 minutes. Add the eggs one at a time, beating just until the yellow disappears.

In a medium bowl combine the mashed bananas, milk, and vanilla. In a separate bowl combine the flour, salt, and baking powder. Add the dry ingredients to the shortening mixture alternately with the banana mixture, beginning and ending with the flour mixture. Beat at low speed just until blended after each addition. Pour the batter into the prepared pan.

Bake at 350° for 1 hour and 20 minutes or until a wooden pick inserted in the center of the cake comes out clean. Cool in the pan on a wire rack for 10 to 15 minutes. Remove the cake from the pan, and cool completely on a wire rack.

MAKES ABOUT 24 SERVINGS.

# Pineapple Sherbet

2 large pineapples, trimmed and cored, the flesh shredded with a fork
2 cups unsweetened pineapple juice
1⅓ to 2 cups superfine sugar (depending on sweetness of pineapple)
6 tablespoons fresh lemon juice

Taste the pineapple to judge its sweetness.

In a medium saucepan combine the pineapple juice with the desired amount of sugar. Heat, stirring constantly, until all of the sugar is dissolved. Allow to cool slightly, then add the lemon juice and fresh pineapple. Add more sugar if the mixture is too tart. Allow to cool, then chill.

Pour the mixture into an ice-cream maker, and freeze until firm according to the manufacturer's directions.

MAKES ABOUT 3 PINTS.

# Strawberry Pineapple Ade

1 6-ounce can frozen lemonade concentrate, thawed
1 6-ounce can frozen pineapple juice concentrate, thawed
1 6-ounce can frozen strawberry daquiri mix concentrate, thawed
5 cups ice cold water
Ice cubes (or ice ring)
1 cup fresh strawberries, hulled and sliced

In a large pitcher stir together the lemonade concentrate, pineapple juice concentrate, and daquiri concentrate. Add cold water, stirring gently. Add ice. Float the strawberries on the top.

MAKES 15 SERVINGS.

# Labor Day Cookout

*This holiday feels like our last chance to wave good-bye to summertime. Don't miss the opportunity to share summer memories and gear up for autumn with your favorite group of friends. The menu celebrates the best of the summer harvest, so take the time to search out the freshest foods and herbs available. Of course, you'll want to celebrate work and the worker: our gratitude for work to perform, and those who take it seriously so that we can spend days like this . . . .*

---

OKRA, ONION, AND TOMATO SALAD

GRILLED SALMON STEAKS

GRILLED CORN WITH BACON-MUSTARD BUTTER

BLACKBERRY BANANA SPLITS

OLD-FASHIONED LEMONADE

OLD-FASHIONED LIMEADE

---

*Oh! You gotta get a glory
In the work you do;
A Hallelujah chorus
In the heart of you.
Paint, or tell a story,
Sing, or shovel coal,
But you gotta get a glory
Or the job lacks soul.*

*The great, whose shining labors
Make our pulses throb,*

*Were men who got a glory
In their daily job.
The battle might be gory
And the odds unfair,
But the men who got a glory
Never knew despair.*

*Oh, Lord, give me a glory,
When all else is gone!
If you've only got a glory
You can still go on.*

# Okra, Onion, and Tomato Salad

1½ pounds small okra
½ cup minced red onion
⅓ cup distilled white vinegar
2 cloves garlic, minced
Salt and freshly ground pepper to taste
1 cup olive oil
2 large tomatoes, seeded and chopped

In a large saucepan of salted water boil the okra for 3 to 5 minutes or until tender. Drain it, and refresh it in a bowl of ice and cold water. Drain the okra well, and place it in a large shallow dish. Add the onion.

In a small bowl whisk together the vinegar, garlic, and salt and pepper to taste. Add the oil in a stream, and whisk until well blended. Pour the dressing over the okra mixture, and toss until well coated. Cover, and refrigerate for 1 hour. Just before serving gently stir the tomatoes into the salad.

MAKES 8 TO 12 SERVINGS.

# Grilled Salmon Steaks

¼ cup butter, softened
2 teaspoons grated lemon peel
1 teaspoon lemon juice
¼ cup olive oil
2 teaspoons dried thyme (or 1 tablespoon fresh)
8 1-inch thick salmon steaks
Salt and pepper to taste

In a small bowl mix the butter with the lemon peel and juice. Place the butter on a piece of plastic wrap and roll to form a 1-inch cylinder. Refrigerate until firm. In a small bowl combine the oil and thyme. Heat the grill. Brush the fish with thyme oil, and sprinkle with salt and pepper. Grill the fish, brushing occasionally with oil, until opaque, 4 or 5 minutes per side. Top each hot steak with 2 thin slices of lemon butter and serve.

MAKES 8 SERVINGS.

# Grilled Corn with Bacon-Mustard Butter

¼ pound smoky sliced bacon, minced
1 cup unsalted butter, softened
3 tablespoons mild, prepared coarse-grained mustard
1 teaspoon freshly ground black pepper
16 ears sweet corn, with husks

In a skillet over medium heat cook the bacon until crisp but tender.

In a small bowl cream together the butter, bacon, and mustard. Stir in the pepper. Transfer the butter to a bowl or small crock.

Do not remove the husks or silks from the corn. Lay the ears on the grill rack and grill for 5 to 7 minutes, turning once or twice, until the outer husks are charred.

Peel the corn (or let the guests peel their own), and serve immediately, accompanied by the bacon-mustard butter and freshly ground pepper.

MAKES 8 SERVINGS.

## Blackberry Banana Splits

2 cups whipping cream
2 cups whole milk
9 egg yolks
⅔ cup sugar
2¼ teaspoons light molasses
2 ripe bananas

3 cups fresh blackberries
¾ cup sugar (or as needed)
1½ tablespoons fresh lemon juice
1½ teaspoons grated lemon peel

8 ripe bananas
Sweetened whipped cream (optional)

*I*n a large heavy saucepan scald the cream with the milk. Remove the pan from the heat. In a small bowl whisk together the yolks with ⅔ cup of sugar and the molasses. Gradually whisk in half of the cream mixture. Return the mixture to the saucepan and stir over medium-low heat for about 7 minutes or until the custard thickens and leaves a path on the back of a spoon when a finger is drawn across. Do not boil. Strain the custard into a bowl.

Peel 2 bananas. In a food processor purée the bananas. Mix the purée into the custard. Cover, and refrigerate the custard until well chilled.

Transfer the custard to an ice cream maker, and process according to the manufacturer's instructions. Freeze in a covered container for several hours.

In a large saucepan combine the blackberries, ¾ cup of sugar, lemon juice, and lemon peel. Cook over medium heat until the sugar dissolves. Increase the heat, and bring to a boil. Taste, adding more sugar if desired. Strain through a sieve set over a medium bowl, pressing on the solids with the back of a spoon. Cover, and refrigerate until well chilled.

Peel 8 bananas and split in half lengthwise. Arrange 2 halves in each bowl. Top each with 3 small scoops ice cream. Pour the blackberry sauce over the ice cream and bananas. Top with whipped cream if desired.

MAKES 8 SERVINGS.

## Old-Fashioned Lemonade

6 or 7 lemons, washed
½ to ¾ cup sugar
4 cups cold water
Ice cubes

*T*hinly slice 2 of the lemons. In a 6-cup pitcher combine the sliced lemons and sugar to taste. Press the sliced lemons with a potato masher or wooden spoon to release the juice.

Squeeze enough of the remaining lemons to make ⅔ cup of juice. Add the juice to the pitcher along with the cold water. Stir to combine. Serve in chilled glasses over ice.

MAKES 6 SERVINGS.

## Old-Fashioned Limeade

10 medium limes, well scrubbed
Water
1¾ to 2 cups sugar
Salt to taste

*R*emove and coarsely chop the peel of 4 limes. In a saucepan combine the lime peel and 2 cups minus 2 tablespoons of water. Cover the pan, and simmer over low heat for about 2 minutes. Remove the pan from the heat, and set aside for 5 minutes. Remove the peel and add the sugar to the flavored water. Simmer over low heat for about 5 minutes or until the sugar has dissolved and a light syrup is formed. Allow to cool.

Juice the remaining limes to get 1¼ cups of mixed juice and pulp. Combine the cooled syrup, juice, and salt. This double-strength limeade will keep in the refrigerator for about a week, and indefinitely in the freezer.

To serve, mix equal parts limeade with water, seltzer or weak tea and serve in a tall glass with lots of ice.

MAKES 12 SERVINGS.

# Fall Menus

# Rosh Hashanah

*Celebrated in September or October, Rosh Hashanah is also known as The Feast of Trumpets. With this feast, Israel begins preparation for the Day of Atonement by self-examination. Commonly used as a biblical motif, trumpets were employed to announce God's presence to Abraham when he laid his son Isaac on the altar, and when He descended upon Mt. Sinai to give the Ten Commandments. The Israelites were instructed to blow them at prescribed times during the overtaking of Jericho and during festal celebrations. Watchmen were often instructed to warn the cities under their protection with trumpets. Poet George Wither (1588-1667) interpreted Psalm 81, a song of self-examination, in the following way:*

CHALLAH

CUCUMBER-ONION SALAD

SWEET APPLESAUCE

CHICKEN SOUP WITH NOCKERLN

GEFILTE FISHBALLS

CHESTNUT AND APPLE-STUFFED ROAST GOOSE

FRUIT AND VEGETABLE TSIMMES

HONEY CAKE

TEIGLACH

PSALM 81

*I*n God our strength, let us rejoice;
To Jacob's God, let us now sing,
And in our psalms, to help the voice,
The timbrel, harp, and psaltery bring.
The moon renewing, trumpets blow,
And when the solemn feastings be:
For Jacob's God, long time ago,
In Israel did this law decree.

This testimony he prepared,
When Joseph came from Egypt land
And lived where he a language heard,
Whose words he did not understand.
From burdens, and the potters task,

Thy hands and shoulders I did free,
I helped, when thou for help didst ask,
And heard thee from the storm, said
    he. Selah.

Even at the waters of debate
I said (that I might prove thee there)
O Israel mark, what I relate,
And to my words incline thine ear.
Thou shalt no other gods at all,
but me the Lord thy God, receive;
For thee I brought from Egypt's
    thrall,
And will thy largest askings give.

But Israel did my words contemn;
Of me, my people would have none:
So, to their pleasures left I them,
Who after their own lusts are gone.
O! Had my people me obeyed,
If Israel had my ways pursued,
I on their foes my hand had laid:
Their haters I had soon subdued.

My foes had then obeyed my power,
And, I had still my folk upheld:
I then had fed with purest flour
And, with rock-honey, them had
    filled.

[ 110 ]

# Challah

3 packages active dry yeast
¼ cup warm water (105 to 110°)
¾ cup corn oil
¾ cup sugar
2 cups hot water
1 teaspoon salt
5 large eggs
9 cups all-purpose flour
½ cup sesame or poppy seeds (optional)

*I*n a large bowl dissolve the yeast in the warm water. Add the oil, sugar, hot water, and salt, and stir well. Mix in 4 of the eggs and gradually stir in 4 cups of the flour. Gradually stir in 4 cups more flour and mix until smooth.

Sprinkle the remaining 1 cup of flour on a work surface. Vigorously knead it into the dough for 10 minutes, until smooth. Return the dough to the bowl, cover with a damp cloth, and set aside to rise in a warm place for 30 to 40 minutes, until slightly risen.

Punch down the dough. Knead for 3 more minutes. Return the bread to the bowl, cover, and set aside to rise for 1 hour, until doubled in size.

Punch down the dough. Knead for 1 minute. Divide the dough in half. Shape each half into a ball and set aside for 10 minutes to rise.

Butter 2 baking sheets. Separate each ball of dough into 3 smaller balls. Roll out each ball into a 10- to 12-inch rope. Braid 3 strands into a loaf, pressing the ends together very firmly. Repeat with the second large ball of dough. Place each loaf on a prepared baking sheet.

In a small bowl beat the remaining egg. Brush the loaves with the egg. Bake at 350° for 30 minutes.

Sprinkle the loaves with the sesame or poppy seeds, if desired. Continue baking for 15 to 20 minutes or until golden brown. Cool on a rack before serving.

Makes 2 loaves.

# Cucumber-Onion Salad

6 medium cucumbers, peeled and thinly sliced
2 red onions, peeled and thinly sliced
⅔ cup white vinegar
¼ cup fresh lemon juice
¼ cup minced dill
1 teaspoon sugar
¼ teaspoon crushed cloves
½ teaspoon salt
Paprika
Freshly ground black pepper
Fresh dill sprigs for garnish

*D*rain the cucumber slices on paper towels, pressing to remove excess liquid. Repeat the procedure if necessary. Transfer to a medium bowl, and add the onions.

In a measuring cup combine the vinegar with lemon juice, minced dill, sugar, and cloves, and blend well. Pour over the salad, and stir. Let the salad stand for at least 30 minutes before serving or cover and refrigerate for several hours, stirring from time to time.

Before serving, sprinkle with salt, and stir to combine. Sprinkle with paprika and pepper. Garnish with dill sprigs.

Makes 8 servings.

## Sweet Applesauce

3 pounds Cortland apples, scrubbed, cored,
    and sliced
¾ cup unsweetened apple juice
6 whole cloves
½ teaspoon ground cinnamon
½ teaspoon ground allspice
2 tablespoons firmly packed dark brown sugar

*I*n a large saucepan combine all of the ingredients. Bring the mixture to a boil. Reduce the heat to simmering. Partially cover, and cook for 20 minutes, stirring twice at equal intervals. Remove the pan from the heat, cover tightly, and let stand for 15 minutes. Uncover, and let stand for 5 minutes.

    Serve warm or chilled.

    MAKES 8 SERVINGS.

## Chicken Soup with Nockerln

1 4-pound chicken, with giblets
7 cups water
2 ribs celery with leaves, cut into ½-inch slices
3 large cloves garlic, minced
3 medium carrots, trimmed, peeled, cut into ½-
    inch slices
2 medium onions, cut into 1-inch chunks
1 medium turnip, peeled, trimmed, cut into
    1-inch chunks
5 sprigs fresh dill
5 sprigs fresh parsley
½ teaspoon ground ginger
1 tablespoon caraway seeds, partially crushed
¼ teaspoon salt
Nockerln (recipe follows)
Minced fresh dill

*I*n a large stockpot combine the chicken and giblets, add the water, and bring to a rolling boil. Reduce the heat, and simmer for 10 minutes, skimming the surface occasionally. Add the celery, garlic, carrots, onion, turnip, dill, and parsley, bring to a boil, and skim as needed. When the liquid looks clear, add the ginger and caraway seeds. Cover, and simmer for 2 hours.

    Remove the chicken pieces from the pot, and chop into small pieces. Pour the remaining contents of the pot through a fine sieve. Pick out and reserve the carrots. Press out the juices from the remaining vegetables and herbs. Rinse and dry the pot. Pour the soup back into the pot and skim off any fat. Drop in the Nockerln, and boil for 10 minutes. Stir in the salt and carrots. Add the chopped chicken.

    To serve, place 1 teaspoon minced dill in each soup plate. Ladle in a serving of soup.

    MAKES 6 SERVINGS.

## Nockerln

2 tablespoons melted chicken fat (or pareve
    margarine)
4 eggs
7 to 8 tablespoons all-purpose flour
Salt to taste

*I*n a medium bowl let the melted chicken fat cool a bit. Add the eggs, one at a time, beating after each addition.

    Add the flour slowly while continually beating with a whisk or spoon. Add salt to taste.

    Drop the Nockerln into boiling soup by placing a small amount on the tip of a teaspoon, putting the spoon in the soup, and leaving it in for a moment.

    MAKES 6 SERVINGS.

# Gefilte Fishballs

One 4- to 5-pound haddock, head, skin, and
    bones reserved
2 quarts plus ½ cup water
1 to 2 large onions, peeled
Several sprigs parsley
6 to 7 large carrots
¼ cup plus 1 tablespoon sugar
3 tablespoons plus 1 teaspoon salt
Freshly ground pepper to taste
1 small onion, grated
1 egg
2 tablespoons matzo meal (or cracker crumbs)

*I*n a large soup pot combine the bones, skin, and
head of the haddock. Cover with about 2 quarts of
water, about 2 inches over the bones. Add the
peeled onions and parsley. Cut the carrots on a
slant and add them to the pot. Bring the water to a
boil. Add the sugar, 3 tablespoons of salt, and pepper to taste. Remove the scum and simmer.

Into a large bowl grind the fillets. Add the
grated onion, egg, matzo meal, 1 teaspoon of salt,
pepper, 1 tablespoon of sugar, and ½ cup of water.
Mix well. Shape into balls 1½ inches in diameter.
Drop the balls in the simmering soup, and bring to
a boil again. Reduce the heat, cover, and simmer
for 1 hour.

Remove the fishballs and carrots carefully,
and place on a serving platter. Reserve the fish
stock for use at another time, if desired.

MAKES ABOUT 20 FISHBALLS.

# Chestnut and Apple-stuffed Roast Goose

1 8 to 10-pound goose
2 cups cooked, peeled, and quartered chestnuts
6 cups peeled, cored, and quartered apples
½ cup raisins
1 cup prunes
Salt to taste

*R*emove the giblets and excess fat from the cavity of the goose. Render the fat to use in cooking.

In a large bowl combine the chestnuts,
apples, raisins, and prunes, and stuff the cavity of
the goose about three-fourths full. Truss the bird
and place it breast-side up on a rack in a roasting
pan. Rub with salt. Place any remaining stuffing in
a baking pan and bake during the last hour of
cooking the goose.

Roast the goose at 400° for 1 hour. Prick the
skin with a fork at ½-inch intervals to let the fat
escape. Reduce the temperature to 350°, and roast
for another hour. As the fat accumulates, remove it
with a bulb baster. To see if the goose is done, prick
the thigh with a fork. It is done if the juices are yel-
lowish. If not, reduce the oven to 325°, and continue cooking.

Let the goose sit for 15 minutes before serving.

MAKES 8 SERVINGS.

# Fruit and Vegetable Tsimmes

3 large carrots, thickly sliced
3 yams or sweet potatoes, peeled and thickly
    sliced
½ pound pitted prunes, soaked until softened
3 Granny Smith apples, peeled and thickly
    sliced
½ cup packed brown sugar
Salt and freshly ground pepper to taste
3 tablespoons schmaltz or butter

*I*n a large saucepan parboil the carrots and yams
in lightly salted water until not quite tender. Drain
the vegetables and prunes. In a casserole dish layer
the carrots, yams, prunes, and apples, sprinkling
the layers with sugar, salt, and pepper, and dotting
with schmaltz. Pour 1 cup of water into the casserole dish. Cover. Bake at 350° for 30 minutes or
until the apples are tender. Uncover and bake for
about 5 minutes or until the top is lightly browned.

MAKES 6 SERVINGS.

# Honey Cake

3½ cups all-purpose flour
1 cup firmly packed dark brown sugar
1 tablespoon baking powder
1 teaspoon baking soda
2 tablespoons cinnamon
½ teaspoon ground allspice
½ teaspoon grated nutmeg
½ teaspoon ground ginger
½ teaspoon salt
4 eggs
1¾ cups honey
1 cup strong black coffee
¼ cup vegetable oil (or melted butter)
All-purpose flour
1 cup coarsely chopped nuts

Grease and flour two 9 x 5-inch loaf pans and set aside.

In a large bowl combine the flour, brown sugar, baking powder, baking soda, and spices, and stir until well combined. Make a well in the center, and add the eggs, honey, coffee, and oil. Stir until smooth. Lightly flour the nuts, and stir the into the batter. Divide the batter between the prepared pans. Bake at 350° for 1 hour or until a toothpick inserted in the center of the cakes comes out clean. Cool in the pans on a wire rack for 10 minutes. Remove the cakes from the pans, and cool completely on a wire rack.

MAKES 8 TO 10 SERVINGS.

# Teiglach

2 cups honey
2 cups sugar
1 tablespoon ground ginger
3 eggs, beaten
1 tablespoon sugar
2 tablespoons vegetable oil
2 cups sifted all-purpose flour
1 teaspoon finely ground almonds
1 teaspoon ground ginger
¼ teaspoon salt (optional)

In a saucepan combine the honey, sugar, and ginger, and set aside. In large bowl combine the eggs, sugar, and oil, and beat well. In a separate bowl combine the remaining ingredients, and work into the egg mixture to form a soft dough. Flour hands, break off pieces of dough, and roll into ½-inch thick ropes. Cut the ropes into ½-inch lengths.

Bring the honey mixture to a boil, and drop in pieces of dough, a few at a time. Cover, and simmer for 30 minutes. Stir gently with a wooden spoon to bring the cookies on the bottom to the surface. Cook until they are lightly browned and dry and crisp inside. Remove with a slotted spoon, and place on waxed paper, not touching, until cool.

MAKES ABOUT 30.

# Back-to-School Brunch

*School has begun, and groups of mothers meet each autumn with very mixed emotions to share relief, plans and projects that may finally be completed without interruption, tidbits about new teachers, and summer highlights. Ready for the children to be back at school? Unqualified yeses! Miss their hugs and spontaneous, bounding energy? Actually, a qualified yes! Does it all pass too quickly? Ask the mothers who have moved on to bridal brunches and grandbaby showers. "Savor, savor . . . ," their shadows whisper.*

---

FRENCH MARKET SANDWICHES

STRAWBERRY OMELETS

PECAN PRALINE BACON

BAKED MAPLE BANANAS

APRICOT-ALMOND COFFEE CAKE

---

## SHEPHERD OF EAGER YOUTH

*Shepherd of eager youth,*
*Guiding in love and truth*
*Through devious ways—*
*Christ, our triumphant King,*
*We come Thy name to sing;*
*Hither Thy children bring*
*Tributes of praise.*

*Thou art our Holy Lord,*
*The all-subduing Word,*
*Healer of strife;*
*Thou dist Thyself abase*
*That from sin's deep disgrace*

*Thou mightests save our race*
*And give us life.*

*Ever be near our side,*
*Our shepherd and our guide,*
*Our staff and song;*
*Jesus, Thou Christ of God,*
*By Thy enduring Word*
*Lead us where Thou hast trod,*
*Make our faith strong.*

*CLEMENT OF ALEXANDRIA (C. 170-220)*
*TRANSLATED BY HENRY MARTYN DEXTER*
*(1821–1890)*

## French Market Sandwiches

12 croissants
1 cup butter, softened
¼ cup prepared mustard
½ teaspoon poppy seeds
2 tablespoons finely minced onion (or shallots)
2 pounds shaved ham
12 slices Swiss cheese, cut to fit

Slice the croissants in half horizontally. In a small bowl mix the butter, mustard, poppy seeds, and onion together. Spread on half of each croissant. Top with 2½ ounces ham and a slice of cheese. Top with the remaining halves. Wrap each sandwich in foil. Bake at 325° for 15 minutes.
MAKES 12 SANDWICHES.

## Strawberry Omelets

16 eggs
8 teaspoons butter
16 large fresh strawberries, sliced
1 cup sour cream
½ cup packed light brown sugar
Fresh lemon juice for sprinkling
Sifted confectioners' sugar

In a medium bowl beat the eggs just until the whites and yolks combine. For each omelet, melt 1 teaspoon of butter in a 6-inch omelet pan, and swirl to cover the bottom and sides. Pour in one-eighth of the egg mixture, and allow it to set for 45 seconds. Lift up the edges, and let the uncooked egg run underneath.

When the omelet has set, arrange 2 sliced strawberries in a fan shape around the edge of half the omelet. Spoon 2 tablespoons of sour cream on top, then sprinkle with 1 tablespoon of brown sugar. Fold the unfilled half over, then slide out onto a warmed plate. Sprinkle with a few drops of lemon juice, and dust with confectioners' sugar.
MAKES 8 OMELETS.

## Pecan Praline Bacon

1½ pounds thick-cut bacon (about 18 slices)
¼ cup sugar
2 tablespoons chili powder
⅓ cup finely chopped pecans

On the rack of a large broiling pan arrange the bacon slices in one layer. Bake at 425° in the middle of the oven for 10 minutes or until they just begin to turn golden.

In a small bowl stir together the sugar and chili powder. Remove the pan from the oven and sprinkle the bacon with the sugar mixture and pecans. Return the pan to the oven, and cook for about 5 minutes, until crisp and browned. Transfer the bacon, praline-side up, to paper towels to drain.
MAKES 8 SERVINGS.

## Baked Maple Bananas

¼ cup butter or margarine
¼ cup plus 2 tablespoons maple syrup
8 bananas, cut in half crosswise, then lengthwise
2 tablespoons lemon juice
½ teaspoon ground cinnamon

In a shallow microwave-proof baking dish melt the butter in the microwave oven at high power. Add the maple syrup, blending well. Add the bananas, spooning the mixture over to coat. Cook on high for 1 minute. Turn the bananas over and cook on high for 1 minute and 30 seconds. Sprinkle with lemon juice and cinnamon. Serve warm.
MAKES 8 SERVINGS.

# Apricot-Almond Coffee Cake

1 cup all-purpose flour
1 cup whole wheat pastry flour
1 teaspoon baking powder
½ teaspoon baking soda
¼ teaspoon salt
¼ teaspoon grated nutmeg
½ cup unsalted butter, softened
1 8-ounce package cream cheese, softened
¾ cup sugar
2 large eggs, at room temperature
1 teaspoon vanilla extract
Finely grated peel of 1 lemon
½ cup milk
1 9- or 10-ounce jar apricot preserves
1 cup slivered almonds

Butter a 9 x 13-inch baking pan.

Into a medium bowl sift the flours, baking powder, baking soda, salt, and nutmeg. In a large bowl cream the butter and cream cheese, gradually adding the sugar. Beat in the eggs, one at a time, beating until smooth after each addition. Blend in the vanilla and lemon peel.

Mix half the dry ingredients into the creamed mixture until smooth. Blend in the milk, then add the rest of the dry ingredients, mixing just until the batter is smooth. Turn the batter into the prepared pan and level the top with a spoon.

Stir the preserves to make a spreadable consistency, adding a little water if necessary. Spoon the preserves here and there over the top of the batter, using the entire jar. Spread the preserves with a spoon so they cover the surface, then sprinkle the almonds evenly over the top. Bake at 350° for 30 to 35 minutes or until a toothpick inserted in the center of the cake comes out clean. Cool in the pan on a rack for 1 hour before serving.

MAKES 12 SERVINGS.

# A Birthday Bash

*"Our family never really celebrated birthdays." You've heard it, and secretly felt sympathy for the friend or coworker who spoke those words. We know that some years pass with greater or less celebration, but no one should ever, ever observe a birthday devoid of any celebration for their unique contributions to the human race. And if at all possible, we should commemorate the anniversaries of birth with Birthday Bashes!!*

SPINACH, BASIL, AND WALNUT SALAD

BUTTERY ONION BISCUITS

SPICY PECAN CHICKEN

SPECIAL OCCASION VEGETABLE CASSEROLE

WHITE BIRTHDAY CAKE

PEACH ICE CREAM

*FROM: RABBI BEN EZRA*

G row old along with me!
The best is yet to be,
The last of life, for which the first was made:
Our times are in his hand
Who saith "A whole I planned,
Youth shows but half; trust God: see all nor be
    afraid!"...

Not on the vulgar mass
Called "work" must sentence pass,
Things done, that took the eye and had the price:
O'er which, from level stand,
The low world laid its hand,
Found straightway to its mind, could value in a
    trice:

But all, the world's coarse thumb
And finger failed to plumb,
So passed in making up the full account:
All instincts immature,
All purposes unsure,
That weighed not as his work, yet sweled the
    man's amount:

Thoughts hardly to be packed
Into a narrow act,

Fancies that broke through language and
    escaped;
All I could never be,
All, men ignored in me,
This, I was worth to God, whose wheel the
    pitcher shaped...

But I need, now as then,
thee, god, who mouldest men;
And since, not even while the whirl was worst,
Did I, - to the wheel of life
With shapes and colours rife,
Bound dizzily, - mistake my end, to slake thy
    thirst:

So, take and use thy work:
Amend what flaws may lurk,
What strains o' the stuff, what warpings past
    the aim!
My times be in thy hand!
Perfect the cup as planned!
Let age approve of youth, and death complete the
    same!

ROBERT BROWNING (1812–89)

# Spinach, Basil, and Walnut Salad

6 cups fresh spinach, washed, dried, and
trimmed
2 cups basil leaves, washed
½ cup olive oil
3 cloves garlic, minced
¼ cup walnuts
4 ounces baked ham, julienned
1 cup grated Parmesan cheese

*I*n a large bowl combine the spinach and basil, and toss well.

In a sauté pan heat the oil over medium heat and sauté the garlic and walnuts until the walnuts begin to brown. Stir in the ham, and cook 1 minute longer. Pour the warm dressing over the greens. Sprinkle with Parmesan cheese. Toss and serve.

Makes 6 to 8 servings.

# Buttery Onion Biscuits

2 cups all-purpose flour
3 teaspoons baking powder
½ teaspoon baking soda
½ teaspoon salt
½ cup plus 3 tablespoons butter
2 green onions, thinly sliced
¾ cup plus 2 tablespoons buttermilk

*I*nto a large mixing bowl sift together the flour, baking powder, baking soda, and salt.

In a small skillet melt 1 tablespoon of the butter over medium low heat, and sauté the green onions for about 3 minutes or until tender but not browned. Remove the pan from the heat, and let cool.

Cut the remaining butter into small pieces, and add to the dry ingredients. Cut the butter into the flour mixture with knives or a pastry cutter until mixture resembles coarse crumbs. Make a well in the center of the mixture, add the green

onions and ¾ cup of the buttermilk, and mix just until a sticky dough forms. Turn the dough out onto a lightly floured surface, and knead 15 to 20 times. Roll or pat the dough into a ½-inch-thick square. Using a sharp knife, cut into sixteen 2-inch squares. Place the biscuits 2 inches apart on a baking sheet, and brush the tops with the remaining buttermilk. Bake at 425° in the center of the oven for 12 to 15 minutes or until the biscuits are well risen and lightly browned on the tops.

Serve warm with butter.

Makes 16 biscuits.

# Spicy Pecan Chicken

2 3-pound chickens, cut up
1½ cups pecans
1 cup all-purpose flour
1 cup yellow cornmeal
4 teaspoons paprika
2 teaspoons salt
2 teaspoons freshly ground black pepper
2 teaspoons cayenne pepper
4 eggs
½ cup water
4 cups corn oil

*R*inse the chicken pieces well, and pat them dry.

In a food processor or blender chop the pecans fine. In a shallow bowl combine the chopped pecans, flour, cornmeal, paprika, salt, pepper, and cayenne and mix well.

In a separate shallow bowl beat the eggs lightly with the water.

Dip the chicken pieces into the egg mixture, and then into the dry mixture. Coat well, shaking off any excess.

In a heavy skillet heat the oil to 375°, until hot, but not smoking. Fry the chicken a few pieces at a time for about 10 to 15 minutes. Drain the chicken on a rack.

Makes 8 servings.

## Special Occasion Vegetable Casserole

2 10-ounce packages frozen green beans
1 10-ounce package frozen lima beans
1 10-ounce package frozen green peas
1 medium onion, chopped
1 green pepper, chopped
1 cup whipping cream, whipped
1½ cups mayonnaise
1 8-ounce can grated Parmesan cheese

Grease a 2-quart casserole dish.

Cook all of the vegetables according to the package directions. Let cool.

In a mixing bowl combine the onion, green pepper, whipping cream, mayonnaise, and half of the Parmesan cheese. In the prepared dish combine the cooked green beans, limas, and peas. Pour the sauce over the vegetables, and sprinkle with the remaining Parmesan cheese. Bake at 350° for 30 minutes or until browned.

MAKES 8 SERVINGS.

## White Birthday Cake

3 cups sifted cake flour
1 tablespoon baking powder
½ teaspoon salt
¾ cup unsalted butter, softened
2 cups sugar
1 teaspoon vanilla extract
1 teaspoon almond extract
1 cup milk
6 large egg whites, room temperature

1 cup boiling water
2¼ cups sugar
1 tablespoon light corn syrup
3 large egg whites, room temperature
1 teaspoon vanilla extract

Grease and lightly flour two 9-inch round cake pans. Set aside.

In a medium bowl sift together the flour, baking powder, and salt. Set aside. In a large bowl cream the butter and 1½ cups of the sugar for about 3 minutes until fluffy. Mix in the vanilla and almond extracts. Add the dry mixture in 4 parts, alternating with the milk.

In a large bowl whisk 6 egg whites until foamy. Gradually add the remaining ½ cup of sugar, continuing to beat until the whites stand in stiff peaks. Fold the whites into the batter with an over-and-under motion. Pour the batter into the prepared pans. Bake at 375° for 35 minutes or until a toothpick inserted in the center comes out clean. Cool slightly, then remove from the pans to cake racks to cool completely.

In a large saucepan combine the boiling water, 2 cups of sugar and the corn syrup over medium heat. Cook at a rolling boil until the mixture reaches the soft-ball stage (238° on a candy thermometer).

In a medium bowl whisk 3 egg whites until foamy. Gradually add the remaining ¼ cup of sugar and 1 teaspoon of vanilla. Continue whisking until the whites stand in stiff peaks.

When the syrup is at the correct temperature, pour it into the beaten whites in a thin, steady stream, beating constantly. Ice between the cake layers, then ice the top and sides of the cake.

MAKES 12 SERVINGS.

## Peach Ice Cream

4 cups mashed fresh peaches
3½ cups sugar
¼ cup fresh lemon juice
2 cups heavy cream
¼ teaspoon salt
Milk

In a large bowl mix together the peaches, sugar, and lemon juice. Slowly blend in the cream and add the salt. Place mixture in ice cream freezer, add milk to the fill line for 1 gallon, and freeze according to the manufacturer's instructions.

MAKES 1 GALLON.

# Yom Kippur

*Yom Kippur, otherwise known as the Day of Atonement, is celebrated as a holy convocation day in September or October. No work is to be done on this holy day; instead, it is to be a day set apart in humility before God. Perhaps a prayer of Daniel, one of God's most humble servants is appropriate before this meal.*

---

CHICKEN BROTH WITH GINGER AND
NUTMEG MATZO BALLS

SOUR RYE BREAD

BAKED CHICKEN LOAF

HONEY-GLAZED CARROTS

HOT FRUIT COMPOTES

DRIED FRUIT DESSERT TSIMMES

---

*O Lord, great and awesome God, who keeps His covenant and mercy with those who love Him, and with those who keep His commandments, we have sinned and committed iniquity, we have done wickedly and rebelled, even by departing from Your precepts and Your judgments. Neither have we heeded Your servants the prophets, who spoke in Your name to our kings and our princes, to our fathers and all the people of the land. O Lord, righteousness belongs to You, but to us shame of face, as it is this day—to the men of Judah, to the inhabitants of Jerusalem and all Israel, those near and those far off in all the countries to which You have driven them, because of the unfaithfulness which they have committed against you. O Lord, to us belongs shame of face, to our kings, our princes, and our fathers, because we have sinned against you. To the Lord our God belong mercy and forgiveness, though we have rebelled against Him. We have not obeyed the voice of the Lord our God, to walk in His laws, which He set before us by His servants the prophets. ... O my God, incline Your ear and hear; open Your eyes and see our desolations, and the city which is called by Your name; for we do not present our supplications before You because of our righteous deeds, but because of Your great mercies. O Lord, hear! O Lord, forgive! O Lord, listen and act! Do not delay for Your own sake, my God, for Your city and Your people are called by Your name.*

DANIEL 9, *SELECTED VERSES*

## Chicken Broth with Ginger and Nutmeg Matzo Balls

    1 6-pound chicken
    1 parsnip, sliced
    1 white turnip, sliced
    ¼ white cabbage, shredded
    ¼ red cabbage, shredded
    ½ rutabaga, sliced
    4 large carrots, cut in chunks
    2 large onions, quartered
    1 28-ounce can tomatoes
    1 handful collard greens
    1 stalk celery, cut in chunks
    2 teaspoons dried thyme
    Salt and freshly ground pepper to taste

    ¼ cup chicken broth
    ¼ cup schmaltz (or melted pareve margarine)
    2 teaspoons salt (or to taste)
    ¼ teaspoon grated nutmeg
    ¼ teaspoon ground ginger
    2 tablespoons grated onion
    2 tablespoons chopped parsley
    2 shakes paprika
    1 cup matzo meal
    4 large eggs
    1 tablespoon salt

In a large stock pot cover the chicken with water 2 inches above the chicken and bring to a boil. Reduce the heat, cover, and simmer for about 2 hours or until tender. Add the parsnip, turnip, cabbages, rutabaga, carrots, onions, tomatoes, collard greens, celery, and thyme, and season with salt and pepper. Cover and simmer for at least 30 minutes, until the vegetables are very tender.

Remove the chicken, and strain the soup. Adjust the seasonings.

In a large bowl combine the broth, schmaltz, 2 teaspoons of salt, nutmeg, ginger, onion, parsley, paprika, and matzo meal, mixing well. Add the eggs with a wooden spoon one at a time until all 4 eggs are incorporated. Refrigerate 3 to 4 hours or overnight.

Bring an 8- to 10-quart pot of water to boil. Add 1 tablespoon of salt. Shape the mixture into balls the size of walnuts, wetting hands with warm water frequently. Drop into boiling water, cover, and simmer for 30 minutes or until the matzo balls are fluffy and floating at the top.

Ladle the chicken broth into serving bowls. Transfer the matzo balls with a slotted spoon to the bowls of hot chicken soup.

MAKES 6 SERVINGS.

# Sour Rye Bread

1 cup light rye flour
1 cup unbleached all-purpose flour
1 package active dry yeast
2 cups warm water (105 to 115°)
1 tablespoon partially crushed caraway seed
1 medium onion, peeled

1½ cups starter
2 cups unbleached all-purpose flour
1 cup warm unsweetened apple juice
1 tablespoon partially crushed caraway seed

1 package active dry yeast
¾ cup warm water (105 to 115°)
1 teaspoon sugar
5 to 5½ cups unbleached flour
2 tablespoons unsulphured molasses
1 teaspoon ground cardamom
2 teaspoons salt
2 tablespoons Italian olive oil
1 tablespoon finely grated orange zest
Stone-ground cornmeal
1 egg (use ½ teaspoon yolk and all the white)
1 tablespoon water
Caraway seeds

Prepare the starter 4 days before bake day. In a large bowl combine 1 cup of rye flour, 1 cup all-purpose flour, the yeast, water, and 1 tablespoon of caraway seed, and beat with a wooden spoon until blended. Prick the onion all over with a sharp-pronged fork. Bury it in the starter. Cover tightly with plastic wrap and set in a warm place (70 to 80°) for 3 days. The mixture will bubble up, rise and fall, and develop a slightly sour but not unpleasant aroma. On the third day, discard the onion and re-cover. Let stand overnight.

Stir the starter on the fourth day. Measure out 1½ cups, and pour into a large mixing bowl. Add 2 cups of unbleached flour, the apple juice, and 1 tablespoon of caraway seed. Stir and recover with plastic wrap. Let stand overnight.

In a small bowl combine the yeast, water, and sugar. Set aside until foamy, about 8 minutes. Pour the yeast mixture into the sponge and stir with a wooden spoon. Add 2 cups of flour, the molasses, cardamom, salt, olive oil, and orange zest. Beat by hand until smooth. With a wooden spoon beat in the remaining flour ½ cup at a time, mixing well after each addition. When the mixture becomes too difficult to handle with a wooden spoon, turn the dough out onto a lightly floured board and knead, adding enough of the remaining flour to make a smooth elastic dough. Add only enough flour to make the dough smooth, elastic, and only slightly sticky.

Shape the dough into a ball. Oil a large warmed, straight-sided bowl. Place the dough in the bowl, and cover tightly with plastic wrap. Let the dough rise at room temperature for about 1 hour and 30 minutes, until doubled in bulk.

Punch down, squeezing out air bubbles. If the dough remains sticky, transfer it to a board, sprinkle with up to 1 tablespoon of flour, and knead until smooth. Place in a bowl, cover again, and let rise until doubled.

Lightly grease a jelly roll pan, and sprinkle it with cornmeal. Punch the dough down. Turn the dough out onto a lightly floured board, and knead briefly. Divide the dough in half. Press or roll each piece into an 8-inch square. Roll up tightly, tucking in and tapering the ends. Place seam-side down in the prepared pan. Cover with an oiled sheet of waxed paper, and let rise for about 45 minutes or until almost doubled.

In a small bowl beat the remaining egg with 1 tablespoon of water. Brush the loaves with the egg wash. Sprinkle with caraway seeds. Bake at 375° in the center section of the oven for 30 minutes. If the bread browns too rapidly, cover loosely with a sheet of aluminum foil.

Remove the bread from the pan, place directly on the oven rack, and bake for 5 minutes. The bread is done when it sounds hollow when tapped on the bottom. Cool completely on a wire rack before slicing.

MAKES 2 LARGE LOAVES.

# Baked Chicken Loaf

1 tablespoon olive oil
1 medium onion, chopped
3 large cloves garlic, halved
14 slender asparagus spears, trimmed and
    chopped
¾ pound snow-white fresh mushrooms,
    chopped
½ teaspoon freshly grated nutmeg
1 teaspoon curry powder
1 teaspoon dried rosemary
¼ teaspoon salt
1¾ pounds boneless, skinless chicken breasts,
    trimmed of fat
1 large egg
1 tablespoon fresh lemon juice
2 ripe plum tomatoes, cored, seeded and cut up
2 teaspoons minced parsley
2 teaspoons sweet pareve margarine
2 cups tomato sauce with mushrooms

*I*n a nonstick skillet heat the oil until very hot and sauté the chopped onion, garlic, asparagus, and mushrooms over medium high heat for 2 minutes, stirring constantly. In a small bowl combine the nutmeg, curry powder, rosemary, and salt. Sprinkle the vegetables with half the seasoning medley. Reduce the heat and cook for 6 to 7 minutes until the onion and asparagus start to wilt and no liquid remains in the pan. Set aside.

Cut the chicken into 1-inch chunks. In a food processor combine the chicken, egg, lemon juice, tomato, parsley, and remaining seasoning medley. Process until chopped but not puréed.

Grease an 8-inch loaf pan with ½ teaspoon of margarine. Spread one-fourth of the chicken mixture across the bottom of the pan. Cover with one third of the sautéed vegetable mixture, smoothing out and pressing into the chicken. Repeat the layer-ing procedure, finishing with the chicken. Cut the remaining margarine into pieces and strew across the top layer. Cover tightly with a sheet of heavy-duty aluminum foil.

Place the loaf pan in a deep-sided broiling pan. Pour 2 inches of boiling water around the loaf pan. Bake in the center of the oven for 45 minutes.

Remove the loaf from the oven, and pour the juices into a saucepan. Re-cover the pan and let the loaf stand for 10 minutes. Pour any remaining juices into the saucepan.

Add the tomato sauce to the saucepan, and heat to simmering. Run a blunt knife around the sides of the loaf. Place a warmed serving plate over it and invert. A sharp rap to the bottom of the pan should loosen the loaf. Spoon some sauce over the loaf. Cut into 1-inch slices. Serve with remaining hot tomato sauce on the side.

MAKES 5 TO 6 SERVINGS.

# Honey-glazed Carrots

2 pounds carrots
1¼ cups water
2 tablespoons cornstarch
½ cup honey
Salt to taste
Ginger to taste

*P*eel and cut the carrots into 1-inch rounds. In a large saucepan place the carrots and 1 cup of water. Cover and simmer for about 20 minutes, until barely tender.

In a cup dissolve the cornstarch in the remaining ¼ cup of water. Add the mixture to the carrots along with the honey, salt, and ginger. Stir over low heat until the mixture thickens.

MAKES 6 TO 8 SERVINGS.

## Hot Fruit Compote

1 16-ounce can sliced peaches, drained, juice
    reserved
1 16-ounce can sliced pears, drained, juice
    reserved
6 ounces dried, pitted prunes
6 ounces dried apricots
1 cup raisins
1 cup slivered almonds
½ teaspoon ground cinnamon
¼ teaspoon grated nutmeg
½ cup brandy
2 tablespoons fresh lemon juice (or to taste)
¼ cup packed dark brown sugar

*I*n a 4-quart casserole dish layer the peaches, pears, prunes, and apricots. Scatter the raisins and almonds over the fruit. Sprinkle with cinnamon and nutmeg. In a 1-cup measure combine the brandy and lemon juice. Stir in the brown sugar until dissolved. Pour the mixture over the fruit. Add enough reserved fruit juice to just cover the fruit. Bake at 350° for 30 minutes or until heated through.

MAKES 8 SERVINGS.

## Dried Fruit Dessert Tsimmes

8 ounces pitted prunes
¼ cup dark seedless raisins
4 ounces dried apricots
½ teaspoon ground cardamom
1 teaspoon ground cinnamon
2 cups unsweetened apple juice
3 tablespoons firmly packed light brown sugar
3 tablespoons water

1 large egg
2 tablespoons fresh lemon juice
½ teaspoon finely minced lemon peel
2 cups commercial matzo farfel
2 teaspoons sweet butter-margarine blend (or
    sweet pareve margarine)
1 tablespoon honey
1 tablespoon warm water

*I*n a medium bowl combine the prunes and raisins. Rinse the apricots under hot running water, and add them to the bowl. Add the cardamom and cinnamon. In a small saucepan heat 1 cup of apple juice to the boiling point. Pour the apple juice over the fruit, stir, and let the mixture stand for 45 minutes, stirring once after about 20 minutes.

In a small saucepan combine the sugar and water, and cook over medium-high heat until the mixture bubbles up and begins to caramelize. Stir in the remaining apple juice and cook over medium heat until any solids that have formed are dissolved. Stir the mixture into the fruit.

In a cup beat the egg and lemon juice with a fork. Add to the fruit with the lemon peel. Fold in the farfel. The mixture will be thick. Let the mixture stand.

Grease an 8-inch square baking pan with ½ teaspoon butter-margarine blend. Spread the dessert evenly in the pan. Cut the remaining shortening into small pieces and scatter over all. Cover with a sheet of aluminum foil. Bake at 375° in the center of the oven for 30 minutes. Uncover and return to the oven for 10 to 15 minutes until set and lightly browned.

In a small bowl combine the honey and water. Remove the pan from oven and immediately drizzle with the honey mixture. Cool for 10 minutes before cutting with a sharp knife into 8 or more serving pieces. Serve warm or at room temperature.

MAKES 8 OR MORE SERVINGS.

# Harvest Patio Dinner

*Here's a celebration of thanksgiving for those who find the November Thanksgiving holiday too rushed (and too close to the Christmas holidays!) to really acknowledge proper gratitude for our blessed abundance. While the schedule isn't quite so hectic, reclaim the opportunity to pause and reflect in thanks for the bounteous harvest and for friends to share it with.*

---

MAKE-AHEAD GREENS

CUCUMBER BUNS

BUTTERED BARBECUED CORNISH GAME HENS

ROASTED VIDALIA "FLOWERS"

GREEN BEANS AND FONTINA IN GARLIC SAUCE

SWEET POTATO PIE WITH CUSTARD

---

## COME, YE THANKFUL PEOPLE, COME

Come, ye thankful people, come, Raise the
　song of harvest home:
All is safely gathered in, Ere the winter storms
　begin;
God, our Maker, doth provide For our wants to
　be supplied:
Come to God's own temple, come, Raise the
　song of harvest home.

All the world is God's own field, Fruit unto His
　praise to yield;
Wheat and tares together sown, Unto joy or
　sorrow grown;
First the blade, and then the ear, Then the full
　corn shall appear:
Lord of harvest, grant that we Wholesome grain
　and pure may be.

For the Lord our God shall come, And shall take
　His harvest home;

From His field shall in that day All offenses
　purge away;
Give His angels charge at last In the fire the
　tares to cast;
But the fruitful ears to store In His garner
　evermore.

Even so, Lord, quickly come To Thy final
　harvest home;
Gather Thou Thy people in, Free from sorrow,
　free from sin;
There, forever purified, In Thy presence to abide:
Come, with all Thine angels, come, Raise the
　glorious harvest home.

HENRY ALFORD (1810-1871)

*Henry Alford and many of his contemporaries offered thanks both before and after meals, as a sign of his great gratitude for God's provisions!*

## Make-Ahead Greens

1 small clove garlic, minced
½ teaspoon salt
¼ teaspoon pepper
¼ teaspoon dry mustard
1 tablespoon tarragon vinegar
¼ cup vegetable oil
1 tablespoon lemon juice
2 small heads Boston lettuce, washed, dried,
       and torn in small pieces
¼ cup grated Parmesan cheese
3 large orange sections

*I*n a large salad bowl combine the garlic, salt, pepper, and mustard, and mash with the back of a spoon. Add the vinegar, oil, and lemon juice, and whisk to combine.

Place the lettuce on top of the dressing. Chill for 2 to 3 hours. To serve, sprinkle with Parmesan cheese and toss the lettuce with the dressing. Top with the orange sections. Serve immediately.

MAKES 6 SERVINGS.

## Cucumber Buns

3¼ to 3¾ cups all-purpose flour
1 package active dry yeast
2 tablespoons snipped fresh chives (or 1
       tablespoon dried)
1 teaspoon snipped fresh dill (or ½ teaspoon
       dried dillweed)

1 medium cucumber, peeled and cut up
½ cup sour cream
¼ cup water
1 tablespoon sugar
1 teaspoon salt

*I*n a large mixing bowl combine 1¼ cups of the flour, the yeast, chives, and dill.

In a food processor purée the cucumber until smooth (there should be ¾ cup). In a saucepan heat and stir the cucumber purée, sour cream, water, sugar, and salt until warm (120 to 130°). The mixture will look curdled. Add the cucumber mixture to the flour mixture, and beat with an electric mixer on low to medium speed for 30 seconds, scraping the bowl. Beat on high speed for 3 minutes. Using a spoon, stir in as much of the remaining flour as possible.

Turn the dough out onto a lightly floured surface. Knead for 6 to 8 minutes, adding enough of the remaining flour to make a moderately stiff dough that is smooth and elastic. Shape into a ball. Place the dough in a lightly greased bowl and turn once. Cover, and let rise for about 45 minutes, until double.

Punch down the dough. Turn out onto a lightly floured surface, cover, and let rest for 10 minutes.

Grease a 9 x 13-inch baking pan. Divide the dough into 12 pieces, and shape each into a ball. Arrange the dough in the prepared pan, allowing space between each ball. Cover, and let rise in a warm place for about 30 minutes, until nearly double. Bake at 350° for 20 to 25 minutes or until light brown. Serve warm or cool.

MAKES 12 ROLLS.

## Buttered Barbecued Cornish Game Hens

6 stalks celery
1½ onions, quartered
6 Cornish game hens
1½ cups butter
1 teaspoon dried thyme
½ teaspoon dried oregano
2 cloves garlic, crushed
¼ to ⅓ cup fresh lemon juice
1 teaspoon paprika
1 tablespoon soy sauce
½ teaspoon freshly ground black pepper

Place a stalk of celery and a wedge of onion in each hen cavity. Tie the wings and legs.

In a saucepan combine the remaining ingredients and heat until the butter is melted. Grill the birds over moderate coals for about 1 hour and 30 minutes, basting frequently with the sauce, until the fat runs yellow (not pink) when pierced.

MAKES 4 SERVINGS.

## Roasted Vidalia "Flowers"

6 large Vidalia onions (about 3½ pounds)
6 tablespoons unsalted butter, melted
¼ cup chopped pecans

Lightly butter a shallow baking dish large enough to let the onions open or "flower."

With a sharp knife trim the root end of each onion carefully so the onion remains intact. Standing each onion on its root end, cut parallel vertical slices at ¼-inch intervals into but not through the onion, stopping about ½ inch above the root end. Rotate each onion 90 degrees and cut parallel vertical slices in the same manner to form a crosshatch pattern, keeping the onions intact. Arrange the onions, root-ends down, in the prepared baking dish, drizzle them with the butter, and season them with salt and pepper. Bake at 350° in the middle of the oven, basting occasionally, for 1 hour.

Sprinkle with the pecans, and bake for 30 minutes more.

MAKES 6 SERVINGS.

## Green Beans and Fontina in Garlic Sauce

1 pound small green beans, washed, trimmed
4 ounces Fontina cheese
1 large clove garlic
½ teaspoon Dijon mustard
¼ cup lemon juice
½ cup olive oil
Salt and pepper to taste

In a saucepan cook the green beans in lightly salted boiling water for about 2 minutes until just tender. Refresh under cold running water. Drain and blot well on paper towels to remove all water.

Cut the cheese into ¼ x 2-inch strips. In a large serving bowl combine the beans and cheese strips.

In a food processor combine the garlic, mustard, and lemon juice, and blend well. With the processor running, slowly add the oil. Pour the sauce over the beans and cheese and toss well. Season with salt and pepper to taste.

MAKES 4 TO 6 SERVINGS.

## Sweet Potato Pie with Custard

3 pounds sweet potatoes
½ cup unsalted butter, room temperature
1 cup packed light brown sugar
3 large eggs, room temperature
1 cup half and half
1 tablespoon all-purpose flour
¾ teaspoon ground cinnamon
½ teaspoon vanilla extract
¼ teaspoon salt
¼ teaspoon ground cloves
¼ teaspoon freshly grated nutmeg
¼ teaspoon ground allspice
⅛ teaspoon ground mace
⅛ teaspoon ground ginger

1½ cups chocolate wafer cookie crumbs
3 tablespoons unsalted butter, melted
Vanilla Custard (recipe follows)
Coarsely chopped pistachios

Pierce the sweet potatoes with a fork several times. Place on baking sheet and bake at 375° until tender, about 1 hour. Cool slightly and peel.

In a food processor purée the sweet potatoes until smooth.

In a large bowl cream ½ cup of butter with the sugar until light. Add the eggs one at a time, beating well after each addition. Beat in 3 cups of sweet potato purée, the half and half, flour, cinnamon, vanilla, salt, cloves, nutmeg, allspice, mace, and ginger.

Lightly butter a 10-inch pie pan. In a medium bowl mix the cookie crumbs and melted butter. Press the mixture into the bottom and up the sides of the prepared pan. Pour the filling into the crust. Bake at 350° for 1 hour or until the center of the pie is set. Transfer to a rack, and cool completely.

Pour custard around each serving and sprinkle with pistachios.

MAKES 8 SERVINGS.

## Pouring Custard

2½ cups milk
½ vanilla bean, split lengthwise
8 large egg yolks
½ cup sugar

In a heavy medium saucepan place the milk. Scrape in the seeds from the vanilla bean and add the pod. Scald the milk. Remove the pan from the heat, cover, and steep for 20 minutes.

In a medium bowl beat the egg yolks and sugar until pale yellow. Strain the milk. Gradually beat the milk into the egg mixture. Return the mixture to the saucepan and stir over low heat until the custard thickens and leaves a path on the back of a spoon when a finger is drawn across, about 12 minutes. Do not boil. Strain into a bowl and refrigerate until cool, stirring occasionally.

MAKES ABOUT 2½ CUPS.

# Pregame Picnic

*Ah, competition! It's the classic story of heroes and heroines and awesome deeds to be recounted ever after. It's not about the event; it's about the quest for glory. Revel in the moments, the shining faces, the smells, the sounds, and the rituals. Your pregame efforts have set the tone for the Heroic Endeavor about to unfold. With this menu, you're assured a victory!*

---

DRAGON'S BREATH DIP

SAUSAGE PASTRIES

DILLED SQUASH SALAD

LEMON CHICKEN

CHOCOLATE APPLESAUCE CAKE

---

## THE PILGRIM SONG

Who would true Valour see,
Let him come hither;
One here will Constant be,
Come Wind, come Weather.
There's no discouragement
Shall make him once Relent
His first avow'd Intent
To be a Pilgrim.

Whoso beset him round
With dismal Stories,
Do but themselves Confound;
His strength the more is.
No Lyon can him fright,

He'll with a Giant fight,
But he will have a right
To be a Pilgrim.

Hobgoblin, nor foul Fiend,
Can daunt his Spirit:
He knows, he at the end
Shall life Inherit.
Then Fancies fly away,
He'll fear not what men say,
He'll labour Night and Day
To be a Pilgrim.

JOHN BUNYAN (1626-1688)

# Dragon's Breath Dip

1 6-ounce can pitted ripe olives, finely chopped
3 ripe firm tomatoes, finely chopped, seeded
    and drained
1 4-ounce can chopped green chilies
3 to 4 cloves garlic, finely chopped
Pinch salt
2 tablespoons wine vinegar
2 tablespoons olive oil
Tortilla chips

*I*n a medium bowl mix the olives, tomatoes, green chilies, garlic, and salt together. Add the vinegar and oil, and mix well.

Serve with tortilla chips.
MAKES 2 CUPS.

# Sausage Pastries

6 ounces cream cheese, softened
1 cup unsalted butter, softened
2 cups all-purpose flour
¼ teaspoon salt

¼ cup spicy mustard
1 12-ounce package kielbasa, thinly sliced
1 egg
2 teaspoons water

*I*n a large bowl beat the cream cheese with the butter until well blended. Add the flour and salt, and mix well. Knead the dough lightly, and shape into a ball. Cut the ball into quarters, and wrap in plastic wrap. Refrigerate for several hours or overnight.

Lightly grease 2 baking sheets. On a lightly floured surface roll out 1 piece of the dough to about ⅛-inch thickness. Cut into 2-inch circles and spread mustard on each.

Place a slice of sausage on half the circles, and top with another circle. Press the edges together to seal. Place the pastries on the prepared cookie sheet. Repeat with the remaining dough, mustard, and sausage.

In a small bowl beat the egg with the water. Brush the egg wash over the pastries. Bake at 375° for 15 to 20 minutes or until lightly browned.
MAKES ABOUT 30 PASTRIES.

# Dilled Squash Salad

1½ pounds zucchini, sliced paper-thin
1½ pounds yellow squash, sliced paper-thin
1 tablespoon salt
⅔ cup distilled white vinegar
1½ teaspoons sugar
2 tablespoons snipped fresh dill

*I*n a colander toss the zucchini and the yellow squash with the salt, and let them drain for 1 hour. Refresh the squash under running cold water and drain it well. In a large ceramic or glass bowl combine the vinegar and the sugar, stirring until the sugar is dissolved. Add the squash and dill, and toss the mixture well. Cover, and chill the salad for at least 2 hours or overnight.

Stir the salad and transfer it to a salad bowl.
MAKES 8 SERVINGS.

# Lemon Chicken

- ¼ cup butter
- 2 tablespoons sugar
- 2 tablespoons prepared mustard
- 3 tablespoons lemon juice
- 2 teaspoons salt
- ¼ teaspoon seasoned salt
- ¼ teaspoon black pepper
- 12 serving pieces chicken
- 1 tablespoon paprika

*I*n a roasting pan large enough to hold all of the chicken melt the butter. Stir in the sugar, mustard, lemon juice, salt, seasoned salt, and pepper, and mix well. Place the chicken in the pan skin-side up, and set aside for several minutes.

Turn the chicken skin-side down, coating the pieces well with the sauce. Sprinkle with half the paprika. Bake at 350° for 30 minutes. Turn the chicken, and sprinkle with the remaining paprika. Return to the oven, and bake for another 30 minutes.

MAKES 6 SERVINGS.

# Chocolate Applesauce Cake

- ½ cup shortening
- 1½ cups sugar
- 2 eggs
- ½ teaspoon ground cinnamon
- 2 tablespoons unsweetened cocoa
- 2 cups all-purpose flour
- 1 teaspoon salt
- 1½ teaspoons baking soda
- 2 cups applesauce

- 2 tablespoons sugar
- 6 ounces chocolate chips
- ½ cup chopped nuts

*B*utter an 8 x 12-inch baking pan.

In a large bowl cream the shortening and 1½ cups of sugar. Add the eggs, and blend thoroughly. Add the cinnamon, cocoa, flour, salt, and baking soda, and mix well. Add the applesauce, and mix well. Pour the batter into the prepared pan. In a small bowl mix together the sugar, chocolate chips, and chopped nuts. Sprinkle the mixture on top of the batter. Bake at 350° for 40 minutes or until done.

MAKES 12 SERVINGS.

# Sir Winston Churchill's Birthday Breakfast

It is a wise person who practices reflection on the characters of men and women whose personalities have so impacted our world as to make it a different place. Sir Winston Churchill was such a man, obviously created for a specific time and place in history, and though certainly not faultless, he lived a life worthy of study and imitation. November 30th is his birthday. Set the tone for discussion with this "veddy" British breakfast.

"Never give in, never give in, never, never, never, never - in nothing, great or small, large or petty - never give in except to convictions of honor and good sense." (Address at the Harrow School, October 29, 1941)

"The destiny of mankind is not decided by material computation. When great causes are on the move in the world...we learn that we are spirits, not animals, and that something is going on in space and time, and beyond space and time, which, whether we like it or not, spells duty."

"Expert knowledge, however indispensible, is no substitute for a generous and comprehending outlook upon a human story with all its sadness—with all its unquenchable hope."

---

MARMALADE TART

KEDGEREE

BACON, TOMATOES, AND FRIED BREAD

HOT CROSS BUNS

---

In the Lord I put my trust;
How can you say to my soul,
"Flee as a bird to your mountain"?
For look! The wicked bend their bow,
They make ready their arrow on the string,
That they may shoot secretly at the upright in
    heart.
If the foundations are destroyed,
What can the righteous do?

The Lord is in His holy temple,
The Lord's throne is in heaven;
His eyes behold,

His eyelids test the sons of men.
The Lord tests the righteous,
But the wicked and the one who loves violence
    His soul hates.
Upon the wicked He will rain coals;
Fire and brimstone and a burning wind
Shall be the portion of their cup.

For the Lord is righteous,
He loves righteousness;
His countenance beholds the upright.

PSALM 11

[ 133 ]

## Marmalade Tart

1 cup all-purpose flour
Pinch salt
Pinch sugar
6 tablespoons butter
1 egg yolk, beaten
Lemon juice

1 cup orange marmalade
2 eggs, separated
Lemon juice to taste

Whipping cream

In a mixing bowl sift the flour, salt, and sugar. Rub in the butter by hand until the mixture is crumbly. Add the egg yolk and enough lemon juice to mix to a stiff paste, adding a few drops of water if necessary. Work on a pastry board until smooth. Roll out on a floured surface and line an 8-inch tart pan. Prick the pastry with a fork. Butter a sheet of aluminum foil, and place the buttered side against the pastry. Partly fill the pastry with dried beans or pie weights. Bake at 400° for 15 minutes. Remove the beans, and bake for 5 minutes. Cool.

If the marmalade has large strips of peel, chop the peel into small pieces. In a medium bowl beat the egg yolks until pale yellow. Mix with the marmalade, and flavor with lemon juice. In a separate bowl beat the egg whites until stiff. Fold the egg whites into the marmalade mixture. Spoon the filling into the pie crust. Bake at 350° for 25 to 30 minutes until the filling has risen and the top is lightly colored. Serve with whipping cream.

MAKES 4 TO 6 SERVINGS.

## Kedgeree

¼ cup butter
1 small onion, chopped
1 teaspoon curry powder
1 cup long grain rice
Salt and pepper to taste

2 cups water
¾ pound smoked haddock (Finnan haddie is best)
2 tablespoons all-purpose flour
½ teaspoon cayenne pepper
1½ cups chicken stock
3 hard-boiled eggs
Chopped parsley
Paprika

In a large skillet melt 2 tablespoons of butter, and sauté the onions until soft. Stir in the curry powder and rice. Sprinkle with salt and pepper. Add the water, cover, and cook over low heat for about 20 minutes until the rice is tender and the liquid is absorbed. Keep the rice warm.

Steam the fish or poach it in milk and water. Flake the fish, and keep it warm. In a medium saucepan melt 2 tablespoons of butter. Add the flour and pepper, mixing well. Blend in the chicken stock, stirring constantly, and cook until the mixture thickens and is reduced to about 1 cup.

Chop the egg whites, and set them aside. Press the egg yolks through a sieve and set them aside. In a medium bowl combine the rice, fish, egg whites, parsley, and sauce. Turn onto a warm dish. Garnish with the sieved yolks and paprika. Serve hot.

MAKES 4 SERVINGS.

## Bacon, Tomatoes, and Fried Bread

4 medium-sized fresh tomatoes, cut in half
2 tablespoons butter
8 bacon slices
4 thick slices bread, crusts removed

Place the tomatoes in a pan, dot them with butter, and cook under the broiler for about 5 minutes until tender but not soggy.

In a skillet fry the bacon. Transfer the bacon to a serving dish, and keep it warm. Increase the heat, and place the bread in the same skillet. Fry the bread until it is golden on both sides and serve immediately with the tomatoes and bacon.

MAKES 4 SERVINGS.

# Hot Cross Buns

4¼ to 4¾ cups all-purpose flour
⅔ cup sugar
1 ¼-ounce envelope rapid-rise yeast
1 teaspoon salt
1 teaspoon ground nutmeg
¼ teaspoon ground cinnamon
1 cup milk
¼ cup water
⅓ cup unsalted butter, cut up
2 large eggs
⅔ cup currants
⅓ cup chopped, mixed candied fruit
1 tablespoon all-purpose flour
1 egg white, slightly beaten

1 cup sifted confectioners' sugar
1 to 1½ tablespoons milk
½ teaspoon vanilla extract

*I*n a large mixing bowl combine 2½ cups of flour, the sugar, yeast, salt, nutmeg, and cinnamon, stirring well. Set aside.

In a small saucepan combine 1 cup of milk, the water, and butter and cook over medium heat, stirring constantly, just until the butter melts. Cool 5 minutes (to 130°).

Pour the milk mixture into the flour mixture, and beat at low speed with an electric mixer until the dry ingredients are moistened. Add the eggs, and beat at medium speed for 3 minutes. Gradually stir in enough of the remaining flour to make a soft dough.

Turn the dough out onto a well-floured surface, and knead until smooth and elastic, about 8 minutes. Place dough in a well greased bowl, turning to grease the top. Cover, and let rise in a warm draft-free place for 1 hour until almost doubled in bulk.

Punch the dough down, and turn it out onto a floured surface. In a small bowl combine the currants, candied fruit, and 1 tablespoon of flour, stirring to coat. Knead about one-fourth of the fruit mixture at a time into the dough until all of the fruit mixture is evenly dispersed.

Grease a 9 x 13-inch baking pan. Divide the dough into 15 equal portions, and shape each portion into a ball. Place the balls in the prepared pan, cover, and let rise in a warm place for 1 hour or until doubled in bulk.

Gently brush tops with beaten egg white. Bake at 375° for 16 minutes or until the buns are deep golden brown and sound hollow when tapped. Cool for 10 minutes in the pan on a wire rack.

In a small bowl combine the confectioners' sugar, 1 to 1½ tablespoons of milk, and vanilla. Pipe the mixture evenly on top of the warm buns, forming a cross.

MAKES 15 BUNS.

# All Saint's Day

*November 1st is All-Saint's day, a day set aside in remembrance of those who have walked before us, often in the most dire circumstances, modeling, preserving, and protecting the faith of the ages.*

---

MINI GRUYÈRE PUFFS

CORNISH HENS WITH BROWN RICE STUFFING

GREEN BEANS WITH SHALLOTS

HAZELNUT TART

---

O Almighty God, who hast knit together thine elect in one communion and fellowship, in the mystical body of thy Son Christ our Lord: Grant us grace so to follow thy blessed Saints in all virtuous and godly living, that we may come to those unspeakable joys, which thou hast prepared for them that unfeignedly love thee; through Jesus Christ our Lord.
Amen.

# Mini Gruyère Puffs

1 cup water
½ cup margarine or butter
¾ teaspoon crushed dried basil
¼ teaspoon garlic salt
⅛ teaspoon ground red pepper
1 cup all-purpose flour
4 eggs
½ cup shredded Gruyère cheese (or Swiss)
2 tablespoons grated Parmesan cheese

Grease a baking sheet. In a medium saucepan combine the water, margarine, basil, garlic salt, and red pepper. Bring the mixture to a boiling. Add the flour all at once, stirring vigorously. Cook and stir until the mixture forms a ball that does not separate. Remove the pan from the heat. Cool for 5 minutes.

Add the eggs one at a time, beating after each addition until smooth. Stir in the Gruyère cheese. Drop the dough by rounded tablespoons onto the prepared baking sheet into 18 equal mounds about 2 inches apart. Sprinkle with Parmesan cheese.

Bake at 400° for 30 to 35 minutes or until golden. Turn off the oven and let the puffs stand in the oven for 10 minutes. Serve hot.

MAKES 18 PUFFS.

# Cornish Hens with Brown Rice Stuffing

5 cups chicken stock
2 cups uncooked brown rice
1 cup unsalted butter
2 small onions, chopped
1 yellow bell pepper, chopped
1 cup dried apricots, chopped
1 cup toasted almonds, slivered or chopped
2 teaspoons salt

½ teaspoon dried thyme
½ teaspoon dried marjoram
Salt and pepper to taste
8 Cornish game hens
8 slices bacon

In a large saucepan bring the chicken stock to a boil. Add the rice. Cover, reduce the heat and cook for 40 minutes or until the stock is absorbed. Set aside.

In a skillet melt the butter, and sauté the onion, bell pepper, and apricots. Remove the skillet from the heat, and add the cooked rice, almonds, salt, thyme, and marjoram. Salt and pepper the hens inside and out. Stuff with the rice mixture, and place one bacon slice on top of each hen. Bake at 325° for 1 hour and 30 minutes to 2 hours, basting often with pan drippings. If the hens are not tender after 1 hour and 30 minutes, cover and steam for the final 30 minutes.

MAKES 8 SERVINGS.

# Green Beans with Shallots

3½ pounds green beans
2 tablespoons olive oil
½ cup minced shallots
2 tablespoons water
1 teaspoon salt
¼ teaspoon pepper

Trim the ends from the beans and remove the strings. Drop the beans into a large stock pot of boiling water and cook for 10 minutes or until tender. Drain.

In a stock pot heat the olive oil over medium heat, and sauté the shallots for 3 minutes or until tender. Add the green beans and water, and cook for 3 minutes or until the beans are tender, stirring occasionally. Remove the pan from the heat, and season with salt and pepper.

MAKES 8 TO 10 SERVINGS.

# Hazelnut Tart

1 cup all-purpose flour
⅛ teaspoon salt
1 tablespoon sugar
7 tablespoons cold butter, cut in pieces
3 to 4 tablespoons cold water

3 ounces semisweet chocolate, melted
¼ cup butter
⅓ cup sugar
½ cup whipping cream
1 tablespoon honey
1¾ cups hazelnuts, lightly toasted, skinned,
    coarsely chopped

*I*n a food processor combine the flour, salt, and 1 tablespoon of sugar, and process to blend. Add the 7 tablespoons of cold butter and process until the mixture resembles coarse meal. Add 3 tablespoons of water, just until the dough holds together and looks moist, adding more water if needed. Do not overprocess. Wrap the pastry in plastic wrap, and chill at least 1 hour.

Roll out the pastry on a floured board to fit a 9½-inch tart pan with removable bottom. Place the pastry in the pan, and trim the excess pastry. Freeze for 20 minutes. Cover the pastry with aluminum foil and fill with dried beans or pie weights. Bake at 425° for 15 minutes.

Remove the foil and beans, and prick the shell thoroughly with fork. Reduce the oven temperature to 350°, and bake 15 minutes longer or until golden. Remove the tart shell from the oven and place on a rack to cool.

Brush the bottom of the tart shell with a thin layer of melted chocolate. Set aside. Reserve the remaining chocolate.

In a small saucepan melt ¼ cup of butter. Add ⅓ cup of sugar, the cream and honey. Bring the mixture to a boil, stirring constantly until the sugar is dissolved. Boil for 2 to 3 minutes. Add the hazelnuts. Pour the mixture into the tart shell.

Bake at 350° for 30 minutes or until golden brown. Remove the tart from the oven and place on a wire rack to cool.

Reheat the reserved chocolate, and drizzle it on top of the tart.

MAKES 10 TO 12 SERVINGS.

# An Elegant Dinner Party with Friends

*The most elegant contributions to the fine table you lay tonight will be the atmosphere of welcome, the special care you have taken to please each friend, and the aromas of faith and peace your home and heart convey. All these intangibles combine with the beauty of taste and presentation arrayed before your fortunate guests to make tonight a memorable evening.*

SAVORY CHEESE BISCOTTI

CAESAR SALAD

PESTO BREAD

CHICKEN, ZUCCHINI, AND MUSHROOM LASAGNA

ESPRESSO-HAZELNUT CHEESECAKE

## THE PRAYERS I MAKE

*The prayers I make will then be sweet indeed,
If Thou the spirit give by which I pray:
My unassisted heart is barren clay,
That of its native self can nothing feed.
Of good and pious works Thou art the seed,
That quickens only where Thou sayest it may;
Unless Thou show to us Thine own true way,
No man can find it: Father! Thou must lead.
Do Thou, then, breathe those thoughts into my mind
By which such virtue may in me be bred,
That in Thy holy footsteps I may tread;
The fetters of my tongue do Thou unbind,
That I may have the power to sing of Thee
And sound Thy praises everlastingly.*

MICHELANGELO (1475-1564)
*The last six lines are attributed to Michelangelo's nephew.*

## Savory Cheese Biscotti

2 cups all-purpose flour
2 tablespoons yellow cornmeal
1 teaspoon baking powder
1 teaspoon salt
1 teaspoon sugar
½ teaspoon dried basil
½ cup sour cream
2 tablespoons margarine, melted
3 egg whites
½ cup shredded Cheddar cheese

*I*n a medium bowl combine the flour, cornmeal, baking powder, salt, sugar, and basil. In a large bowl combine the sour cream, margarine, and egg whites, stirring with a wire whisk until blended. Fold in the Cheddar cheese. Add the flour mixture, stirring until well blended. The dough will be crumbly.

Coat a baking sheet with baking spray. Turn the dough out onto a lightly floured surface and knead lightly 7 or 8 times. Shape the dough into a 16-inch long roll. Place the roll on the prepared baking sheet. Flatten to 1-inch thickness. Bake at 350° for 30 minutes. Remove the roll from the baking sheet to a wire rack. Cook for 10 minutes.

Cut the roll diagonally into 24 ½-inch slices. Place cut-side down on the baking sheet. Reduce the oven temperature to 325° and bake for 15 minutes. Turn the biscotti over and bake an additional 15 minutes. The biscotti will be slightly soft in the center but will harden as they cool. Remove from the baking sheet and cool completely on a wire rack.

MAKES 24 BISCOTTI.

## Caesar Salad

3 tablespoons butter
5 slices bread
Garlic powder to taste
Celery salt to taste
Thyme to taste
¾ cup oil
¼ cup fresh lemon juice
1 2-ounce can anchovies, drained and mashed
2 cloves garlic, crushed
2 teaspoons mustard
Romaine lettuce, torn

*B*utter the bread and season with garlic powder, celery salt, and thyme. Place on a baking sheet. Bake at 200° for 30 minutes. Cut up the bread into crouton-size pieces, and bake for 10 to 15 more minutes. Let cool.

In a salad bowl combine the oil, lemon juice, anchovies, garlic, and mustard. Set aside.

At serving time remove the garlic from the dressing. Add the lettuce to the dressing. Add the croutons. Toss well.

MAKES 4 TO 6 SERVINGS.

## Pesto Bread

¼ cup unsalted butter, softened
1 tablespoon oil
2 tablespoons sugar
3 eggs
1 cup milk
1 cup all-purpose flour
1 cup whole wheat flour
1 tablespoon baking powder
1½ teaspoons salt
1 cup coarsely ground almonds
2 teaspoons dried basil leaves
2 teaspoons parsley flakes
1 teaspoon garlic powder

*G*rease an 8½ x 4½-inch loaf pan. In a large bowl combine the butter, oil, and sugar and beat well. In a separate bowl combine the eggs and milk, and beat well. Add the egg mixture to the butter mixture, mixing well.

In a medium bowl combine the flour, baking powder, and salt. Add the dry ingredients to the batter, beating well. Stir in the almonds, basil, parsley, and garlic. Spoon the batter into the prepared pan. Bake at 350° for 55 minutes or until a toothpick inserted in the center comes out clean. Remove the loaf from the pan, and cool on a wire rack.

MAKES 1 LOAF.

## Chicken, Zucchini, and Mushroom Lasagna

5 tablespoons unsalted butter
1½ pounds leeks, thinly sliced
1 pound whole skinless boneless chicken breasts, chopped
Salt and pepper to taste
1 pound mushrooms, thinly sliced
1¼ pounds (about 4) zucchini, scrubbed
2 tablespoons all-purpose flour
2½ cups milk
1 cup cottage cheese
1 16-ounce box lasagna noodles
⅓ cup freshly grated Parmesan cheese
½ cup heavy cream, chilled

In a stockpot melt 3 tablespoon of the butter and sauté the leeks over low heat, stirring occasionally, for 30 minutes or until they are softened. Pat the chicken dry and season it with salt and pepper. In a heavy skillet melt the remaining 2 tablespoons of butter over moderately high heat and sauté the chicken for 5 minutes on each side or until just firm to the touch. Transfer the chicken with a slotted spatula to a plate. In the same skillet sauté the mushrooms over moderate heat, stirring and adding any juices from the chicken that have accumulated on the plate, until all of the liquid the mushrooms give off is evaporated.

Cut the zucchini lengthwise with a vegetable peeler into thin strips. In a large saucepan of boiling water blanch the zucchini strips, stirring constantly, for 30 seconds. Drain them well.

In the stockpot with the leeks stir in the flour and cook the mixture over moderately low heat for 3 minutes, whisking constantly. Whisk in the milk. Bring the liquid to a boil, stirring constantly, and simmer for 5 minutes. Stir in the cottage cheese, chicken, and salt and pepper to taste. Remove the pot from the heat.

Butter a 9 x 13-inch baking dish. In a large pot of boiling salted water cook the lasagna for 10 to 12 minutes or until al dente. Drain, refresh the lasagna under cold water, and drain well. Arrange a single layer of the lasagna strips in the prepared dish. Sprinkle ¼ cup of the Parmesan over it, and arrange half the zucchini strips on top. Sprinkle half the mushrooms over the zucchini, and spread half the chicken mixture on top. Repeat the layers of lasagna strips, zucchini, mushrooms, and chicken mixture, ending with a layer of lasagna strips.

In a medium bowl beat the cream with an electric mixer until it holds soft peaks. Season with salt and pepper to taste, and spread the cream over the lasagna. Sprinkle with the remaining Parmesan. Bake at 375° for 30 minutes or until the top is golden brown. Cool for 15 minutes.

MAKES 8 SERVINGS.

# Espresso-Hazelnut Cheesecake

8½ ounces butter biscuit cookies
½ cup toasted hazelnuts, husked
2 tablespoons sugar
1 teaspoon ground cinnamon
5 tablespoons unsalted butter, melted

4 8-ounce packages cream cheese, softened
1¼ cups sugar
4 large eggs
1 cup sour cream
½ cup plus ⅔ cup chilled whipping cream
3 tablespoons instant espresso powder
2 tablespoons warm water
2 teaspoons vanilla extract
¾ cup toasted hazelnuts, husked, and coarsely
    chopped
Chocolate-covered espresso beans for garnish

Generously butter the bottom and sides of a 9-inch-diameter springform pan. Wrap the outside of the pan with a double layer of foil. In a food processor finely chop the cookies, hazelnuts, sugar, and cinnamon. Add the butter and process until moist clumps form. Press the crumb mixture onto the bottom and up the sides of the pan. Refrigerate until chilled.

In a large bowl beat the cream cheese with an electric mixer until smooth. Add the sugar and beat until well blended. Add the eggs one at a time, beating just until blended and scraping down the sides of the bowl after each addition. Beat in the sour cream and ½ cup of whipping cream. In a small bowl stir together the espresso powder and 2 tablespoons of warm water until the powder dissolves. Add the espresso mixture to the filling and beat until blended. Beat in the vanilla. Stir in the hazelnuts. Pour the filling into the prepared pan. Place the pan in a large baking pan. Pour enough hot water into baking pan to come halfway up sides of the springform pan. Bake at 350° for about 1 hour and 15 minutes or until the top is puffed and the center is almost set. Turn off the oven, and open the door slightly. Leave the cheesecake in the oven with the door ajar for 1 hour. Remove the pan from the water and transfer to a rack. Cool. Wrap in foil and chill overnight.

Remove the cheesecake from the pan. In a medium bowl beat ⅔ cup of whipping cream until stiff peaks form. Pipe the whipped cream through a large star tip around the top of the cheesecake. Garnish with chocolate covered espresso beans.

MAKES 8 SERVINGS.

# Election Day Dinner

You may not find yourself at party headquarters tonight, unless of course, your house becomes Party Headquarters! This is one night the conversation will flow easily, as everyone's favorite candidate, issue, and party's position is up for grabs. We can assure you of at least one outcome—you'll be at the top of the opinion polls when you lay out this spread!

---

WHITE BEAN AND FETA SALAD

PAN-FRIED TROUT WITH PECAN SAUCE

SQUASH CHEESE BAKE

HOT MILK SPONGE CAKE WITH PENUCHE ICING

---

*LORD, WHILE FOR ALL MANKIND WE PRAY*

L ord, while for all mankind we pray,
Of every clime and coast,
O Hear us for our native land,
The land we love the most.

O guard our shores from every foe;
With peace our borders bless,
Our cities with prosperity,
Our fields with plentiousness.

Unite us in the sacred love
Of knowledge, truth, and Thee;
And let our hills and valleys shout
The songs of liberty.

Lord of the nations, thus to Thee
Our country we commend;
Be Thou her refuge and her trust,
Her everlasting friend.

## White Bean and Feta Salad

1 pound dried small white beans, soaked
    overnight
6 cups water
3 carrots, diced
2 bay leaves

2 cloves garlic, minced
1½ tablespoons coarse-grained mustard
⅓ cup fresh lemon juice
1¼ cups olive oil
Salt and freshly ground pepper to taste

1 medium red onion, chopped
1 cup crumbled feta cheese
½ cup toasted pine nuts
1 bunch parsley, chopped

Drain the beans. In a large saucepan combine the beans, water, carrots, and bay leaves and bring the water to a boil. Skim the surface as needed. Reduce the heat and simmer for 25 to 30 minutes until the beans are just tender. Remove the pan from the heat and drain, discarding the carrots and bay leaves.

In a small bowl combine the garlic, mustard, and lemon juice. Whisk in the oil. Season with salt and pepper to taste.

In a serving bowl combine the beans, onion, feta cheese, pine nuts, and parsley. Pour the dressing over the salad mixture, and toss well.

MAKES 8 SERVINGS.

## Pan-Fried Trout with Pecan Sauce

1 cup pecans
½ cup unsalted butter, softened
4 shallots, coarsely chopped
2 small cloves garlic, minced
1 teaspoon fresh lemon juice
Pinch lemon peel
½ teaspoon hot sauce

8 fresh trout fillets
½ cup all-purpose flour
¼ cup finely ground pecans
1½ teaspoons salt
½ teaspoon white pepper
Dash cayenne pepper
½ cup unsalted butter
¼ cup oil
Large pecan halves for garnish

Spread 1 cup of pecans on a baking sheet and toast in a 350° oven for 7 to 8 minutes. In a blender combine the toasted pecans, ½ cup of butter, shallots, garlic, lemon juice, lemon peel, and hot sauce. Blend on high until smooth, about 2 minutes, scraping down the sides of the container occasionally.

Rinse the trout fillets and dry well on paper towels.

In a shallow pan combine the flour, ¼ cup of ground pecans, salt, pepper, and cayenne. Dredge the fillets in the flour mixture.

In a large saucepan melt ½ cup of butter with the oil over medium-high heat, and sauté the fillets for 2 to 3 minutes on each side or until golden brown, turning once. Drain on paper towels. Immediately transfer the fillets to serving plates and top each with a generous 2 tablespoons of pecan sauce. Sprinkle with pecan halves, and serve at once.

MAKES 8 SERVINGS.

## Squash Cheese Bake

2 pounds yellow squash, sliced
4 eggs, beaten
½ cup finely chopped onion
1 teaspoon sage
2 cups grated Cheddar cheese
1 teaspoon salt
Paprika

Grease a 1½-quart casserole dish.

Steam the squash until tender. Drain. In a large bowl blend together thoroughly the squash, eggs, onion, sage, ½ cup of the cheese, and salt. Pour the mixture into the prepared dish. Sprinkle with the paprika and the remaining cheese. Bake at 350° for 20 to 25 minutes or until brown.

MAKES 8 SERVINGS.

## Hot Milk Sponge Cake with Penuche Icing

4 large eggs
1¾ cups sugar
2 cups cake flour
2 teaspoons baking powder
¼ teaspoon salt
1 cup hot milk
6 tablespoons unsalted butter, cut into bits and softened
1½ teaspoons vanilla extract

1½ cups firmly packed dark brown sugar
½ cup sugar
1 tablespoon light corn syrup
¼ cup unsalted butter, cut up
½ cup heavy cream
1 teaspoon vanilla extract

Butter and flour a 10-inch round cake pan. In a large bowl beat the eggs and sugar with an electric mixer until well mixed. Sift in the flour, baking powder, and salt and beat the mixture until smooth. Add the milk, butter, and vanilla, and beat until combined. Pour the batter into the prepared pan. Bake at 350° in the middle of the oven for 50 minutes to 1 hour or until a toothpick inserted in the center of the cake comes out clean. Let the cake cool in the pan for 10 minutes. Invert onto a rack set over a shallow baking pan to cool completely.

In a heavy saucepan combine the brown sugar, sugar, corn syrup, ¼ cup of butter, and cream to a boil over medium heat, stirring constantly. Brush the sides of the pan with a brush dipped in cold water, dissolving the sugar clinging to the pan. Boil the mixture until it reaches the soft-ball stage, 238° on a candy thermometer.

Remove the pan from the heat, and stir in the vanilla. Set aside to cool for 5 to 10 minutes.

Stir the icing for 1 to 2 minutes or until it reaches a spreadable consistency. Working quickly, pour the icing over the cake, smoothing the top and sides with a spatula. Let the icing cool.

MAKES 8 SERVINGS.

# Claude Monet's Birthday

*One way to increase our cultural literacy is to observe the birthdays of those who have made significant contributions in a given discipline. Read aloud from a biographical sketch, peruse a book of paintings, intone a speech in best oratorical style—these things impress upon us our cultural heritage. Then, bless the food and eat a meal your character from history might have partaken. We may be sure Monsieur Monet would have gladly joined us for this impression of his Fete D'Anniversaire! November 14th is his birthday. Claude Monet (1840-1926) was a French painter whose work gave birth to the Impressionist movement. We contrast the serene work of Monet with the forceful theology of his fellow countryman, Blaise Pascal.*

---

SOUPE À L'OIGNON GRATINÉE
(Onion Soup with Cheese Crusts)

POULET DE BRESSE RÔTI
(Roast Bresse Chicken)

GATEAU DE POMMES DE TERRE
(Potato Cake)

BROUILLADE AUX LÉGUMES
(Mixed Vegetable Dish)

TARTE AUX POIRES ET CHOCOLAT
(Chocolate Pear Tart)

---

*O Lord, open my heart; enter into this rebellious place that my sins have possessed. They hold it in subjection; do Thou enter, as into the strong man's house; but first bind the strong and powerful enemy, who is the tyrant over it, and take to Thyself the treasures which are there. Lord, take my affections, which the world has robbed me of: spoil Thou the world of this treasure; or rather, resume it to Thyself, for to Thee it belongs; it is a tribute I owe Thee, for Thine own image is stamped upon it.*

## Soupe à l'Oignon Gratinée
### (Onion Soup with Cheese Crusts)

3 tablespoons butter
3 cups diced onions
2 tablespoons all-purpose flour
6 cups beef broth
¼ teaspoon freshly ground black pepper
Sliced French bread, lightly toasted
1 cup grated Gruyère cheese (or Swiss)
Grated Parmesan cheese (optional)

*I*n a large saucepan melt the butter and sauté the onions over low heat until browned and tender. Blend in the flour. Gradually add the broth, stirring constantly. Add the pepper. Cook over low heat for 30 minutes. Taste and adjust the seasonings.

In individual serving bowls place a slice of bread, and sprinkle each with Gruyère cheese. Pour the soup around the bread. Set the bowls of soup under a hot broiler until the cheese melts.

Serve with grated Parmesan cheese if desired.

MAKES 6 SERVINGS.

## Poulet de Bresse Rôti
### (Roast Bresse Chicken)

1 large roaster chicken, with giblets
1 large clove garlic, halved
Salt and freshly ground black pepper
1 teaspoon dried or finely chopped fresh mixed herbs
½ cup butter, softened
1 onion, quartered
1 carrot, quartered
1 bouquet garni (parsley, thyme, and bay leaf tied in cheesecloth)
Strip of lemon peel
1 teaspoon all-purpose flour

*W*ipe the chicken inside and out. Rub with the cut surface of the clove of garlic, and then with salt and pepper and the herbs. Place a small pat of the butter inside the cavity.

Lay the chicken on its side on a rack in the roasting pan, and brush the side that is turned up liberally with some of the softened butter. Roast in a 425° oven for 15 minutes. Turn the chicken over and rub with half of the remaining butter. Return to the oven for another 15 minutes. Turn the chicken breast-side up and brush the breast with all but a pat of the remaining butter. Reduce the oven temperature to 375° and continue to roast for 30 to 40 minutes, basting frequently with the pan juices.

In a saucepan combine the giblets, onion, carrot, bouquet garni, and lemon peel. Cover with water, and bring to a boil. Leave to simmer while the chicken is cooking.

The chicken is ready when the juice that runs out is just clear when the thickest part of the drumstick is pierced. Place the chicken on a heated serving platter and wrap in foil to keep warm. Let the chicken rest for at least 5 minutes before carving.

Skim any excess fat from the roasting pan. In a saucepan bring the remaining juice to a boil. Strain ¾ cup of the giblet stock into the pan and bring the mixture rapidly to a boil.

Make a beurre manié by working the flour into the remaining butter. Remove the saucepan from the heat and add the beurre manié to the pan. Stir to make a smooth sauce, adjust the seasoning, and bring to a boil. Simmer for 1 minute. Strain into a heated sauceboat. Serve the sauce with the chicken.

MAKES 6 SERVINGS.

## Gateau de Pommes de Terre
*(Potato Cake)*

¼ cup unsalted butter
2 pounds large baking potatoes, peeled and
    thinly sliced
Salt to taste
1 tablespoon unsalted butter
1 large clove garlic, finely chopped
1 tablespoon finely chopped fresh flat-leaf
    parsley

*I*n a large cast-iron skillet melt 3 tablespoons of butter. Add the potato slices, and season well with salt. Cover partially and cook over moderate heat, tossing gently with a metal spatula from time to time for about 25 minutes or until the potatoes are golden and tender. Turn the potatoes out on a platter, arrange the nicest slices in overlapping concentric rings in the skillet, and then top with the remaining potatoes. Firmly press the potatoes down.

Bake at 400° for about 20 minutes until crisp and evenly browned. Spear the remaining butter on a fork and run it around the side of the hot pan, letting it melt underneath potatoes. Invert the potato cake onto a large round plate. Sprinkle with garlic and parsley, and serve.

MAKES 6 SERVINGS.

## Brouillade Aux Légumes
*(Mixed Vegetable Dish)*

3¼ pound young fava beans, shelled
1 bunch small scallions
2 bundles asparagus
18 small purple artichokes
1 lemon, halved
1 10-ounce slice ham
3 tablespoons olive oil

1 large onion, peeled and diced
1 medium carrot, peeled and diced
1 cup Côte de Provence white wine
4 unpeeled cloves of garlic
Salt and pepper to taste
1 teaspoon fennel seeds

*I*n a large pot of boiling water cook the shelled fava beans for 20 seconds. Trim the scallions, leaving 1½ to 1¾ inches of the green part.

Trim the asparagus and cut diagonally into ¾-inch long pieces. Leave the asparagus tips in one piece even if some are longer than ¾-inch and separate them from the remaining asparagus pieces.

Trim the artichoke leaves by cutting off about 1 inch from the tip, depending on the size of each leaf. Remove the little leaves attached to the artichoke stem, as well as the outer leaves at its base. With a vegetable peeler, peel the stem until you reach the thin, white, tender heart. Split the artichokes into 4 pieces and rub the insides with half a lemon. This prevents them from turning brown. Do not squeeze all the juice out of the lemon as it will be used again later.

Cut the ham into long strips, leaving the fat on. In a large frying pan heat the oil over a medium heat. Add the strips of ham and fry for 3 minutes or until golden on each side. Remove the ham and keep it warm. In the same pan gently fry the diced onion and carrot for 5 minutes. Stir frequently, so the onion turns golden but does not brown.

Add the artichokes and white wine. Squeeze the remaining juice from the lemon into the pan. Cook for 10 minutes. Throw in the scallions and garlic, and cook for 5 minutes. Add the asparagus pieces, but not the tips, and cook for 6 to 7 minutes. Season with salt and pepper to taste, add the asparagus tips, and cook for 2 minutes. Add the fava beans, stirring gently.

Sprinkle with fennel seeds, and cook for 5 minutes over low heat. Stir in the ham and continue cooking for another minute. Serve on a heated serving platter.

MAKES 6 SERVINGS.

## *Tarte aux Poires et Chocolat*
### *(Chocolate Pear Tart)*

1½ cups all-purpose flour
7 tablespoons unsalted butter
1 egg yolk
¾ teaspoon salt
3 tablespoons sugar
3 tablespoons cold water
2 to 3 tablespoons sugar (for sprinkling)

1 egg
1 egg yolk
½ cup light cream
½ teaspoon vanilla extract

4 ounces semisweet chocolate, chopped finely
3 ripe dessert pears (about 1 pound)
Sugar for sprinkling

Sift the flour onto a work surface, and make a large well in the center. Pound the butter with a rolling pin to soften it. Put the butter, egg yolk, salt, sugar, and water in the well. Work together by hand until partly mixed. Gradually draw in the flour with a pastry scraper or metal spatula, pulling the dough into large crumbs using the fingertips of both hands. If the crumbs are dry, sprinkle with another tablespoon of water. Press the dough together. It should be soft but not sticky. Work small portions of dough, pushing away from you on the work surface with the heel of your hand, then gathering it up with a scraper. Continue until the dough is smooth and pliable. Press the pâté brisé into a ball. Wrap, and refrigerate for 30 minutes or until firm.

Butter a 10- to 11-inch tart pan generously, then sprinkle with sugar. Roll out the dough to 1/8 inch thickness and line the tart pan.

In a medium bowl beat 1 egg, the egg yolk, cream, and vanilla until thoroughly mixed.

Sprinkle the bottom of the tart with the chopped chocolate. Peel and thinly slice the pears crosswise. Flatten the slices lightly. Arrange the slices in an overlapping flower petal design on the chocolate. Spoon the custard over the pears and gently spread to coat. The custard should be just visible between the pear slices. Sprinkle with sugar.

Bake at 400° near the bottom of the oven for 10 minutes. Reduce the heat to 350° and bake for 15 to 20 minutes longer or until the crust is brown and the custard is set. If the pears are not caramelized, brown them under a hot broiler for 2 to 3 minutes.

MAKES 8 TO 12 SERVINGS.

# A Southern Thanksgiving

*It may have been a cold winter and a sparse feast that first year, honey, but no one ever said it had to stay that way! Southern cookin' is synonymous with good cookin', and we cheerfully admit that the meal we present for Thanksgiving barely resembles the humble repast in Plymouth of old. Y'all hush up now and eat for all those poor hungry Pilgrims.*

BENNE SEED ANGEL BISCUITS

ROAST TURKEY WITH HAM AND
APRICOT DRESSING AND GRAVY

CRANBERRY DELIGHT

THANKSGIVING POTATOES

OLD-FASHIONED GREEN BEANS

COMPANY CARROTS

PUMPKIN PIE BARS

GEORGIA PECAN PIE

## FIVE KERNELS OF CORN

*T'was the year of the famine in Plymouth of old,
  The ice and the snow from the thatched roofs had
    rolled;
Through the warm purle skies steered the geese o'er
    the seas,
  And the woodpeckers tapped in the clocks of the
    trees;
And the boughs on the slopes to the south winds lay
    bare,
  And dreaming of summer, the buds swelled in
    the air.
And pale Pilgrims welcomed each reddening morn;
  There were left but for rations Five Kernels of
    Corn.
  Five Kernels of Corn!
  Five Kernels of Corn!
But to Bradford a feast were Five Kernels of Corn!*

*"Five Kernels of Corn! Five Kernels of Corn!
  Ye people, be glad for Five Kernels of Corn!"
So Bradford cried out on bleak Burial Hill,
  And the thin women stood in their doors, white
    and still.
"Lo, the harbor of Plymouth rolls bright in the
    Spring,
  The maples grow red, and the wood robins sing,
The west wind is blowing, and fading the snow
  And the pleasant pines sing, and arbutuses blow.
  Five Kernels of Corn!
  Five kernels of Corn!
To each one be given Five Kernels of corn!"*

O Bradford of Austerfield haste on thy way.
　The west winds are blowing o'er Provincetown
　　Bay,

The white avens bloom, but the pine domes are chill,
　And new graves have furrowed Precisioners'
　　Hill!
"Give thanks, all ye people, the warm skies have
　　come,
　The hilltops are sunny, and green grows the
　　holm,
And the trumpets of winds, and the white March is
　　gone,
　And ye still have left you Five Kernels of Corn.
　Five Kernels of Corn!
　Five Kernels of Corn!
Ye have for Thanksgiving Five Kernels of Corn!

The raven's gift eat and be humble and pray,
　A new light is breaking, and Truth leads your
　　way;
One taper a thousand shall kindle: rejoice
　That to you has been given the wilderness voice!"
O Bradford of Austerfield, daring the wave,
　And safe through the sounding blasts leading the
　　brave,
Of deeds such as thine was the free nation born,
　And the festal world sings the "Five Kernels of
　　Corn."
　Five Kernels of Corn!
　Five Kernels of Corn!
The nation gives thanks for Five Kernels of Corn!
To the Thanksgiving Feast bring Five Kernels of
　　Corn!

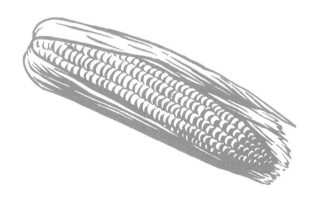

# Benne Seed Angel Biscuits

1 package active dry yeast
¼ cup warm water (about 105°)
3 tablespoons sugar
5½ cups cake flour
1 tablespoon baking powder
1 teaspoon baking soda
2 teaspoons salt
½ cup chilled vegetable shortening
½ cup cold unsalted butter, cut into pieces
1¼ cups buttermilk plus additional for
	brushing biscuits
3 tablespoons benne (sesame) seeds, toasted
	lightly and cooled

*I*n a small bowl stir together the yeast, water, and a pinch sugar. Let the mixture stand for about 5 minutes, until foamy.

In a large bowl stir together the flour, baking powder, baking soda, salt, and remaining sugar. Cut in the shortening and butter until the mixture resembles coarse meal. Add the yeast mixture and 1¼ cups of buttermilk, stirring until a sticky dough just forms. Gather the dough into a ball. On a lightly floured surface knead the dough gently 6 times. Pat out into a 10-inch round about ½-inch thick. Wrap the dough in plastic wrap, and refrigerate for at least 8 hours.

Lightly butter a large baking sheet. With a 2-inch round cutter cut out as many rounds as possible and arrange, sides just touching, on the prepared baking sheet. Gather the scraps into a ball, pat out, and continue to cut out rounds. Brush the biscuits with additional buttermilk and sprinkle with benne seeds. Bake at 425° in the middle of the oven for 10 minutes or until golden.

MAKES ABOUT 24 BISCUITS.

# Roast Turkey and Gravy

1 12- to 15-pound turkey, giblets reserved for
	making stock
Salt and freshly ground pepper to taste
½ cup unsalted butter, softened
4 cups turkey giblet stock or chicken broth
¼ cup all-purpose flour

*R*inse the turkey and pat it dry. Season it inside and out with salt and pepper. Fold the neck skin under the body, and fasten with a skewer. Truss the turkey. Spread with ¼ cup of butter. Place the turkey on the rack of a roasting pan. Roast at 425° in the middle of the oven for 30 minutes.

Reduce the oven temperature to 325°. Baste the turkey with the pan juices, and drape it with a piece of cheesecloth soaked in 1 cup of the stock and the remaining ¼ cup of melted butter. Continue to roast the turkey, basting every 20 minutes, for 2 hours and 30 minutes to 3 hours more or until the juices run clear when the fleshy part of a thigh is pricked with a skewer and a meat thermometer inserted in the fleshy part of a thigh registers 180°.

Discard the cheesecloth, skewer, and trussing strings, and transfer the turkey to a platter. Keep it warm, covered loosely with foil.

Skim off all but ¼ cup of the fat from the pan juices. Add the flour and cook the mixture over moderately low heat, stirring constantly, for 5 minutes. Add the remaining 3 cups of stock in a stream, stirring constantly. Simmer for 20 minutes, stirring occasionally, or until reduced to 2½ cups. Season the gravy with salt and pepper, and strain it into a heated gravy boat. Serve the gravy with the turkey and the stuffing.

MAKES 8 SERVINGS.

# Ham and Apricot Stuffing

1 cup yellow cornmeal
1 cup all-purpose flour
4 teaspoons baking powder
¼ teaspoon baking soda
½ teaspoon salt
¼ cup plus 1 teaspoon chilled vegetable
    shortening
1 cup buttermilk
1 large egg, beaten lightly

⅓ cup oil
4 cups chopped onion
2 cups chopped celery
3 garlic cloves, minced
Salt and freshly ground pepper to taste
2 cups chopped dried apricots
½ pound smoked ham, finely chopped
½ cup minced fresh parsley leaves
3 tablespoons minced fresh sage (or 1
    tablespoon dried, crumbled)
2 tablespoons minced fresh marjoram (or
    2 teaspoons dried, crumbled)
1 tablespoon minced fresh rosemary (or
    1 teaspoon dried, crumbled)
½ teaspoon freshly grated nutmeg
½ cup unsalted butter, melted and cooled

In a medium bowl combine the cornmeal, flour, baking powder, baking soda, and salt. Add ¼ cup of the shortening, cut into bits. Blend until the mixture resembles coarse meal. Stir in the buttermilk and the egg until combined but still slightly lumpy.

In an 8-inch square baking pan heat the remaining 1 teaspoon of shortening in a 425° oven until melted. Tilt the pan to coat the bottom and sides well with the shortening. Pour the batter into the pan. Bake at 425° in the middle of the oven for 20 to 25 minutes or until the top is golden and a toothpick inserted in the center comes out clean. Cool in the pan for 5 minutes.

Crumble the corn bread coarsely into 2 jelly-roll pans. Bake at 325° in the middle of the oven, stirring frequently, for 30 to 40 minutes or until dry and deep golden. Let the cornbread cool.

In a large skillet heat the oil and sauté the onion, celery, garlic, and salt and pepper over moderate heat, stirring constantly, until softened. In a large bowl combine the corn bread and the sautéed mixture. Add the remaining ingredients, and toss gently to combine well. Cool completely.

Spread the mixture into a 9-inch square pan. Bake in a 325° oven for 1 hour.

MAKES 8 SERVINGS.

# Cranberry Delight

1 16-ounce can wholeberry cranberry sauce
1 8-ounce carton sour cream
1 cup whole pecans
1 15½-ounce can crushed pineapple, well-
    drained

In an 8-inch square pan or ring mold combine all of the ingredients. Mix well and smooth out. Freeze for 5 to 7 hours. Unmold before serving.

MAKES 6 TO 8 SERVINGS.

# Thanksgiving Potatoes

9 large baking potatoes, peeled and diced
½ cup unsalted butter, softened
12 ounces cream cheese, softened
¾ cup sour cream
½ teaspoon ground nutmeg
Salt and pepper to taste

In a large stock pot place the potatoes in water to cover. Bring the water to a boil, reduce the heat, and simmer over medium heat until tender. Drain.

In a large bowl combine the potatoes, butter, and cream cheese, and beat until fluffy. Beat in the sour cream. Season with nutmeg, salt, and pepper.

MAKES 8 SERVINGS.

# Old-fashioned Green Beans

4 to 6 slices bacon
1 large onion, chopped
1½ to 2 pounds green beans, snapped
½ cup water
Salt and pepper to taste
1 cube chicken bouillon
¼ teaspoon sugar

*I*n a heavy pot fry the bacon until crisp over medium heat. Remove the bacon, and place on paper towels. Add the onion to the bacon grease and sauté until limp. Add the green beans, water, salt, pepper, and bouillon cube, and sugar. Cover, and simmer the mixture for 45 minutes or until tender. Transfer the green bean mixture to a serving dish and crumble the bacon over the top of the beans.

MAKES 8 SERVINGS.

# Company Carrots

2½ pounds carrots, cut in strips
½ cup mayonnaise
1 tablespoon minced onion
1 tablespoon horseradish
Salt and pepper to taste
6 saltine crackers, crumbled
1 tablespoon parsley flakes
Paprika
Butter

*I*n a saucepan cook the carrots in boiling salted water until tender. Drain the carrots and reserve ¼ cup of the liquid. In a shallow 1½-quart baking dish arrange the carrots. In a small bowl combine the carrot liquid, mayonnaise, onion, horseradish, salt, and pepper. Pour the mixture over the carrots. Sprinkle with the cracker crumbs, parsley flakes, and paprika, and dot with butter. Bake at 375° for 20 to 25 minutes.

MAKES 8 SERVINGS.

# Pumpkin Pie Bars

¼ cup cake flour
1½ cups sugar
1 tablespoon baking powder
1 teaspoon salt
10 tablespoons chilled unsalted butter, cut into pieces
1 large egg, beaten to blend

1 cup chopped walnuts
¼ cup firmly packed light brown sugar
½ teaspoon ground cinnamon
2 tablespoons chilled unsalted butter, cut into pieces

2 large eggs
¼ cup firmly packed light brown sugar
1 29-ounce can solid pack pumpkin
⅔ cup whole milk
½ teaspoon ground cinnamon
½ teaspoon ground allspice
¼ teaspoon ground cloves
¼ teaspoon ground ginger
¼ teaspoon salt
⅛ teaspoon freshly grated nutmeg
½ cup finely chopped walnuts

1 cup chilled whipping cream
1 tablespoon sugar
1 teaspoon vanilla extract
½ teaspoon ground cinnamon
2 teaspoons grated orange peel

*L*ightly butter a 9 x 13-inch baking dish. Into a large bowl sift the flour, sugar, baking soda, and salt. Cut in 10 tablespoons of butter until the mixture resembles fine crumbs. Transfer 1 cup of the crumb mixture to a small bowl and reserve for topping. Stir 1 egg into the remaining crumb mixture. Spoon the mixture into the bottom of the prepared baking dish, and press to form an even layer. Bake at 350° for about 15 minutes, until golden brown. Cool.

Add the walnuts, ¼ cup of brown sugar, and ¼ teaspoon of cinnamon to the reserved crumb mixture. Cut in 2 tablespoons of butter until crumbly.

In a large bowl whisk 2 eggs until foamy. Add ¼ cup of brown sugar and stir until dissolved. Gradually add the pumpkin and milk, and mix until smooth. Stir in the cinnamon, allspice, cloves, ginger, salt, and nutmeg. Pour the filling into the prepared crust. Crumble the topping over the filling. Bake at 350° for about 30 minutes or until the filling is set in the center and the topping is golden brown. Transfer to a rack and cool.

Sprinkle ½ cup of walnuts over the pie.

In a large bowl beat the whipping cream, sugar, vanilla, and ½ teaspoon of cinnamon until soft peaks form. Fold in the orange peel.

Cut the pumpkin pie into squares, and serve with spiced whipped cream.

MAKES 8 TO 12 SERVINGS.

## Georgia Pecan Pie

1 cup sugar
2 tablespoons butter, melted
1 cup dark corn syrup
1 teaspoon vanilla extract
1 9-inch pie crust
3 eggs
1½ cups coarsely chopped pecans
Sweetened whipped cream

In a saucepan combine the sugar, butter, corn syrup, and vanilla. Simmer, stirring constantly, until the sugar melts. Cool briefly.

In a medium bowl beat the eggs. Add the cooled mixture to the beaten eggs, and mix well. Stir in the pecans. Pour the filling into the prepared pie crust. Bake at 375° for 30 minutes or until the pie is well puffed. Remove and place on a rack to cool.

Serve with sweetened whipped cream on top.

MAKES 8 SERVINGS.

# A Portable Thanksgiving:
## A Blessing in Deed

*Who among us is not often aware of our own responsibility to share our abundance with others? Thanksgiving is a time when we pause to name the reasons for our gratitude. If all your friends, family, and acquaintances have enough, a simple call to your church, The American Red Cross, Goodwill, The Salvation Army, or another like-minded organization will produce the name of a needy family with whom your family can share its bounty by taking a Thanksgiving meal for their family to enjoy. Make arrangements to humbly and discreetly share your blessings with another family. Don't forget to enclose a copy of a blessing for their meal!*

---

PUMPKIN BREAD

BAKED TURKEY WITH CORN BREAD DRESSING

MUSTARD GREEN BEANS

SWEET POTATO CASSEROLE

BAKED CRANBERRY SAUCE

APPLE CRANBERRY CRUMB BARS

---

### A SONG OF THANKSGIVING

O gracious God whose bounteous hand,
Has blessed this year our native land,
We thank Thee for the hope of spring,
When trees did bud, and birds did sing.
We thank Thee for the summer time,
Of sun and rain, and days sublime.
But most of all we sing Thy praise,
For mellow Autumn's harvest days,
When fruit and grains our bins did fill,
Obedient to Thy bounteous will.
Thy promises in bud and flower,
Redeemed to us this day and hour.

If we have suffered in the past,
Let bitterness from us be cast,
That crushing sense of grief and pain,
That scorched the heart and seared the brain.
Pour in rich floods of Thy dear love,
That falls, like dew, from heaven above.
Let smiles be seen above the feast,
So bounteous for man and beast.
Let us uphold that Pilgrim faith,
That trusted Thee through life and death.
Let gratitude in every way,
Abide with us Thanksgiving Day.

# Pumpkin Bread

⅔ cup oil
2⅔ cups sugar
4 eggs
2 cups canned pumpkin
3⅓ cups all-purpose flour
½ teaspoon baking powder
2 teaspoons baking soda
1½ teaspoons salt
1 teaspoon ground cinnamon
½ teaspoon ground cloves
⅔ cup water
⅔ cup chopped pecans
⅔ cup chopped dates

Grease two 9 x 5-inch loaf pans. In a large bowl beat the oil with the sugar. Add the eggs one at a time, beating after each addition. Stir in the pumpkin. In a separate bowl sift together the flour, baking powder, baking soda, salt, cinnamon, and cloves. Beat the dry ingredients into the creamed mixture. Beat in the water. Toss the pecans and dates lightly with flour, and add them to the batter. Pour the batter into the prepared pans. Bake at 350° for 1 hour.

MAKES 2 LOAVES.

# Baked Turkey

1 10- to 12-pound turkey
Salt to taste
¼ cup butter, softened
1 onion
1 rib celery

Remove the giblets, rinse the turkey, and pat dry. Sprinkle inside the cavity with salt. Brush the outside of the turkey with softened butter. Place the onion and celery inside the cavity. Place the turkey in a roasting pan and cover. Bake at 350° for about 3 to 3 1/2 hours or 20 minutes per pound. After baking, discard the onion and celery and reserve the pan broth for dressing.

MAKES 8 SERVINGS.

# Corn Bread Dressing

3 eggs
3 cups self-rising cornmeal
2 cups buttermilk
½ cup oil (or bacon drippings)
½ cup chopped celery
½ cup chopped onion
1 tablespoon dried sage
2 teaspoons black pepper
2 to 3 cups turkey broth

Grease a 12-inch skillet. In a large bowl combine the eggs, cornmeal, buttermilk, and oil, mixing well. Pour into the prepared skillet. Bake at 425° for 20 minutes or until golden brown.

Grease a 9 x 13-inch glass baking dish. Crumble the corn bread into a large bowl. Add the celery, onion, sage, and black pepper. Stir in 2 or more cups of broth or just enough to moisten. Pour the dressing mixture into the prepared dish. Bake at 425° for about 35 to 40 minutes or until golden brown.

MAKES 8 SERVINGS.

## Mustard Green Beans

3 9-ounce packages frozen green beans (or 1½ pounds fresh)
2 slices bacon
¾ cup thinly sliced onion
2 cloves garlic, minced
1 tablespoon brown mustard
½ teaspoon lemon-pepper seasoning (or ¼ teaspoon pepper)
⅛ teaspoon salt

*I*n a large saucepan combine the beans and a small amount of water. Bring the water to a boil, cover, and simmer for 20 to 25 minutes or until crisp-tender. Drain.

In a medium skillet cook the bacon until crisp. Drain, reserving the drippings in the skillet. Crumble the bacon and set aside. In the drippings sauté the onions and garlic over medium heat for 3 minutes or until tender. Stir in the mustard, lemon-pepper, and salt, and cook about 30 seconds more. In a serving dish toss the onion mixture with the beans and sprinkle with bacon.

MAKES 8 SERVINGS.

## Sweet Potato Casserole

3 large sweet potatoes, quartered
¼ cup sugar
1 tablespoon ground cinnamon
1 teaspoon grated nutmeg
½ cup butter
2 eggs, beaten
½ cup packed brown sugar
3 tablespoons all-purpose flour
3 tablespoons butter
½ cup chopped pecans

*I*n a stock pot boil the sweet potatoes in water to cover until tender. Remove the skins. In a large bowl mash the potatoes. Add the sugar, cinnamon, nutmeg, ½ cup of butter, eggs, and brown sugar, and beat well. Transfer the mixture to a 1½-quart casserole dish. In a small bowl combine the flour, 3 tablespoons of butter, and pecans, and sprinkle over the top. Bake at 350° for 30 minutes.

MAKES 8 SERVINGS.

## Baked Cranberry Sauce

1 pound cranberries
1 12-ounce jar orange marmalade
1 cup chopped pecans
1 cup coconut
¾ cup sugar
½ cup water

*I*n a large bowl stir together all of the ingredients. Spread the mixture into a 9 x 13-inch baking dish. Bake, uncovered, at 350° for about 30 minutes. Transfer to small attractive jars. Seal and label. Store in the refrigerator.

MAKES ABOUT 4 CUPS.

# Apple Cranberry Crumb Bars

6 tablespoons butter
¾ cup brown sugar
1 egg
2 cups all-purpose flour
1 teaspoon baking powder
½ teaspoon salt

1 tablespoon butter
2 tart apples, peeled and finely chopped
½ cup sugar
1 tablespoon all-purpose flour
1 tablespoon lemon juice
1 tablespoon orange juice
½ cup canned whole cranberry sauce
Dash ground cinnamon

6 tablespoons butter
½ cup sugar
¾ cup all-purpose flour
Pinch salt
¼ cup chopped walnuts

In a medium bowl cream 6 tablespoons of butter with the brown sugar. Add the egg and blend well. In a separate bowl stir together 2 cups of flour, the baking powder, and salt. Add the dry ingredients to the creamed mixture, and blend well.

Pat the dough evenly into a greased 11 x 7-inch pan, pressing it about ¼ inch up the sides.

In a saucepan melt 1 tablespoon of butter. Add the chopped apples, and cook at low heat for about 3 minutes until the apples soften. Add ½ cup of sugar, 1 tablespoon of flour, and lemon juice, stirring well. Bring the mixture to a boil. Reduce the heat and cook, stirring constantly, for 5 minutes. Set the filling aside to cool.

In a medium bowl blend 6 tablespoons of butter, ½ cup of sugar, ¾ cup of flour, and the salt until crumbly. Add the chopped walnuts and blend briefly.

Spread the cooled apple-cranberry filling over the dough in the pan. Sprinkle the crumb topping over the filling.

Bake at 350° for 30 minutes. Cool on a wire rack.

MAKES 12 BARS.

# Stir-Up Sunday

*Stir-Up Sunday, more commonly known as the Sunday before Advent,
usually falls on the Sunday after our American Thanksgiving.
A holiday borrowed from the Victorians, it provides a wonderful way to
make the transition into the Christmas season. Gather the whole family into
the kitchen, assign various chopping, stirring, measuring, and clean-up tasks
and bake the Christmas plum pudding together. Then, pudding baked and
ageing nicely in a cool, dark spot, relax with the feeling of satisfaction that
although the busy Christmas season is upon us, at least some of the
preparation for Christmas dinner is completed!*

ROAST DUCK WITH ORANGE SAUCE

BAKED TOMATOES WITH FRESH BASIL

POTATO PUDDING

APPLE FRITTERS

VICTORIAN CHRISTMAS PUDDING WITH BRANDY BUTTER

*Stir up, we beseech thee, O Lord,
the wills of thy faithful people;
that they, plenteously bringing forth
the fruit of good works,
may by thee be plenteously rewarded.*

# Roast Duck with Orange Sauce

2 5½-pound ducks
Salt and pepper to taste
1 medium onion, cut into wedges
1 stalk celery, cut in pieces
1 small carrot, cut in pieces
1 cup red wine
2 tablespoons sugar
¼ cup red wine
¾ cup fresh orange juice
¼ cup red currant jelly
Dash cayenne pepper
Juices from the roasting pan
1 large orange
1 tablespoon arrowroot
¼ cup Grand Marnier
4 drops red food color (optional)

*R*emove the giblets and liver from the ducks and reserve the liver for pâté if desired. Set the giblets aside. Rinse the ducks and pat them dry. Remove all excess fat. Season the duck inside and out with salt and pepper. Poke the duck skin all over with a trussing needle or knife, especially around the legs, to enable the fat to escape during roasting. Truss with white kitchen string and set them on their side in a roasting pan.

Roast the ducks at 450° for 10 minutes or until they sizzle. Reduce the heat to 350° and roast for 30 minutes on each side.

Drain all of the fat from the pan, and turn the ducks breast-side up in the pan. Arrange the onion, celery, carrot, giblets, and neck pieces around the ducks. Roast at 350° for 10 minutes.

Add 1 cup of wine. Reduce the heat to 325° and roast for 35 minutes. Baste with the pan juices every 10 minutes. Insert a knife into the leg joint, and if the juices run clear, remove the ducks from the oven. If the juices are pink or red, return the ducks to the oven and roast 10 to 15 minutes before checking again.

When the ducks are cooked, remove them to the platter, breast-side down, and let them rest in a warm (not hot) spot for at least 15 to 20 minutes before carving. Place the roasting pan over medium heat and reduce the cooking juices until a brown syrupy liquid.

In a saucepan cook the sugar over medium-low heat until the sugar is a light brown caramel color. Add ¼ cup of red wine and simmer until the sugar is dissolved. Add the orange juice, jelly, cayenne, and juices from the roasting pan and bring the mixture to a low simmer. Simmer for 10 minutes.

Peel one half of the orange, leaving the bitter white. Cut the peel into very fine, thin strips with a paring knife. In a small saucepan cover the orange peel strips with water, and bring to a boil over medium high heat. Boil for 5 minutes. Strain through a fine-mesh sieve, and reserve the strips.

Peel the rest of the orange, cut into sections, and reserve.

In a small bowl blend the arrowroot and Grand Marnier until a smooth paste. Remove the sauce from the heat and whisk in the arrowroot mixture. Set the saucepan back over the heat and stir until the sauce simmers. Add the blanched orange peel and let the sauce simmer over low heat for 3 minutes. Add red food coloring if desired.

Place the ducks on a serving platter and arrange the orange sections around them. Pour the sauce into a serving dish and pass separately.

MAKES 6 SERVINGS.

## Baked Tomatoes with Fresh Basil

8 ripe tomatoes
1 teaspoon salt
½ teaspoon pepper
1 tablespoon brown sugar
1 cup fresh breadcrumbs
3 tablespoons butter, cut into small cubes
½ cup minced fresh basil

Butter a shallow baking dish.

Cut a thin slice off the tops and bottoms of the tomatoes. Cut each tomato in half. Arrange the tomato halves in the prepared dish. Sprinkle with salt, pepper, and brown sugar, and cover with breadcrumbs. Dot with butter and sprinkle basil over all. Bake at 350° for 30 to 40 minutes or until done to taste.

MAKES 8 SERVINGS.

## Potato Pudding

3 pounds Idaho or russet potatoes, peeled
1 cup butter
½ cup sugar
2 teaspoons salt
1 teaspoon grated nutmeg
12 eggs
½ cup sherry
¼ cup all-purpose flour
2 teaspoons orange essence
1 cup sliced almonds

In a large pot bring the potatoes to a boil in water to cover. Boil them for 20 minutes or until tender. Mash the potatoes. Stir in the softened butter, sugar, salt, and nutmeg, and blend well. In a medium bowl beat the eggs, and stir them into the potatoes. In a small bowl blend the sherry, flour and orange essence into a paste and add this mixture to the potatoes. Stir in the almonds. Transfer the mixture to a soufflé dish. Bake at 350° for 40 to 45 minutes.

MAKES 8 SERVINGS.

## Apple Fritters

1½ cups all-purpose flour
⅓ cup sugar
½ teaspoon grated nutmeg
2 eggs, separated
1 tablespoon butter, softened
¾ cup flat ale
4 large apples, peeled, cored, and cut into
    ½-inch slices
¼ cup confectioners' sugar
Sugar and cinnamon for sprinkling
Oil

In a large bowl sift together the flour, sugar, and nutmeg. In a separate bowl beat together the egg yolks, butter, and ale. Gradually add the liquid mixture to the dry ingredients, and blend until smooth. Set aside for 2 hours.

In a deep fryer heat the oil to about 360°. In a shallow bowl toss the apples with the confectioners' sugar. In a medium bowl beat the egg whites until stiff, and fold them into the batter. Dip the sugared apple slices in the batter. Fry in hot oil for 5 to 7 minutes or until golden brown and puffy. Drain well. Serve sprinkled with sugar and cinnamon. Serve very hot.

MAKES 6 SERVINGS.

# Victorian Christmas Pudding

2 cups raisins, coarsely chopped
2 cups currants, coarsely chopped
½ cup almonds, blanched and chopped
1 teaspoon grated nutmeg
1 teaspoon ground cinnamon
1 teaspoon grated allspice
1 cup all-purpose flour
1 teaspoon salt
½ cup ground almonds
12 ounces fresh brown breadcrumbs
1 pound suet, shredded
1⅓ cups packed dark brown sugar
8 eggs, beaten
½ cup brandy
½ cup sherry
½ cup milk
Brandy Butter (recipe follows)

*I*n a large bowl mix the chopped raisins, currants, and almonds with the spices. Add the flour, salt, and ground almonds and mix well. Work in the breadcrumbs, suet, and brown sugar until thoroughly mixed together. In a separate bowl beat the eggs lightly, and add them to the mixture. Add the brandy, sherry, and milk, stirring until the pudding is a soft paste. Refrigerate overnight.

In the morning pour the mixture into a large, well-buttered pudding basin or 2 small basins (pyrex or corningware works well), cover with greased waxed paper and cloth, and tie tightly around the rim of the basin. Set the basin in a large open roasting pan filled to the sides with boiling water. Steam the pudding for 8 hours, adding hot water as necessary.

Remove the wet cloths and cover the pudding with fresh greased paper and fresh muslin. Store in a cool, dark place for 4 weeks.

On Christmas Day, steam the pudding an additional 2 hours. Unmold and serve with Brandy Butter.

MAKES 8 SERVINGS.

# Brandy Butter

½ cup unsalted butter, softened
1 cup confectioners' sugar
¼ cup brandy

*I*n a medium bowl beat the butter vigorously until creamy. Gradually beat in the confectioner's sugar until pale and fluffy. Add the brandy a tablespoon at a time.

Brandy butter may be made a few days beforehand, and stored in the refrigerator.

MAKES 8 SERVINGS.

# Winter Menus

# A Jane Austen Holiday Luncheon
## with Friends

*William Cowper corresponded regularly with his contemporary, Jane Austen. Although Cowper rhapsodizes about friendship in the following selection, Austen's readership will find to their great delight that her views display more common sense than rhyme! While enjoying the fine luncheon you have prepared, perhaps you and your friends would enjoy a discussion about the myths and realities of true friendship!*

STILTON AND ONION SOUP

HERB TART

WESTMORELAND ASPARAGUS PUFFS

BAKED APRICOT CASSEROLE

WHIPPED CREAM POUND CAKE

FRIENDSHIP

Who seeks a friend, should come dispos'd
T' exhibit in full bloom disclos'd
The graces and the beauties
That form the character he seeks,
For 'tis an union that bespeaks
Reciprocated duties.
And all the world admits them.

Oh Friendship! If my soul forego
Thy dear delights while here below;
To mortify and grieve me,
May I myself at last appear
Unworthy, base, and insincere,
Or may my friend deceive me!

*Selected verses*
WILLIAM COWPER (1731-1800)

Contrast this with Austen's frank portrayal of Mrs. Norris' "friendly" advice to Fanny in Mansfield Park:

"The nonsense and folly of people's stepping our of their rank and trying to appear above themselves, makes me think it right to give you a hint, Fanny, now that you are going into company without any of us; and I do beseech and intreat you not to be putting yourself forward, and talking and giving your opinion as if you were one of your cousins....That will never do, believe me. Remember, where-ever you are, you must be the lowest and last...."

# Stilton and Onion Soup

6 onions (about 2 pounds), minced
½ cup unsalted butter
¼ cup all-purpose flour
4 cups milk
12 ounces Stilton cheese, crumbled
Salt and freshly ground pepper to taste

In a large heavy saucepan melt the butter and cook the onions over moderately low heat, stirring occasionally, for 15 to 20 minutes, or until they are softened. Stir in the flour. Cook the mixture over moderately low heat, stirring constantly, for 3 minutes. Add the milk in a stream, whisking constantly. Bring the mixture to a boil, stirring constantly, and simmer it for 10 to 12 minutes, or until thickened. Stir in the Stilton cheese, stirring until melted. Season with salt and pepper.

MAKES 8 SERVINGS.

# Herb Tart

4 eggs
½ cup heavy cream
½ cup milk
4 tablespoons Parmesan cheese
Salt and freshly ground pepper to taste
Grated nutmeg to taste
2 tablespoons butter
¼ cup finely chopped onion
1 head lettuce, washed and cut in slivers
1 tablespoon finely chopped fresh chives
1 tablespoon finely chopped fresh tarragon
1 tablespoon finely chopped fresh dill
2 tablespoons finely chopped fresh parsley
½ teaspoon finely chopped fresh rosemary
1 11-inch tart pastry shell, partially baked

In a large bowl beat the eggs with the cream and milk. Beat in the Parmesan cheese and season with salt, pepper, and nutmeg.

In a skillet melt the butter, and sauté the onion until tender and browned. Add the lettuce, and toss quickly, about 30 seconds. Add the lettuce and onion mixture to egg mixture, and blend in the herbs. Transfer the mixture to a blender, and blend well. Pour the filling into the pie shell. Bake at 325° for 30 to 40 minutes. Serve hot, lukewarm, or cold in wedges.

MAKES 6 TO 8 SERVINGS.

# Westmoreland Asparagus Puffs

6 fresh asparagus spears, blanched, drained, and finely chopped
¾ cup finely chopped pimiento-stuffed green olives
4 ounces Swiss cheese, finely chopped
6 ounces cream cheese, room temperature
¼ cup fine dry breadcrumbs
2 egg yolks, room temperature
1 tablespoon fresh lemon juice
¼ teaspoon freshly ground pepper
8 5 x 5-inch squares puff pastry, ⅛-inch thick
24 fresh asparagus spears, cooked crisp-tender and trimmed to 5-inch lengths

Grease a baking sheet.

In a large bowl combine the chopped asparagus, olives, Swiss cheese, cream cheese, breadcrumbs, egg yolks, lemon juice, and pepper. Blend well. Spread some of the cheese mixture over ⅔ of each pastry square, leaving a small strip for sealing the puffs. Arrange 3 asparagus spears over the filling on each square. Brush the uncovered strip of the square with water. Roll each square up, pressing the moistened edge to seal. Place seam-side down on prepared baking sheet. Cover, and refrigerate for 1 hour.

Bake at 325° for about 20 minutes or until the pastry is puffed and golden brown. Serve immediately.

MAKES 6 SERVINGS.

## Baked Apricot Casserole

2 17-ounce cans apricot halves, drained
2 cups firmly packed light brown sugar
3 cups butter cracker crumbs
1 cup butter

*I*n a greased 2-quart casserole dish arrange the apricot halves cut-side up. Sprinkle first the brown sugar and then the cracker crumbs over the apricots. Dot the crumbs with butter. Bake at 350° for 35 minutes, or until the casserole has thickened and is crusty on the top.

MAKES 8 SERVINGS.

## Whipped Cream Pound Cake

2 cups all-purpose flour
2 teaspoons baking powder
1 teaspoon salt
1 cup heavy cream
4 large eggs

1½ cups sugar
1 teaspoon vanilla extract
3 drops almond extract
2 tablespoons firmly packed light brown sugar
Grated zest of 1 orange
Confectioners' sugar for sprinkling

*G*rease and flour a 10-inch tube pan. Onto a sheet of waxed paper sift together the flour, baking powder, and salt. In a medium bowl beat the heavy cream until stiff. Set aside.

In a large bowl beat the eggs with an electric mixer at high speed until blended. Slowly add the sugar and beat until pale and fluffy. Add the vanilla and almond extracts. At low speed of the mixer gradually beat in the flour mixture, mixing just until blended. Gently fold in the whipped cream with a spatula. Pour the batter into the prepared pan. Sprinkle with brown sugar and orange zest. Bake at 350° for 1 hour or until a toothpick inserted in the center comes out clean. Cool in the pan on a wire rack for 15 minutes. Remove the cake from the pan and cool completely on the rack. Sprinkle lightly with confectioners' sugar.

MAKES 8 TO 12 SERVINGS.

# An Advent Dinner

*The Advent season begins four Sundays before Christmas, and is typically celebrated with the lighting of one candle in the advent wreath each Sunday, accompanied by an appropriate scripture reading and prayer. If each year you find yourself vowing that next year will focus more on the real meaning of Christmas and less on the brouhaha, this is the place to begin to set the tone for the holidays. Providing the opportunity to share this unhurried meal further instills the traditions and focus you are trying to emphasize this season.*

---

GREEN SALAD WITH BASIL DRESSING

CHICKEN AND ARTICHOKES

BROWN RICE

FRIED APPLES

CHOCOLATE CRANBERRY TORTE
WITH CHOCOLATE BUTTERCREAM

---

*COME, THOU LONG-EXPECTED JESUS*

*Come, Thou long-expected Jesus,*
*Born to set Thy people free;*
*From our fears and sins release us;*
*Let us find our rest in Thee.*
*Israel's strength and consolation,*
*Hope of all the earth Thou art;*
*Dear desire of every nation,*
*Joy of every longing heart.*

*Born Thy people to deliver,*
*Born a child and yet a King,*
*Born to reign in us forever,*
*Now Thy gracious kingdom bring.*
*By Thine own eternal spirit*
*Rule in all our hearts alone;*
*By Thine all sufficient merit,*
*Raise us to Thy glorious throne.*

CHARLES WESLEY (1707-1788)

# Green Salad with Basil Dressing

2 extra large eggs
1 cup tightly packed basil leaves
3 tablespoons finely minced shallots
3 tablespoons basil vinegar (or red wine)
¾ cup olive oil
Freshly ground black pepper
6 cups mixed salad greens

*I*n a large saucepan boil the eggs in water to cover for 3 to 4 minutes until the yolks are still soft and runny but the whites are firm enough to mince. Rinse the basil, and remove the leaves from the stems. Shell the eggs, and scoop the yolks into a processor or blender. Add the shallots, vinegar, and basil leaves. Process to finely mince the basil. Add ¼ cup of the oil, and process for 2 to 3 minutes, until the ingredients are smooth. Pour in the remaining oil slowly with the machine running. Season with pepper. The dressing will be thick, creamy, and pale green. Pour the dressing into a large salad bowl. Mince the egg whites, and fold gently into the dressing. Add the salad greens, and toss to mix well.

MAKES 6 SERVINGS.

# Chicken and Artichokes

4 tablespoons butter
1 tablespoon oil
4 chicken breasts, boned but not skinned, cut into 1-inch pieces
16 canned artichoke hearts (2 cans)
2 cups sliced mushrooms
½ cup finely chopped shallots
½ garlic clove, minced
1 cup dry white wine
1 tablespoon arrowroot

*I*n a large heavy skillet heat 2 tablespoons of the butter and the oil. Add the chicken pieces, and sauté over medium heat for about 5 minutes, turn-

ing once, or until golden brown. Transfer to a heated platter.

Add another tablespoon of the butter to the skillet, add the artichoke hearts, and sauté for about 5 minutes, turning occasionally, until lightly browned. Transfer to the platter with the chicken.

Add the remaining butter to the skillet, and add the mushrooms, shallots, and garlic, and stir well. Reduce the heat, and sauté for 5 minutes, stirring constantly.. Return the chicken and artichoke hearts to the skillet. Add the wine, increase the heat to medium, and simmer for 10 minutes or until the chicken is tender.

Transfer the chicken, mushrooms, and artichoke hearts back to the platter. Blend the arrowroot into the sauce and simmer for about 5 minutes until thickened. Pour the sauce over the chicken, and serve immediately.

MAKES 6 SERVINGS.

# Brown Rice

2½ cups water
2 cups brown rice, rinsed and drained
2 teaspoons chicken base (or bouillon)
2 tablespoons sherry
2 teaspoons freshly ground pepper

*I*n a saucepan bring the water to a boil. Add the rice, chicken base, sherry, and pepper. Cover, reduce the heat, and simmer for 40 minutes. Do not stir or peek.

MAKES 6 SERVINGS.

# Fried Apples

3 tablespoons butter
6 tart cooking apples, peeled and sliced
⅓ cup sugar
¼ teaspoon grated nutmeg
¼ teaspoon ground cinnamon

*I*n a large skillet melt the butter over medium heat. Add the apples and cook until slightly soft. Add the sugar and spices. Reduce the heat and simmer for about 15 minutes or until the apples are soft, ,stirring occasionally.

MAKES 6 SERVINGS.

# Chocolate-Cranberry Torte

¾ cup unsweetened cocoa powder
6 tablespoons unsalted butter
1 cup hot espresso or strong coffee
1½ cups coarsely chopped fresh or frozen
    cranberries
2 cups all-purpose flour
1½ teaspoons baking soda
½ teaspoon salt
2 cups sugar
½ cup buttermilk
2 large eggs, beaten
1 teaspoon vanilla extract
1 cup whipping cream
2 tablespoons confectioners' sugar
1 tablespoon framboise
Chocolate Buttercream (recipe follows)
Mint leaves and cranberries rolled in sugar for
    garnish

*G*rease and flour two 9-inch cake pans. In a large bowl melt the cocoa and butter in the espresso. In a medium bowl toss the cranberries with ½ cup of the flour, and set aside.

In a separate bowl sift together the remaining flour, the baking soda, salt, and sugar. Gradually add the sifted dry ingredients to the espresso mixture alternately with the buttermilk. Beat in the eggs and vanilla until smooth. Fold in the cranberries, and divide the batter evenly between the two pans. Bake at 375° for 25 to 30 minutes or until a cake tester inserted near the center of the layers comes out clean. Cool the cakes for 10 minutes in the pans and then turn out onto wire racks and cool to room temperature. Wrap the cakes well, and freeze.

Unwrap and thaw the cakes for 10 minutes.

In a medium bowl combine the whipping cream and confectioners' sugar and beat until stiff. Add the framboise and blend well.

Using a long serrated knife split each cake into 2 layers. Place one layer of the cake on a cake plate. Spread the layer with some of the buttercream. Place the second layer over the first, and spread it with some of the flavored whipped cream. Top with the third layer, and spread with some of the remaining buttercream. Finish with the final layer. Spread the remaining buttercream over the sides and top of the torte, forming swirls and peaks with the knife. Transfer the remaining flavored whipped cream into a pastry bag fitted with a star-shaped tip, and decorate the top and around the base of the torte. Garnish with cranberries rolled in granulated sugar and whole mint leaves.

MAKES 6 TO 8 SERVINGS.

# Chocolate Buttercream

12 ounces semisweet chocolate, broken into
    bits
1 tablespoon instant espresso powder
¼ cup boiling water
6 large egg yolks
3 cups sifted confectioners' sugar
2 cups unsalted butter, softened

*I*n the top of a partially covered double boiler melt the chocolate over barely simmering water. Dissolve the espresso in the boiling water and set aside. In a medium bowl beat the egg yolks with the confectioners' sugar for about 5 minutes until thick. Gradually add the chocolate, and then the espresso, and beat until smooth. Add the softened butter a little at a time, beating after each addition until smooth. Beat for 1 to 2 minutes more.

MAKES 4 CUPS.

# A Country Christmas

*Simple pleasures complement the simple message of Christmas. Handcrafted decorations, the sounds of silence, and nature's sweet surprises are always there for those who seek them. Only a country Christmas can provide all these things. Unless, of course, the hostess plans ahead and makes it all happen! While we can't supply nature's sweet surprises, we can help you with the planning for bounteous country fare that will get you thinking about your entry in next summer's county fair . . .*

TART CRANBERRY PUNCH

FLUFFY ROLLS

BAKED VIRGINIA HAM

STUFFED ONIONS

CORN PUDDING

GLAZED CARROTS AND BRUSSELS SPROUTS

SPICED PEACHES

BLACKBERRY JAM CAKE

ORANGE GINGERBREAD WITH GINGER CREAM

*THE HYMN*

It was the winter wild
While the heaven-born Child
All meanly wrapt in the rude manger lies;
Nature in awe to Him
Had doff'd her gaudy trim,
With her great Mater so to sympathize:
It was no season then for her
To wanton with the sun, her lusty paramour.

Only with speeches fair
She woos the gentle air
To hide her guilty front with innocent snow;
And on her naked shame,
Pollute with sinful blame,
The saintly veil of maiden white to throw;
Confounded, that her Maker's eyes
Should look so near upon her foul deformities.

But see! The Virgin blest
Hath laid her Babe to rest;
Time is, our tedious song should here have
    ending:
Heaven's youngest-teemed star
Hath fix'd her polishíd car,
Her sleeping Lord with hand-maid lamp
    attending:
And all about the courtly stable
Bright-harness'd Angels sit in order serviceable.

JOHN MILTON (1608–1674)

[ 172 ]

# Tart Cranberry Punch

3 (3-inch) sticks cinnamon
24 whole cloves
1 teaspoon whole allspice
1 medium orange, sliced
2 quarts apple cider
2 cups water
3 cups fresh cranberries
Orange peel strips (optional)
Cinnamon sticks (optional)

*I*n a piece of cheesecloth combine the cinnamon sticks, cloves, and allspice, and tie the cheesecloth to make a spice bag. In a large stockpot combine the spice bag, orange slices, apple cider, water, and cranberries. Bring the mixture to a boil. Reduce the heat, and simmer for 5 minutes. Remove and discard the spice bag and orange slices. For garnish, gently tie the orange peel strips around the cinnamon sticks and place in individual cups, if desired. Serve warm.

MAKES 10 TO 12 SERVINGS.

# Fluffy Rolls

1¼ cups milk
¼ cup vegetable shortening
¾ cup sugar
1 teaspoon salt
1 package active dry yeast
¼ cup lukewarm water (105 to 115°)
2 eggs, lightly beaten
4 cups all-purpose flour
¾ cup butter, melted

*I*n a medium saucepan combine the milk, shortening, sugar, and salt and cook over medium heat, stirring constantly, until the sugar dissolves. Remove the pan from the heat and set aside to cool.

In a large bowl dissolve the yeast in the lukewarm water. Set aside for about 10 minutes or until foamy.

Pour the milk mixture into the yeast. Stir in the eggs. Gradually add the flour, stirring with a wooden spoon until a stiff dough forms, then continue by hand. The dough will be sticky, so grease your hands with a little butter. Brush a small amount of butter on the inside of a large bowl and on one side of a sheet of waxed paper. Place the dough in the bowl, cover with buttered wax paper, and lay a damp dishcloth on top. Set aside to rise for at least 3 hours or until doubled in bulk.

Turn the dough out onto a lightly floured surface, and knead until elastic. Roll out to ½-inch thickness and cut with a 3-inch biscuit cutter. Dip each round into melted butter, and fold in half. Line up, round edges up, sides touching, on a cookie sheet. Butter a sheet of waxed paper and place it over the rolls. Set the rolls aside to rise for at least 2 hours and 30 minutes.

Bake at 350° for about 15 minutes until golden. Serve warm.

MAKES ABOUT 20 ROLLS.

## Baked Virginia Ham

1 16- to 20-pound smoked Virginia ham
2 teaspoons whole cloves
1 8-ounce jar Dijon mustard
1 11-ounce jar red currant jelly
1 cup apple juice

*T*ightly wrap the ham in heavy foil, and place it in a shallow roasting pan. Bake at 325° for 2 hours and 30 minutes.

Remove the ham from the oven, and insert a meat thermometer, making sure it does not touch the fat or bone. Score the fat in a diamond pattern, and stud with cloves.

In a medium bowl stir together the mustard, jelly, and apple juice, mixing well. Pour the mixture over the ham. Cover the ham, and return it to the oven for 1 hour and 30 minutes.

Remove the cover from the ham. Baste the ham, and continue to bake for 1 hour or until the meat thermometer reaches 160°, basting every 15 minutes. If the ham gets too brown, recover it with foil.

MAKES 12 TO 18 SERVINGS.

## Stuffed Onions

12 large onions (about 8 pounds)
1 cup butter
8 medium scallions, with 2 inches green tops, finely chopped
2 cloves garlic
8 dashes Tabasco
6 cups finely chopped fresh mushrooms
4 cups finely chopped cooked ham
1 cup finely chopped parsley
Dash rubbed sage
Dash ground cinnamon
1 cup heavy cream
Salt and freshly ground pepper to taste

4 cups beef broth
½ cup minced fresh parsley

*R*emove the skin from each onion, and cut off and discard a thick slice from the stem end. Scoop out the centers of each with a melon-ball scoop or sturdy spoon, leaving a ¼-inch shell. Finely chop enough of the centers to measure 1 cup.

Bring a kettle of salted water to the boil, add the onion shells, and cook over moderately high heat for 5 minutes. Invert the onions on paper towels and drain.

In a large skillet heat ½ cup of butter. Add the chopped onions, scallions, garlic, and Tabasco, and sauté over low heat for 5 minutes, stirring constantly. Add the remaining butter, mushrooms, ham, parsley, sage, and cinnamon, increase heat to moderate, and continue sautéeing, stirring, for about 5 minutes or until mushrooms are soft. Add the cream, sherry, and salt and pepper to taste, stir well again, and let cook for 5 minutes.

Sprinkle the onion shells with salt and pepper to taste, arrange them open-side up in a casserole or baking dish just large enough to hold them, and divide the stuffing among them, mounding it. Pour enough broth around the onions to reach 1 inch up the sides. Cover with foil. Bake at 350° oven for 1 hour, basting once or twice.

Transfer the onions with a slotted spoon to a heated serving platter and sprinkle the tops with parsley.

MAKES 12.

## Corn Pudding

4 tablespoons butter
2 16-ounce cans whole kernel corn, drained
2 eggs
2 cups milk
1 cup sugar
1 teaspoon salt, or to taste

Butter an ovenproof 1½-quart casserole dish with part of the butter. In a large bowl combine the corn, eggs, milk, sugar, and salt. Pour into casserole and dot with remaining butter. Bake uncovered for 1 hour.

MAKES 8 TO 12 SERVINGS.

## Glazed Carrots and Brussels Sprouts

2 teaspoons salt
2 pounds baby carrots, peeled
2 pounds Brussels sprouts, trimmed, with an X
    cut in the root end
1½ cups canned chicken broth
6 tablespoons unsalted butter
⅓ cup firmly packed dark brown sugar
1 tablespoon freshly ground black pepper

Bring a large pan of water to a boil. Add the salt and the carrots and cook for about 4 minutes until crisp but tender. With a slotted spoon, transfer the carrots to a large bowl of ice water. Return the water to a boil, add the Brussels sprouts, and cook for about 5 minutes or until crisp-tender. With a slotted spoon, transfer the Brussels sprouts to a bowl of ice water. When the vegetables are cool, drain thoroughly.

In a large, heavy skillet over medium heat combine the chicken broth, butter, and brown sugar. Bring to a boil, stirring to dissolve the sugar. Lower the heat slightly and cook hard for about 7 minutes or until reduced by half. Add the carrots and cook for about 6 minutes, shaking the pan occasionally, until they are almost tender and the sauce begins to coat them. Add the Brussels sprouts and the pepper, and cook for about 4 minutes or until just heated through, stirring occasionally. Serve immediately.

MAKES 8 SERVINGS.

## Spiced Peaches

2 29-ounce cans extra large peach halves
¾ cup cider vinegar
¾ cup sugar
1 stick cinnamon
½ to 1 teaspoon whole cloves

Reserve ½ of the syrup from the peaches. In a saucepan combine the syrup, vinegar, sugar, cinnamon, and cloves. Boil for 5 minutes. Arrange the peaches in a flat casserole. Pour the hot mixture over the peaches, and refrigerate overnight.

Note: It is important to buy the large, better-quality peach halves.

MAKES 14 PEACH HALVES.

## Blackberry Jam Cake

1 cup butter
1½ cups sugar
3 eggs
1 cup seedless blackberry or raspberry jam
3 cups all-purpose flour
2 teaspoons grated nutmeg
2 teaspoons ground cloves
2 teaspoons ground cinnamon
1 teaspoon baking soda
1 cup buttermilk
2 teaspoons vanilla extract

Grease well a 9-inch angel food or bundt pan. In a large bowl cream together the butter and sugar until light and fluffy. Beat in the eggs one at a time. Fold in the jam. In a separate bowl stir together the flour, nutmeg, cloves, cinnamon, and baking soda. Add the dry ingredients to the egg mixture alternately with the buttermilk, folding in lightly. Fold in the vanilla. Spoon the batter into the greased pan. Bake at 350° for 35 to 45 minutes.

Cool the cake for 10 minutes before turning it out of the mold.

MAKES 8 TO 10 SERVINGS.

# Orange Gingerbread with Ginger Cream

⅓ cup butter, melted
⅔ cup milk
1 cup dark molasses
1 large egg, lightly beaten
3 cups sifted all-purpose flour
½ teaspoon baking soda
2 teaspoons baking powder
½ teaspoon salt
1 tablespoon ground ginger
1 teaspoon ground cinnamon
½ teaspoon ground cloves
2 tablespoons grated orange peel

1 cup heavy cream
Pinch salt
Pinch cream of tartar
1 tablespoon finely chopped preserved ginger
1 tablespoon syrup from preserved ginger

Grease a 9 x 12-inch baking pan. In a large mixing bowl stir together the melted butter, milk, molasses, and beaten egg until well mixed. In a separate bowl sift together the flour, baking soda, baking powder, salt, and spices. Gradually add this mixture to the liquid mixture, stirring constantly until completely blended. Stir in the grated orange peel. Pour the batter into the prepared pan. Bake at 350° for about 50 minutes, or until a knife inserted in the center comes out clean. Cool in the pan. Cut into 3-inch squares.

In a chilled bowl beat the cream with the salt and cream of tartar until stiff peaks form. Gently fold in the chopped ginger and syrup.

MAKES 12 SERVINGS.

# An English Christmas Dinner

*The table is groaning with the English feast before you. You have laid the table with your most beautiful pieces. Use burnished, winter colors, and make sure the atmosphere is embellished with background music of, perhaps, Christmas hymns sung by an English boy's choir. The great day of celebration has finally arrived. Your Christmas dinner is fit for the occasion!*

OYSTER SOUP

ROAST BEEF WITH HORSERADISH SAUCE

YORKSHIRE PUDDING

ROASTED GOOSE WITH SAGE AND SCALLION DRESSING

AND GRAVY

GRILLED TOMATOES

GRATIN DE POMMES DE TERRE

PEASE PUDDING

TRIFLE WITH VANILLA CUSTARD

(AND OF COURSE, THE PUDDING, PAGE 000)

*A HYMN FOR CHRISTMAS DAY*

Christians awake, salute the happy morn
Whereon the Saviour of the world was born;
Rise, to adore the Mystery of Love,
Which hosts of angels chanted from above.
With them the joyful tidings first begun
Of God incarnate and the Virgin's Son.
Then to the watchful shepherd it was told,
Who heard the angelic herald's voice: "Behold!
I bring good tidings of a Saviour's birth
To you, and all the nations upon earth;
This day hath God fulfilled his promised word;
This day is born a saviour, Christ the lord:
In David's city, Shepherds, ye shall find
The long foretold Redeemer of mankind;
Wrapped up in swaddling clothes, the Babe
        divine

Lies in a manger; this shall be your sign."
He spake, and straighway the celestial choir
In hymns of joy, unknown before, conspire.
The praises of redeeming Love they sung,
And Heaven's whole orb with Hallelujahs rung.
God's highest glory was their anthem still;
Peace upon earth, and mutual good will.
To Bethlehem straight the enlightened shepherds
        ran,
To see the wonder God had wrought for man;
And found, with Joseph and the blessed Maid,
Her Son, the Saviour, in a manger laid.
Amazed, the wondrous story they proclaim,
The first apostles of his infant fame.
While Mary keeps, and ponders in her heart
The heavenly vision, which the swains impart,

[ 177 ]

They to their flocks, still praising God, return,
And their glad hearts within their bosoms burn.
Let us, like these good shepherds then, employ
Our grateful voices to proclaim the joy:
Like Mary, let us ponder in our mind
God's wondrous love in saving lost mankind.
Artless, and watchful, as these favoured swains,
While virgin meekness in the heart remains,
Trace we the Babe, who has retrieved our loss,
From his poor manger to his bitter cross;

Treading his steps, assisted by his grace,
Till man's first heavenly state again takes place.
Then may we hope, the angelic thrones among,
To sing, redeemed, a glad triumphal song.
He that was born, upon this joyful day,
Around us all his glory shall display;
Saved by his love, incessant we shall sing
Of angels, and of angel-men, the King.

JOHN BYROM (1692-1763)

# Oyster Soup

3 to 4 pounds fresh fish heads and bones
1 cup white wine
2 carrots, cut up
Parsley to taste
1 or 2 onions, studded with cloves
Lemon juice to taste
Mushroom stalks and peelings
1 strip orange peel
Pinch thyme
2 quarts boiling water
Salt and peppercorns to taste
6 dozen oysters in their shells
2 quarts strained seasoned fish stock
¼ cup all-purpose flour
¼ cup butter
Juice of a half lemon

Wash and drain the fish heads and bones. In a large pot place the fish and the wine. Bring to a boil, and cook for a moment to reduce the wine. Add the carrots, parsley, an onion or two, lemon juice, mushroom stalks and peelings, orange peel, and a pinch of thyme. Add 2 quarts of boiling water and return to a boil. Boil for 20 to 30 minutes. During the last 10 minutes add salt to taste, and a few peppercorns. Strain, and reserve the stock.

In a large pan heat the oysters on top of the stove just until the shells open. Remove, reserve the oysters, and strain the juice into a clean saucepan. Add 2 quarts of the fish stock and bring the mixture just to a simmer. In a small bowl blend the flour with the butter. Add the mixture to the stock, blending well. Simmer for 15 minutes.

Add the lemon juice and oysters, heat through, and serve at once.

MAKES 8 SERVINGS.

# Roast Beef

1 8-pound standing 3-rib roast

Place the beef fat-side up, in a large shallow roasting pan. Insert a meat thermometer into the thickest part of the beef, being careful not to let the tip of the thermometer touch any fat or bone. Roast the beef undisturbed at 450° in the middle of the oven for 20 minutes. Reduce the heat to 325°, and continue to roast, without basting, for about 90 minutes or until the beef is cooked to taste. (A meat thermometer will register 130° to 140° when the beef is rare, 150° to 160° when medium, and 160° to 170° when it is well done.) If you are not using a thermometer, start timing the roast after you reduce the heat to 325°. Estimate approximately 12 minutes per pound for rare beef, 15 minutes per pound for medium, and 20 minutes per pound for well done.

Transfer the beef to a heated platter, and let it rest for at least 15 minutes for easier carving.

To carve, first remove a thin slice of beef from the large end of the roast so it will stand firmly on this end. Insert a large fork below the top rib and carve slices of beef from the top, separating each slice from the bone. Serve with the pan juices and a horseradish sauce.

MAKES 6 TO 8 SERVINGS.

## Horseradish Sauce

¼ cup bottled horseradish, drained and
    squeezed dry in a kitchen towel
1 tablespoon white wine vinegar
1 teaspoon sugar
¼ teaspoon dry English mustard
½ teaspoon salt
½ teaspoon white pepper
½ cup chilled heavy cream

In a small bowl stir the horseradish, vinegar, sugar, mustard, salt, and white pepper together until well blended. In a medium bowl beat the cream with a whisk or an electric beater until stiff peaks form. Pour the horseradish mixture over the cream and fold together lightly but thoroughly with a rubber spatula. Taste for seasoning. Pour into a sauceboat and serve with Roast Beef.

MAKES 6 TO 8 SERVINGS.

## Yorkshire Pudding

2 eggs
½ teaspoon salt
1 cup all-purpose flour
1 cup milk
2 tablespoons roast beef drippings (or
    substitute 2 tablespoons lard)

In a blender combine the eggs, salt, flour, and milk, and blend at high speed for 2 to 3 seconds. Turn off the machine, scrape down the sides of the jar, and blend again for 40 seconds. (To make the batter by hand, beat the eggs and salt with a whisk or a rotary or electric beater until frothy. Slowly add the flour, beating constantly. Then pour in the milk in a thin stream, and beat until the mixture is smooth and creamy.) Refrigerate for at least 1 hour.

In a 10 x 15-inch roasting pan heat the roast beef drippings over moderate heat until it splutters. Briefly beat the batter again and pour it into the pan. Bake at 400° in the middle of the oven for 15 minutes. Reduce the heat to 375°, and bake for

15 minutes longer or until the pudding has risen over the top of the pan and is crisp and brown. With a sharp knife divide the pudding into portions, and serve immediately.

MAKES 6 TO 8 SERVINGS.

## Roast Goose with Sage and Scallion Dressing

1 cup butter
12 scallions, white and green parts only, thinly
    sliced
1 medium onion, chopped
1 cup chopped celery
1 small apple, coarsely chopped
6 cups coarse dry breadcrumbs
½ teaspoon salt
1 teaspoon freshly ground black pepper
2 tablespoons chopped fresh sage (or
    1 tablespoon dried sage)
1 teaspoon dried thyme
2 tablespoons chopped parsley
1 12- to 14-pound goose
½ cup chicken stock
2 large eggs, lightly beaten
Cider, for basting

In a skillet melt the butter and sauté the scallions, onion, celery, and apple for 10 minutes or until the onion is transparent and golden brown. Transfer to a large mixing bowl and add the bread crumbs, salt, pepper, and herbs. Toss to combine all ingredients. Add a bit more stock if the stuffing seems too dry.

Rinse and dry the goose and season the cavity with salt and pepper. Stuff the goose loosely with the dressing and truss using trussing skewers and string. Prick the exterior of the goose all over with a sharp-tined fork to allow excess fat to escape during roasting.

Place the goose on a rack in a large, deep roasting pan, breast-side up. Roast at 450° for 15 minutes. Reduce the oven temperature to 350° and continue roasting for about 20 minutes per pound, or until the goose is very well browned and the leg joints move up and down easily. During the roasting time remove any fat that accumulates in the pan and baste with cider.

When the goose is done, remove it to a board and let it rest, loosely covered with aluminum foil, for 30 minutes before carving. Make the gravy while the goose is resting.

MAKES 8 TO 10 SERVINGS.

## Goose Gravy

¼ cup goose fat
¼ cup all-purpose flour
4 cups chicken stock
Pan drippings and scrapings
Salt and freshly ground black pepper to taste

When removing the goose fat from the pan during roasting, reserve ¼ cup. In a heavy saucepan heat the goose fat, over medium heat. Slowly stir in the flour. Cook slowly, stirring frequently, until a brown roux has formed. Add the chicken stock a cup at a time, stirring constantly. Simmer about 5 to 7 minutes or until the flour is cooked and the gravy is thickened.

When the goose comes out of the pan, pour off the fat, then pour off the remaining drippings and any scraped browned bits from the pan into the gravy. Stir to blend thoroughly and season with salt and pepper to taste.

MAKES 6 TO 8 SERVINGS.

## Grilled Tomatoes

4 to 5 medium tomatoes
¼ cup (½ stick) butter
¼ cup grated Parmesan cheese
Dried thyme
Salt and freshly ground black pepper

Slice the tomatoes in half horizontally. Place the halves cut-side up on a broiling pan. Dot the surface of each half with butter, a sprinkling of Parmesan cheese, a pinch of thyme, and salt and pepper to taste. Broil for about 7 to 10 minutes until the tops are bubbly and golden brown.

MAKES 6 TO 8 SERVINGS.

## Gratin de Pommes de Terre

6 cups peeled, sliced russet potatoes
1 cup milk
¼ cup heavy cream
1 chicken bouillon cube
1 large clove garlic
1 tablespoon unsalted butter
Freshly ground black pepper
1 to 2 tablespoons Gruyère cheese, grated

In a small saucepan combine the milk, cream, and bouillon cube, and simmer for 3 to 5 minutes, stirring occasionally, until the bouillon cube has dissolved. Set aside. Cut the garlic clove in half. Remove the skin and use the cut side of each half to rub the baking pan. Add the garlic to the simmering milk mixture.

Use half the butter to grease the baking dish. Layer the potato slices in the pan, grinding a little pepper over each layer. Remove and discard the garlic from the milk mixture, and pour it over the potatoes. Sprinkle the top of the potatoes with the Gruyère cheese. Cut the remaining butter into small cubes and scatter over all. Bake at 400° for about 60 to 70 minutes or until golden brown and tender when pierced with a sharp knife tip. If the surface becomes very browned before the potatoes are tender, cover it loosely with foil. Serve hot.

MAKES 6 SERVINGS.

## Pease Pudding

2 cups dry green split peas (1 pound)
2 cups water
1 teaspoon salt
4 tablespoons butter
¼ teaspoon white pepper

Wash the split peas. Pick over the peas and discard any discolored ones. In a large, heavy saucepan, bring the water to a boil and drop in the peas slowly so that the water continues to boil. Reduce the heat and simmer partially covered for 1 hour and 30 minutes, or until the peas can be easily mashed against the side of the pan with a spoon. Drain the peas. In a blender or food processor purée the peas. Return the peas to the pan and cook over low heat, stirring constantly, until the purée is heated through. Stir in the salt, butter and pepper, and taste for seasoning. Serve at once from a heated vegetable dish.
MAKES 6 TO 8 SERVINGS.

## Trifle with Vanilla Custard

1 trifle spongecake
½ cup apricot jam
½ cup seedless raspberry jam
6 almond macaroons, crumbled
6 zwieback biscuits, crumbled
¼ cup medium-dry Sherry
2 tablespoons brandy

2 cups milk
¼ cup sugar
3 large eggs
⅛ teaspoon salt
½ teaspoon vanilla extract
1 cup well chilled heavy cream
¼ cup blanched whole almonds, toasted lightly
Candied fruit and silver dragées for garnish, if
      desired

Slice the spongecake in half horizontally, and then in half crosswise. Spread the top of one piece with apricot jam, and top with another piece. Spread the top of a third piece with raspberry jam and top with the remaining piece. Cut the cakes into 4 x ½-inch fingers and line the sides of a 2½-quart glass bowl with some of the fingers, arranging them so that the jam filling shows, alternating the apricot and the raspberry. Cube the remaining cake fingers.

In a bowl combine the remaining cake fingers, macaroons, and zwieback, and sprinkle the mixture with the Sherry and the brandy. Transfer the mixture to the cake-lined bowl. Cover with plastic wrap.

In a saucepan heat the milk with the sugar over moderate heat, stirring constantly, until it is hot. In a medium bowl beat the eggs with the salt. Add the milk mixture in a stream, stirring constantly. Return the mixture to the saucepan and cook over moderately low heat, stirring constantly, for 10 minutes or until it is thick enough to coat the spoon (175° on a candy thermometer). Do not let it boil. Stir in the vanilla. Strain the custard over the spongecake mixture in the bowl, and let it cool. Cover and refrigerate for at least 3 hours or overnight.

In a chilled bowl beat the cream until stiff peaks form. Transfer it to a pastry bag fitted with a decorative tip, and pipe it onto the top of the trifle. Decorate the trifle with the almonds and, if desired, garnish it with the candied fruit and the dragées.
MAKES 6 TO 8 SERVINGS.

## Victorian Christmas Pudding
*(recipe found with Stir-up Sunday)*

# Boxing Day: A Blessing in Deed

*December twenty-sixth is an official holiday in Britain known as Boxing Day. On this day boxes of food are to be delivered to the needy, and in days gone by were given to servants from their employers. With a little forethought, your church or community organization can provide you with the name of a family who might greatly appreciate a box of food today! It's a helpful reminder that benevolence doesn't have to cease with Christmas Day.*

IRISH SODA BREAD

BUBBLE AND SQUEAK WITH WOW-WOW SAUCE

MINCE PIES

*J esus, Lord, we look to thee,*
*Let us in thy name agree;*
*Show thyself the Prince of Peace;*
*Bid our jarring conflicts cease.*

*Let us for each other care,*
*Each the other's burden bear,*
*To thy church the pattern give,*
*Show how true believers live.*

*Make us one of heart and mind,*
*Courteous, pitiful, and kind,*
*Lowly, meek in thought and word,*
*Altogether like our Lord.*

CHARLES WESLEY (1707-1788)

# Irish Soda Bread

1½ cups all-purpose flour
1 cup whole wheat flour
1 teaspoon baking soda
½ teaspoon salt
¼ cup currants
1¼ to 1½ cups buttermilk
1 tablespoon butter, melted

Grease a baking sheet. In a large bowl combine the flour, baking soda, and salt. Stir in the currants. Add 1¼ cups of buttermilk and stir just until the dry ingredients are moistened. (Add more buttermilk, if necessary, to make a soft dough.) Turn the dough onto a lightly floured surface and knead gently for 1 to 2 minutes. Shape into a ball and place on a greased baking sheet. Pat into an 8-inch circle. Using a sharp knife or razor blade, cut a ½-inch deep X in the top of the dough. Bake at 425° for about 45 minutes or until golden. Transfer to a wire rack, and brush with melted butter. Serve hot or at room temperature.

MAKES 1 LOAF

# Bubble and Squeak

1 medium onion, chopped
3 tablespoons bacon drippings (or butter)
2½ cups cooked shredded cabbage
2 cups mashed potatoes
1 cup chopped leftover cooked beef (or corned beef)
½ teaspoon salt
Freshly ground black pepper to taste

In a 10-inch skillet heat the bacon drippings and sauté the onion over medium heat for about 5 minutes or until soft. Place the cabbage in a colander and press to remove the excess liquid. Add the cabbage to the onions and stir in the potatoes. Cook, stirring frequently, for about 5 minutes or until the vegetables begin to brown. Stir in the meat, and season with salt and pepper. Continue cooking without stirring for about 10 minutes or until golden on bottom. Invert the mixture onto a large serving plate. Cover with foil and keep warm in a 225° oven while preparing Wow-Wow Sauce. Cut into wedges and serve with Wow-Wow Sauce.

MAKES 6 SERVINGS.

# Wow- Wow Sauce

2 tablespoons butter
2 tablespoons minced onion
2 tablespoons all-purpose flour
1 cup beef broth
1 tablespoon white wine vinegar
1 tablespoon Worcestershire sauce
1 tablespoon English-style mustard
½ teaspoon prepared horseradish
Salt and freshly ground black pepper to taste
2 tablespoons finely chopped fresh parsley

In a 1½-quart saucepan melt the butter over medium heat and sauté the onion, stirring constantly, for about 3 minutes or until onion is soft but not browned. Stir in the flour and cook for 1 minute, stirring constantly. Add the broth all at once and whisk until smooth. Stir in all of the remaining ingredients except the parsley. Bring to a boil. Reduce the heat to medium-low and simmer, stirring frequently, for about 10 minutes, until the sauce is thickened. Stir in the parsley.

MAKES 6 SERVINGS.

# Mince Pies

8 teaspoons butter, softened
Short-crush pastry
1½ cups mincemeat (recipe follows)

Preheat the oven to 375°. Butter the bottom and sides of eight 2½-inch tart tins with the softened butter, allowing 1 teaspoon of butter for each tin.

On a lightly floured surface, roll out the pastry into a circle about ⅛-inch thick. With a cookie cutter or the rim of a glass, cut sixteen 3½-inch rounds of pastry. Gently press 8 of the rounds, 1 at a time, into the tart tins. Then spoon about 3 tablespoons of mincemeat into each pastry shell. Dampen the outside edges of the pastry shells with water and carefully fit the remaining 8 rounds over them. Crimp the edges of the pastry together with fingers or the tines of a fork. Trim the excess pastry from around the rims with a sharp knife, and cut 2 small slits about ¼ inch apart in the top of each of the pies. Arrange the pies on a large baking sheet. Bake at 375° in the middle of the oven for 10 minutes. Reduce the heat to 350° and bake for 20 minutes longer or until the crust is golden brown. Run the blade of a knife around the inside edges of the pies to loosen them slightly, and set them aside to cool in the pans. Turn out the pies with a narrow spatula, and serve.

MAKES 8 INDIVIDUAL PIES.

## Mincemeat

½ pound fresh beef suet, finely chopped
4 cups seedless raisins
2 cups dried currants
1 cup coarsely chopped almonds
½ cup coarsely chopped candied citron
½ cup coarsely chopped dried figs
½ cup coarsely chopped candied orange peel
¼ cup coarsely chopped lemon peel
4 cups peeled, cored, and coarsely chopped
    Granny Smith apples
1¼ cups sugar
1 teaspoon grated nutmeg
1 teaspoon ground allspice
1 teaspoon ground cinnamon
½ teaspoon ground cloves
2½ cups brandy
1 cup pale dry sherry

*I*n a large bowl combine the suet, raisins, currants, almonds, citron, dried figs, candied orange peel, candied lemon peel, apples, sugar, nutmeg, allspice, cinnamon, and cloves, and mix thoroughly. Pour in the brandy and sherry, and mix with a large wooden spoon until all the ingredients are well moistened. Cover the bowl and set the mincemeat aside in a cool place (not the refrigerator) for at least 3 weeks.

Check the mincemeat once a week. As the liquid is absorbed by the fruit, replenish it with sherry and brandy, using about ¼ cup at a time. Mincemeat can be kept indefinitely in a covered container in a cool place, without refrigeration, but after a month or so refrigerate it if desired.

MAKES ABOUT 3 QUARTS.

# New Year's Eve Open House

*An open house can be elegant and understated at the same time. By including this celebration in your holiday entertaining, your message is loud and clear. "Come and go as you please; we wanted to make sure we didn't let the holiday season pass without impressing upon you the important place you hold in our lives." The combination of traditional favorites with classic newcomers in the menu kind of reminds us of the friends who will be coming . . .*

---

HERB CHEESECAKE

GOOD LUCK SOUP

PORK LOIN STUFFED WITH FRUITCAKE

ROASTED NEW POTATOES

CONFETTI CAULIFLOWER

CHOCOLATE SURPRISE BARS

CROQUEMBOUCHE

---

*GOD'S AID*

*God to enfold me,*
*God to surround me,*
*God in my speaking,*
*God in my thinking.*

*God in my sleeping,*
*God in my waking,*
*God in my watching,*
*God in my hoping.*

*God in my life,*
*God in my lips,*
*God in my soul,*
*God in my heart.*

*God in my sufficing,*
*God in my slumber,*
*God in mine ever-living soul,*
*God in mine eternity.*

*TRADITIONAL CELTIC*
*COLLECTED BY ALEXANDER CARMICHAEL,*
*19TH CENTURY*

# Herb Cheesecake

1 cup all-purpose flour
½ cup unsalted butter, chilled
½ teaspoon salt
1 large egg yolk
2 teaspoons grated lemon peel

2 cloves garlic
1 large onion, coarsely chopped
⅔ cup chopped fresh parsley
3 ounces freshly grated Parmesan cheese
      (¾ cup)
3 8-ounce packages cream cheese, softened
3 tablespoons all-purpose flour
4 large eggs
2 teaspoons salt
½ teaspoon Tabasco sauce
2 tablespoons fresh lemon juice
1 tablespoon chopped fresh oregano (or 1
      teaspoon dried)
1 tablespoon chopped fresh tarragon (or 1
      teaspoon dried)
1 tablespoon chopped fresh basil (or 1 teaspoon
      dried)
½ tablespoon chopped fresh rosemary (or ½
      teaspoon dried)
½ cup chopped pepperoni

Fresh herbs for garnish
Wafer crackers

In a food processor blend 1 cup of flour, butter, salt, egg yolk, and lemon peel to a cornmeal-like consistency. Turn onto a floured surface and knead lightly. Shape into a ball, wrap in waxed paper, and refrigerate until slightly chilled.

Evenly press ⅓ of the dough into bottom of an 8-inch springform pan, and press the remaining dough around the sides. Store in the freezer while preparing the filling.

In a food processor chop the garlic. Add the onion, then the parsley, and Parmesan cheese. Add the cream cheese one package at a time, and process. Add 3 tablespoons of flour and 1 egg, and continue processing until smooth. Add the remaining 3 eggs one at a time, blending well after each addition. Add the salt, Tabasco, lemon juice, and herbs, processing just until blended. Stir in the pepperoni and pour into the dough-lined pan. Bake at 400° for 10 minutes. Reduce the oven temperature to 325°, and bake 50 minutes longer. Let stand 1 hour before serving.

Garnish with fresh herbs and serve with plain wafer crackers.

MAKES 10 TO 12 SERVINGS.

# Good Luck Soup

2 pounds dried black-eyed peas
4 quarts chicken stock
1 ham hock
1 pound smoked ham, cubed
4 medium yellow onions, chopped
2 green bell peppers, chopped
2 stalks celery, chopped
4 cloves garlic, minced
1 teaspoon ground red pepper
2 10-ounce packages frozen cut okra, thawed
2 teaspoons salt or to taste

In a large stockpot combine the peas, chicken stock, ham hock, ham, onions, bell peppers, celery, garlic, and red pepper. Cover and bring to a boil over high heat, stirring occasionally. Reduce the heat to low and simmer for 1 hour, stirring occasionally.

Stir in the okra and salt, cover, and simmer for 30 minutes, stirring frequently to prevent scorching. Remove the cover and cook, stirring constantly, for 10 minutes or until thickened and creamy. Remove the ham hock, and serve hot.

MAKES 10 TO 12 SERVINGS.

# Pork Loin Stuffed with Fruitcake

⅓ cup chopped onion
1 clove garlic, minced
1 tablespoon olive oil
3 cups crumbled fruitcake
1 5-pound boneless rolled pork loin roast
¼ teaspoon salt
¼ teaspoon pepper
2 tablespoons dried thyme
1 cup apple juice
1 cup chicken broth
¼ cup plus 2 tablespoons Bourbon
¼ cup honey
2 tablespoons butter or margarine
2 tablespoons all-purpose flour
¼ cup whipping cream

Fresh grapes, kumquats, thyme sprigs, canned
    crabapples for garnish

*I*n a skillet heat the olive oil and sauté the onion and garlic over medium-high heat, stirring constantly, until tender. Remove the skillet from heat, add the fruitcake, and stir well.

Remove the pork loin from the elastic net. (There should be 2 pieces.) Trim the excess fat. Make a cut lengthwise down the center of each piece, cutting to, but not through, the bottom. Starting from the center cut of each piece, slice horizontally toward each side, stopping ½ inch from each edge. Unfold each piece of meat so that it lies flat. Flatten to ½-inch thickness using a meat mallet or rolling pin. Sprinkle salt, pepper, and 1 tablespoon of thyme evenly over the pork. Sprinkle the fruitcake mixture over the pork. Roll up each loin half starting with the the long side. Secure with string, and place seam-side down in a shallow roasting pan. Pour apple juice and chicken broth around the rolled pork loins in the pan.

In a small bowl combine ¼ cup of bourbon and the honey. Brush lightly over the rolled pork loins. Sprinkle with the remaining thyme. Bake at 350° for 50 minutes or until a meat thermometer inserted in the thickest portion registers 160°, basting with the bourbon mixture at 20 minute intervals.

Remove the pork loins from the pan, reserving the pan drippings. Keep the pork warm. In a saucepan bring the pan drippings to a boil, and cook about 10 to 15 minutes or until the mixture is reduced to 1 cup. Set aside.

In a heavy saucepan melt the butter over low heat. Add the flour, stirring until smooth. Cook for 1 minute, stirring constantly. Gradually add the reduced dripping and 2 tablespoons of bourbon, and cook over medium heat; stirring constantly, until the mixture thickens and boils. Remove the pan from the heat and stir in the whipping cream.

Serve the sauce with the sliced pork.
MAKES 10 SERVINGS.

# Roasted New Potatoes

½ cup extra virgin olive oil
16 large cloves garlic, flattened
50 new potatoes, halved
2 tablespoons chopped fresh rosemary (or
    1 tablespoon dried)
Salt and coarsely ground pepper to taste
Fresh rosemary for garnish

*I*n a small bowl combine the olive oil and garlic, and allow the flavors to blend for at least 1 hour.

Place the potatoes in a baking dish and sprinkle with rosemary, salt, and pepper. Pour the oil and garlic over the potatoes and toss well. Roast at 400° for 45 minutes or until the potatoes are tender and crusty, stirring occasionally.

Serve hot, garnished with fresh rosemary sprigs.
MAKES 10 TO 12 SERVINGS.

## Confetti Cauliflower

7 cups cauliflower florets (about 1¾ pounds)
1 tablespoon olive oil
2 cloves garlic, minced
½ cup diced green bell pepper
½ cup diced red bell pepper
½ cup diced yellow bell pepper
2 tablespoons sliced green onion
¼ cup chopped fresh dillweed
1 teaspoon lemon pepper
2 teaspoons white wine vinegar

*I*n a steamer cover the the cauliflower, and steam for 8 minutes or until crisp-tender. Drain and set the cauliflower aside.

In a medium nonstick skillet heat the oil over medium-high heat. Add the garlic, peppers, and onion, and sauté for 2 minutes. Stir in the dillweed, lemon pepper, and vinegar, and cook for 1 minute. Spoon over the cauliflower.

MAKES 7 SERVINGS.

## Chocolate Surprise Bars

½ cup butter, at room temperature
1 egg yolk
2 tablespoons water
1¼ cups all-purpose flour
1 teaspoon sugar
1 teaspoon baking powder
⅛ teaspoon salt

1 12-ounce package chocolate chips

2 eggs
¾ cup sugar
6 tablespoons melted butter
2 cups finely chopped pecans or walnuts
1¼ teaspoons vanilla extract
Confectioners' sugar

*G*rease a 9 x 13-inch pan. In a large bowl cream ½ cup of butter. Beat in the egg yolk and water and mix well. In a separate bowl sift together the flour, 1 teaspoon of sugar, baking powder, and salt. Add the dry ingredients to the creamed mixture and mix well. Press the mixture into the prepared baking pan. Bake at 350° for about 10 minutes.

Remove the pan from the oven and sprinkle the chocolate chips evenly over the dough. Return the pan to the oven for about 2 minutes, or until the chocolate melts. Spread the chocolate evenly over the crust.

In the same mixing bowl beat 2 eggs until thick. Beat in ¾ cup of sugar and blend well. Stir in the butter, nuts, and extract. Mix well and pour evenly over the chocolate layer.

Return the pan to the oven, and bake at 350° for about 30 to 35 minutes more or until a light golden brown, and the dough springs back when touched lightly in the center with the fingers. Cool on a rack and cut into bars. Sprinkle with confectioners' sugar.

MAKES ABOUT 4 DOZEN.

# Croquembouche

¾ cup unsalted butter
1½ cups water
¼ teaspoon salt
1 teaspoon sugar
1½ cups all-purpose flour
6 large eggs

1 egg beaten with 1 teaspoon water

6 egg yolks
½ cup sugar
½ cup sifted flour
2 cups milk, scalded
3 tablespoons butter
1 tablespoon vanilla extract
Pinch salt

2 cups sugar
⅔ cup water
2 tablespoons corn syrup

*I*n a saucepan melt ¾ cup of butter in 1½ cups of water with salt and 1 teaspoon of sugar over low heat. Remove the pan from the heat and beat in 1½ cups of flour with a wooden spoon until completely mixed. Return to the heat and stir vigorously for 2 to 3 minutes. The mixture will form a ball, and a film will form on the bottom of the pan. Remove the pan from the heat, and add the eggs one by one, beating vigorously after each addition. Transfer the mixture to a pastry tube with a ½-inch opening, and form puffs on a buttered baking sheet. In a small bowl beat 1 egg with 1 teaspoon of water and glaze each puff with the mixture using a pastry brush. Smooth the top of each puff. Bake at 425° for 20 minutes. Remove the pan from the oven and pierce each puff with a sharp knife. (This allows the steam to escape so that the interior of the puff is not soggy.) Return to the oven for 10 minutes more. Cool the puffs on a rack.

In a large bowl beat the egg yolks, gradually adding the sugar, until the mixture is thick and pale yellow. Beat in the flour. Add the hot milk in dribbles, reserving ½ cup for thinning. Return to the pot in which the milk was scalded, and bring to a boil over high heat, stirring constantly. It will become lumpy first and then will smooth out with vigorous stirring. Be careful not to scorch the bottom of the pot. The cream should be thick, but add milk if too thick to pipe. Add the butter 1 tablespoon at a time. Blend in the vanilla and salt. Cool completely. Inject the pastry cream into the puffs with a ¼-inch pastry tip.

In a saucepan combine 2 cups of sugar, 2 cups of water, and the corn syrup. Bring the mixture to a boil over high heat. Do not stir. Cover the pan (allowing the steam to dissolve any crystals that might form). Uncover the pan and boil several more minutes, until the syrup is amber. Reduce the heat to the keep syrup from hardening.

Dip the filled cream puffs one by one into the caramel syrup and arrange on the base, forming a cone resembling a pyramid. The caramel holds the cream puffs together.

Note: *Croquembouche* means "crunch in the mouth." Guests pluck off the puffs with their fingers.

Makes about 70 puffs, enough for a small pyramid.

# Burns Night

No one could accuse Robert Burns, the national bard of Scotland, of leading a sedate and contemplative life. A poet who was a true common man, and a Christian who wasn't quite virtuous, he seemed to take great satisfaction in shattering stereotypes. Although Burns Night, January 25th, is commonly celebrated by drinking oneself under the table while quoting Burns' poetry, it could be observed equally well with the realization that the truly creative spirit sometimes crosses lines drawn by others, and that the sinner in all of us is not as easily hidden as we would like it to be. Perhaps upon reading his dying thoughts, we might reflect on our own pitiful excuses for improprieties.

SELKIRK BANNOCK

SHEPHERD'S PIE

DATE BARS

## A PRAYER IN THE PROSPECT OF DEATH

O Thou unknown, Almighty Cause
Of all my hope and fear!
In whose dread presence, ere an hour,
Perhaps I must appear!

If I have wandered in those paths
Of life I ought to shun;
As something loudly in my breast
Remonstrates I have done;

Thou know'st that Thou hast formed me
With passions wild and strong;
And list'ning to their witching voice
Has often led me wrong.

Where human weakness has come short,
Or frailty stept aside,
Do thou, All Good! For such Thou art,
In shades of darkness hide.

Where with intention I have erred,
No other plea I have,
But, Thou art good; and goodness still
Delighteth to forgive.

## Selkirk Bannock

3 cups bread flour or as needed
2 tablespoons sugar
1 package fast-rising dry yeast
½ teaspoon salt
¾ cup milk
½ cup unsalted butter
2½ cups golden raisins
1 egg yolk, beaten with 1 tablespoon water

*I*n a large bowl mix 2½ cups of flour, the sugar, yeast, and salt. In a medium saucepan bring the milk and butter to a simmer, stirring until the butter melts. Cool to 125 to 130°. Stir the mixture into the dry ingredients. Mix in enough remaining flour to form a soft dough. Turn out onto a floured surface and knead until smooth and elastic, about 5 minutes. Lightly oil a large bowl. Add the dough, turning to coat. Cover and let rise in a warm draft-free place for 1 hour and 30 minutes or until doubled in volume.

Lightly grease a baking sheet. Punch down the dough and knead in the raisins. Shape the dough into a 7-inch-diameter round. Place on the prepared sheet. Cover with a towel and let rise in a warm area for about 40 minutes, until almost doubled in volume.

In a small bowl beat 1 egg yolk with 1 tablespoon of water. Brush the bread with the egg glaze. Bake at 375° for about 45 minutes until the bread is golden and sounds hollow when tapped on the bottom. Transfer to a rack and cool.

MAKES 1 LOAF.

## Shepherd's Pie

3 tablespoons oil
2 medium-sized onions, finely chopped
2 garlic cloves, finely chopped
1½ pounds ground lamb (or ground beef)
1 6-ounce can tomato paste
2 bouillon cubes
1 heaped tablespoon all-purpose flour
1 cup white wine
½ cup water
½ teaspoon tarragon
Salt and freshly ground black pepper to taste
3 large potatoes, peeled
6 tablespoons butter
1 cup milk
½ cup cooked corn
2 tablespoons Parmesan cheese

*I*n a large frying pan heat the oil over low heat. Add the onion and garlic and cook until soft. Turn up the heat and add the meat, stirring until it is well browned.

Drain off any fat, and add the tomato paste, bouillon cubes, and flour. Mix well, and cook for 1 minute before adding the wine and water. Add the tarragon and season well with salt and pepper. Simmer gently for 15 minutes.

Meanwhile cook and mash the potatoes. Add the butter and milk, and season with salt and pepper. Transfer the meat mixture to a large well-greased soufflé or baking dish. Spread the corn over the meat, and top with the mashed potatoes, covering the meat and corn completely. Sprinkle the Parmesan cheese over the potatoes. Bake at 350° for 35 minutes. Place under the broiler for a few minutes to brown the top.

MAKES 6 SERVINGS.

## Date Bars

1 cup all-purpose flour
1 teaspoon baking powder
¼ teaspoon salt
½ cup butter, softened
1 cup sugar
3 large eggs, separated
1 cup chopped dates
1 cup chopped pecans
Confectioners' sugar for dusting

*G*rease a 9 x 13-inch baking pan. In a bowl combine the flour, baking powder, and salt, and mix well. In a large bowl beat the butter and sugar with an electric mixer at high speed until light and fluffy. Add the egg yolks one at a time, beating well after each addition. Fold in the flour mixture, dates, and pecans. In a small bowl with an electric mixer beat the egg whites at high speed until stiff peaks form. Fold them into the batter and spread it into the prepared baking pan. Bake at 375° for 12 minutes.

While the mixture is hot, cut it into bars in the pan, and sprinkle them with the confectioners' sugar.

MAKES ABOUT 2 DOZEN.

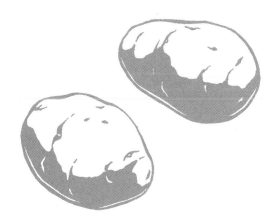

# After-Game Buffet Supper

*The pregame anticipation is over, and the results are in. Along with a hearty winter meal, we have provided a blessing that just about covers all possible outcomes and gently realigns perspectives. "Comfort food" goes a long way toward cheering the defeated and reinvigorating the victor. Returning home to this winter balm ensures an unqualified victory for the cook!*

---

CHILI IN PASTRY CUPS

CHEDDAR CHEESE STRAWS

FRESH POTATO SOUP WITH SWISS CHEESE

DILL POT ROAST

BRUSSELS SPROUTS AND BABY CARROTS
WITH TWO MUSTARDS

TEX-MEX BROWNIES

LEMON CORNMEAL COOKIES

---

## THE TWENTIETH PSALM

*A*nd let his help come down from heaven for
thee,
The Lord give ear to thee in thy distress,
And be thy shield when troubles thee oppress,

And strength from Sion hill imparted be;
Let him remember and accept withal
Thine offerings, and thy sacrifices all,
And of his bounty evermore fulfill
Thy heart's desire, and satisfy thy will.
But we will glory in our great God's name,
And joy in our salvation through the same,

And pray unto the Lord our God that he
The effect of all thy prayers will grant to thee.
He now I know will hear, and help will bring,
With his strong hand to his anointed kind;
On chariots some, on horses some rely,
But we invoke the name of God most high.
Those others are bowed down, and fall full low,
When we are risen and upright do go;
Save us O Lord of heaven, and hear us thence,
When we invoke thy name for our defence.

INTERPRETED BY JOHN DAVIES (1569–1626)

# Chili in Pastry Cups

1¾ cups all-purpose flour
¼ cup cornmeal
½ teaspoon salt
½ cup shortening
4 to 6 tablespoons cold water

¾ pound ground beef
⅓ cup chopped green bell pepper
⅓ cup chopped onion
1 7½-ounce can tomatoes, puréed
1 4-ounce can chopped green chilies, drained
¼ cup tomato paste
1 teaspoon sugar
¼ teaspoon salt
¾ teaspoon chili powder

Grease 48 1¾-inch tart pans. In a medium bowl combine the flour, cornmeal, and salt. Cut in the shortening with a pastry blender until the mixture resembles coarse meal. Sprinkle cold water over the surface 1 tablespoon at a time. Stir with a fork until the dry ingredients are moistened. Shape into 48 balls. Place in the prepared tart pans, shaping to form shells. Bake at 350° for 20 minutes or until lightly browned. Cool on wire racks. Remove the shells from the pans.

In a large skillet cook the ground beef, green pepper, and onion until the meat is browned, stirring to crumble the meat. Drain. Add the tomatoes, chilies, tomato paste, sugar, salt, and chili powder, stirring well. Simmer for 10 minutes. Spoon hot chili into the pastry cups.

MAKES 48 APPETIZERS.

# Cheddar Cheese Straws

4 cups grated sharp Cheddar cheese
½ cup butter, softened
½ teaspoon paprika
¼ teaspoon cayenne pepper
½ teaspoon salt
3 cups sifted all-purpose flour

In a large bowl cream the cheese and butter together with an electric mixer. Add the remaining ingredients and mix until well blended. Turn the dough onto a floured board and roll into a rectangle ¼-inch thick. Cut the dough into strips approximately ½ x 4 inches. Twist the strips several times and placed them 1 inch apart on ungreased baking sheets. Bake at 400° for about 5 to 7 minutes or until golden brown. Remove to wire racks to cool.

MAKES ABOUT 6 DOZEN.

# Fresh Potato Soup with Swiss Cheese

6 slices bacon, chopped
1 medium onion, chopped
3 cups shredded white cabbage
2 to 3 Idaho potatoes, chopped
2 13¾-ounce cans chicken broth
Salt and pepper to taste
2 cups half and half or milk
1 cup grated Swiss cheese

In a skillet cook the bacon until brown. Remove the bacon, and sauté the onions in the fat until golden. Remove and drain. In a soup pot combine the onion, cabbage, potatoes, chicken broth, salt, and pepper, and cook for about 40 minutes. Stir in the half and half, Swiss cheese, and bacon, and heat through.

MAKES 6 SERVINGS.

# Dill Pot Roast

4½ to 5 pounds rump, arm, or chuck roast
1 teaspoon salt
¼ teaspoon pepper
1 teaspoon dill seed
¼ cup water
1 tablespoon wine vinegar
3 tablespoons all-purpose flour
1 teaspoon dillweed
1 cup sour cream

Season the beef with salt, pepper, and dill seed. Place in an ovenproof dish. Add the water and vinegar, and cover. Bake at 200° for 5 hours.

Remove the meat. To the liquid in the pan add the flour and dillweed. Cook and stir to thicken. Add the sour cream. Spoon the sauce over the sliced beef.

MAKES 8 TO 10 SERVINGS.

# Brussels Sprouts and Baby Carrots with Two Mustards

1½ pounds Brussels sprouts
1½ pounds baby carrots
¼ cup butter
2 tablespoons grainy mustard
1 tablespoon Dijon mustard
Salt and freshly ground black pepper to taste
2 tablespoons chopped parsley

Trim the ends of the Brussels sprouts, and score an X into each end to ensure even cooking. Remove any tough outer leaves and wash carefully under cold running water to remove any sandy particles.

Peel the carrots (if using large carrots, cut into half lengthwise, then cut the halves into 1½-inch lengths. Place the carrots in a vegetable steamer, and steam over medium heat for 10 to 15 minutes or until they are just beginning to become tender.

Add the Brussels sprouts to the steamer, and steam for an additional 7 to 10 minutes, or until the sprouts are crisp-tender and a vivid green.

Carefully remove the steamer basket of vegetables from the pan and pour off the steaming water. Add the butter, mustards, salt, and pepper to the pan, and stir until the butter has melted. Add the vegetables and cover tightly. Lift up the pan and shake vigorously, holding the cover on, to combine the vegetables and coat them evenly with the butter and mustards.

Remove to a vegetable dish, and garnish with chopped parsley.

MAKES 8 TO 10 SERVINGS.

# Tex-Mex Brownies

½ cup butter
2 1-ounce squares unsweetened chocolate
½ to 1 teaspoon ground red pepper
2 eggs
1 cup sugar
½ cup all-purpose flour
1 teaspoon vanilla extract
1 cup semisweet chocolate chips

Grease and flour an 8-inch square pan. In a small heavy saucepan melt the butter and unsweetened chocolate over low heat. Remove the pan from the heat, and stir in the red pepper.

In a medium bowl beat the eggs until light. Add the sugar, beating well. Blend in the chocolate mixture. Stir in the flour and vanilla. Spread the batter evenly in the prepared pan. Bake at 325° for 30 minutes or until firm in the center. Remove the pan from the oven, and sprinkle the chocolate chips over the top. Let the brownies stand until the chocolate is melted, then spread evenly. Cool completely in the pan on a wire rack. Cut into 2-inch squares.

MAKES 16 SQUARES.

# Lemon Cornmeal Cookies

1 cup butter, softened
1 cup sugar
2 egg yolks
1 teaspoon grated lemon peel
1½ cups all-purpose flour
1 cup yellow cornmeal
Sugar for sprinkling

In a medium bowl cream the butter and sugar with an electric mixer until lighter in color and well blended. Add the egg yolks and mix well. Stir in the lemon peel, flour, and cornmeal, and mix well. Wrap the dough, and refrigerate for 3 to 4 hours.

Roll the dough on a lightly floured surface and cut into shapes. Place on an ungreased baking sheet, and sprinkle with additional sugar. Bake at 350° in the center of the oven until the edges are browned.

MAKES 3 DOZEN.

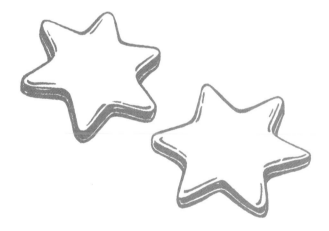

# Valentine's Day

*What a blessing to live in a society with the leisure to celebrate love! If you're in it or out of it, glowing with its sentiment or glowering from its sting, celebrate Valentine's Day! Pamper your loved one with time, words, and true affection, or gather together fellow singles and perform a deed of unselfish love for someone else (then watch a Cary Grant movie and eat lots of chocolate). Whatever the general mood—passionate or petulant—a great meal like this one will go a long way toward accomplishing your personal, shall we say, goals for the evening.*

> BRIE TART
>
> OLIVE BREAD
>
> BROILED FISH WITH FENNEL
>
> POTATO, CARAMELIZED ONION, AND GOAT CHEESE GRATIN
>
> PROVENÇAL TOMATOES
>
> COFFEE PROFITEROLES WITH CHOCOLATE SAUCE AND
>
> WHIPPED CREAM
>
> COEUR Á LA CRÈME

A view of the highest form of love:

*Father, into thy hands I give the heart*
*Which left thee but to learn how good thou art.*

GEORGE MACDONALD (1824-1905)

And of the more worldly hue:

*If thou must love me, let it be for naught*
*Except for love's sake only. Do not say,*
*"I love her for her smile—her look her way*
*Of speaking gently,—for a trick of thought*
*That falls in well with mine, and certes brought*
*    A sense of pleasant ease on such a day"—*
*    For these things in themselves, Beloved, may*
*Be changed, or change for thee—and love, so*
*wrought,*
*May be unwrought so. Neither love me for*
*    Thine own dear pity's wiping my cheeks dry:*
*A creature might forget to weep, who bore*
*    Thy comfort long, and lose thy love thereby!*
*But love me for love's sake, that evermore*
*    Thou mayst love on, through love's eternity.*

ELIZABETH BARRETT BROWNING (1806–1861)
FROM SONNETS FROM THE PORTUGUESE

# *Brie Tart*

3 cups all-purpose flour
¼ teaspoon salt
½ cup butter
6 to 8 tablespoons ice water
½ cup cold vegetable shortening

2½ cups heavy cream
¼ pound Brie, peel discarded
1 teaspoon saffron threads, crushed
1 teaspoon sugar
½ teaspoon ground ginger
Salt and pepper to taste
3 large eggs
2 large egg yolks

*I*n a large bowl combine the flour and the salt. Cut in half of the butter with a pastry blender until the mixture resembles coarse crumbs. Add the ice water 1 tablespoon at a time, mixing with a fork until the pastry holds together. On a lightly floured surface roll the pastry into a 5-inch wide strip. Dot two-thirds of the length of the surface of the pastry with half of the shortening, and fold the dough crosswise into thirds as for folding a letter, with the plain end of the pastry folded first over the shortening on the middle of the pastry strip. Sprinkle the pastry with flour, wrap it in plastic wrap, and refrigerate it for 20 minutes.

When chilled, roll out the pastry into a 5-inch-wide strip, dot two-thirds of the length of the surface with the remaining butter, fold up the dough as for the first rolling, and roll it out again into a 5-inch-wide strip. Dot two thirds of the length of the surface with the remaining shortening, fold it into thirds, sprinkle it with flour, and chill it, covered, for 20 minutes.

Roll out the pastry, fold it into thirds again, cover, and refrigerate until ready to make the tart.

In a small baking dish combine the heavy cream, Brie, and saffron, and cover. Bake at 200° for 20 to 30 minutes, or until the cheese has just melted and the saffron has dissolved and colored the cream.

While the cheese mixture bakes, roll out the pastry on a lightly floured surface, fit it into a 10-inch quiche dish, and prick it lightly with a fork. When the cheese mixture is out of the oven, bake the pastry shell at 425° for 10 minutes.

Transfer the cheese mixture to a blender or food processor and blend it until smooth. Add the sugar and ginger, and blend well, seasoning carefully with salt and pepper. In a bowl beat the eggs and egg yolks until blended. Add the cheese mixture and beat until blended. Pour the cheese mixture into the partially baked pastry shell. Bake at 350° for 30 minutes, or until the filling is set and puffy.

MAKES 6 SERVINGS.

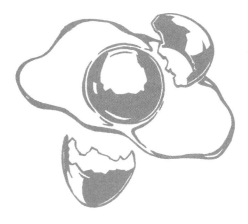

## Olive Bread

3 to 3½ cups unsifted bread flour
1 package active dry yeast
2 tablespoons sugar
1 cup warm water (115 to 120°)
⅓ cup pitted, chopped, oil-cured ripe olives
2 tablespoons olive oil
1 teaspoon salt
Boiling water

In a large bowl combine ½ cup of flour, the yeast, and sugar. Add the warm water, stir to blend, and let stand for 10 minutes or until the surface is bubbly. Add the olives, oil, salt, and 2 cups of the remaining flour. Stir until well combined.

Turn the dough out onto a lightly floured surface. Knead the dough for about 10 minutes, adding the remaining flour if necessary, until smooth and elastic. Lightly oil a mixing bowl. Place the dough in the bowl, turning to grease the dough. Cover with a clean cloth, and let the dough rise in a warm place for about 1 hour or until doubled in bulk.

Lightly oil a large baking sheet. When the dough has doubled, roll it into a 12 x 8-inch oval. Starting from the long side, roll the edge of the dough over 1 turn, and pinch to make a tight seam. Continue rolling the dough, pinching the seam with each turn, to form a 12-inch long roll. Pinch the edges and ends tightly to seal. Gently pull and taper the ends of the rolled dough. Place the loaf on an oiled baking sheet, cover loosely with a clean cloth, and let rise in a warm place for about 40 minutes until doubled in size.

Place a deep roasting pan filled with 1 inch of boiling water on the bottom rack of the oven. When the dough has doubled, brush the top with additional warm water. Make three ½-inch-deep slits on the top. Bake at 400° for 35 to 40 minutes or until lightly browned and the bread sounds hollow when tapped on the top. Cool on a wire rack for at least 15 minutes before serving.

MAKES 1 LOAF.

## Broiled Fish with Fennel

2 ounces frozen spinach, thawed and drained well
1 bunch watercress
1 small bunch fresh parsley
2 sprigs fresh tarragon
2 tablespoons capers
6 anchovy fillets
3 hard-boiled egg yolks
½ cup butter
1 tablespoon olive oil
Lemon juice to taste
Freshly ground black pepper to taste

6½ pounds bass (or similar fish)
1 bunch fresh fennel
Salt and freshly ground black pepper to taste
Lemon juice
2 tablespoons olive oil

In a saucepan blanch the spinach, watercress, parsley, and tarragon for 1 minute. In a food processor or blender combine the blanched vegetables and herbs, capers, anchovies, and egg yolks, and blend to a fine paste. Blend in the butter, and then the oil a few drops at a time until blended. Add the lemon juice, and season with pepper to taste. Set the butter sauce aside.

Cut deep diagonal slashes in the side of the fish, and insert a sprig of fennel in each. Place a sprig of fennel in the cavity of each fish and season with salt and pepper. Place the fish on a grill rack or on a rack in a broiler pan. Drizzle lemon juice and olive oil over each, place a sprig of fennel on each piece, and place over hot coals or under the broiler. Cook for about 7 to 10 minutes on one side. Turn carefully and sprinkle again with lemon juice and oil, topping with sprigs of fennel. Cook for another 7 to 10 minutes or until done. Pour the cooking juices over the fish to serve, and accompany with the butter sauce.

MAKES 6 SERVINGS.

## Potato, Caramelized Onion, and Goat Cheese Gratin

2 tablespoons olive oil
2 pounds medium onions (about 7), halved
    lengthwise and sliced thin crosswise
1 teaspoon minced fresh thyme leaves or ¼
    teaspoon dried, crumbled
2½ pounds large red potatoes (about 7)
½ cup chilled soft mild goat cheese, crumbled
1½ tablespoons cold unsalted butter, cut into
    pieces
1 cup milk

*I*n a heavy stockpot heat the olive oil over moderate heat until hot but not smoking, and sauté the onions with thyme and salt and pepper to taste for about 15 minutes, stirring occasionally, until tender. Reduce the heat to moderately low and cook, stirring frequently to keep from scorching, until golden brown. Remove the pot from the heat.

Meanwhile, bring a large saucepan of salted water to a boil. Peel the potatoes and cut crosswise into ¼-inch thick slices. Add the potatoes to the boiling water, return to a boil, and cook for 5 minutes. Drain the potatoes well.

Lightly oil a 2½-quart casserole dish or other shallow baking dish. Arrange half of the potatoes overlapping slightly in the prepared dish and season generously with salt and pepper. Cover the potatoes with the onions, spreading evenly, and top with the goat cheese. Arrange the remaining potatoes overlapping slightly over the cheese, and season generously with salt and pepper. Dot the gratin with butter. Pour the milk evenly over the potatoes. Bake at 425° for 35 minutes or until the potatoes are tender and the top is golden.

MAKES 6 SERVINGS.

## Provençal Tomatoes

1 tablespoon olive oil
15 small ripe tomatoes, cut in half crosswise
¼ cup finely chopped parsley
¼ cup finely chopped garlic
Salt and freshly ground black pepper to taste

*I*n a large thick-bottomed skillet heat the olive oil. Arrange the tomato halves cut-side up in the pan and cook over high heat for 20 minutes. Turn the tomato halves over and cook for 20 minutes more. Then turn the tomatoes cut-side up again and sprinkle with finely chopped parsley, garlic, salt, and pepper to taste. Cover the pan and cook for 2 minutes more. Serve immediately.

MAKES 6 SERVINGS.

# Coffee Profiteroles with Chocolate Sauce and Whipped Cream

½ cup butter
1 teaspoon sugar
½ teaspoon salt
1 cup water
1 cup all-purpose flour
4 large eggs

8 ounces semisweet chocolate morsels
¼ cup packed light brown sugar
¼ cup light cream (or half and half), heated
1 tablespoon grated orange peel
1 teaspoon Grand Marnier (optional)

Coffee ice cream

In a small saucepan combine the butter, sugar, salt, and water. Bring the liquid to a boil, and add all of the flour at once. Cook the mixture over low heat, beating briskly and constantly with a wooden spoon until smooth, cleanly leaves the sides of the pan, and forms a ball. Remove the pan from the heat, and beat in the eggs one at a time, beating until the dough is smooth and glossy.

Drop the dough from a teaspoon or tablespoon onto a parchment-lined baking sheet in mounds about 2 inches apart. Bake at 425° for 15 to 18 minutes. Reduce the heat to 375°, and bake until golden brown and light in the hand. If the profiteroles start to brown too quickly, cover with a sheet of aluminum foil. Cool on a rack.

In a food processor combine the chocolate and sugar, and with the processor running pour in the hot light cream, and process the mixture until the chocolate melts. Pour the sauce into a bowl, and set aside to cool. Stir in the Grand Marnier.

Slit the profiteroles and fill with the ice cream. Refrigerate or freeze the profiteroles until ready to serve.

Serve them covered with the chocolate sauce.

MAKES 6 SERVINGS.

# Coeur a la Crème

2 tablespoons sour cream or buttermilk
2½ cups heavy cream

1 cup cottage cheese
2 tablespoons superfine sugar
2 egg whites
1¼ cups light cream

In a saucepan stir the sour cream into the heavy cream and heat very gently until lukewarm (85°). The cream should feel slightly cool. Pour into an earthenware bowl, cover, and leave in a warm place for 5 to 24 hours to thicken, depending on the room temperature. Measure 1¼ cups of the thickened crème fraîche. Store the unused crème fraîche in the refrigerator.

Press the cottage cheese through a nylon sieve into a large bowl. In a medium bowl lightly whip 1¼ cups of crème fraîche with the sugar. Mix the crème fraîche mixture with the sieved cheese. In a separate bowl beat the egg whites until stiff. Fold the egg whites into the cheese mixture.

Line a heart-shaped mold (or colander or seive) with cheesecloth or paper towels, and add the cheese mixture. Place the mold in a larger pan and drain overnight in the refrigerator.

Unmold and serve with the light cream.

MAKES 6 SERVINGS.

# *Mardi Gras*

*Mardi Gras, or Fat Tuesday, is really a quite a festival. Parades are probably the most famous element, with all they entail—masks, royalty, and gaudy costumes. Now for your contribution: Creole-inspired foods that embody that Mardi Gras spirit.*
*Laissez-Bon Temps Rouille!*

---

MARDI GRAS SALAD

SPICY DEEP-FRIED CORNMEAL FRITTERS

SEAFOOD GUMBO

CHICKEN JAMBALAYA

KING CAKE

---

## LIGHT SHINING OUT OF DARKNESS

God moves in a mysterious way,
His wonders to perform;
He plants his footsteps in the sea,
And rides upon the storm.

Ye fearful saints fresh courage take,
The clouds ye so much dread
Are big with mercy, and shall break
In blessings on your head.

Judge not the Lord by feeble sense,
But trust him for his grace;
Behind a frowning providence,
He hides a smiling face.

Blind unbelief is sure to err,
And scan his work in vain;
God is his own interpreter,
And he will make it plain.

WILLIAM COWPER (1731–1800)

## Mardi Gras Salad

2 teaspoons chopped onion
½ cup cider vinegar
¼ cup sugar
1 teaspoon dry mustard
1 teaspoon salt
⅔ cup oil

1 head lettuce, shredded
1 10-ounce bag spinach leaves, stemmed and
    shredded
10 slices bacon, fried and crumbled
1 red onion, slivered
1½ cups mandarin orange sections
1 8-ounce package mushrooms, sliced

*I*n a blender combine the onion, cider vinegar, sugar, dry mustard, and salt. Start on low speed and slowly add the oil. Refrigerate the dressing until needed.

In a salad bowl mix and toss the remaining ingredients. Briefly blend the dressing and pour over the salad.

MAKES 8 SERVINGS.

## Spicy Deep-fried Cornmeal Fritters

1 cup grated onion
1 cup grated sharp Cheddar cheese
2 tablespoons chopped red or green bell
    pepper
1 cup cornmeal (or as needed)
1 teaspoon cayenne
1 teaspoon black pepper
¾ teaspoon salt
Vegetable shortening (or oil or lard)

*I*n a bowl toss together well the onion, Cheddar cheese, bell pepper, cornmeal, cayenne, black pepper, and salt. Stir in ¾ cup of boiling water, and combine the batter well. In a deep fryer or large deep kettle heat 2 inches of shortening over moder-

ately high heat until it registers 350° on a deep-fat thermometer. Test the batter by frying a heaping teaspoon of it in the fat for 2 to 3 minutes or until golden brown. If the fritter falls apart in the fat stir in some of the additional cornmeal. Fry heaping teaspoons of the batter in batches, making sure the fat returns to 350° before adding each new batch. Fry each batch for 2 minutes or until the fritters are golden brown. Drain on paper towels or brown paper. Serve immediately.

MAKES 8 SERVINGS.

## Seafood Gumbo

5 tablespoons bacon drippings
6 tablespoons all-purpose flour
2 onions, chopped
1½ cups chopped celery
2 cloves garlic, minced
1 28-ounce can tomatoes, chopped
1 8-ounce can tomato sauce
6 cups water
1 tablespoon salt
1 teaspoon Creole seasoning (or to taste)
10 drops hot pepper sauce
1 pound package frozen cut okra
3 pounds raw medium shrimp, peeled
1 pound crab meat
4 gumbo crabs (optional)
1 pint oysters (optional)
3 tablespoons Worcestershire sauce

*I*n a saucepan heat the bacon drippings and blend in the flour, stirring constantly for 30 minutes or until very dark. Add the onions, celery, and garlic, and sauté for 5 minutes. Add the tomatoes, tomato sauce, water, and seasonings, and simmer for 1 hour.

Add the okra and cook over low heat for 1 hour.

Add the shrimp, crab meat, crabs, and oysters, and cook for 20 minutes. Add the Worcestershire sauce and stir well. Serve over rice.

MAKES 8 SERVINGS.

# Chicken Jambalaya

½ cup butter
1 3-pound frying chicken, cooked and
    deboned, stock reserved
¾ pound country-style ham, cubed
3 cloves garlic, minced
1 large onion, chopped
2 green bell peppers, chopped
½ cup chopped celery
1 bunch scallions, sliced, including green tops
¼ cup chopped parsley
1 large tomato, peeled, seeded, and chopped
2 cups reserved chicken stock
Salt and pepper to taste
Red pepper sauce to taste
1½ cups uncooked rice

*I*n a large skillet melt the butter, and sauté the chicken, ham, garlic, onion, green pepper, and celery until the vegetables are golden. Stir in the scallions, parsley, tomato, and chicken stock. Season with salt, pepper, and red pepper sauce, and simmer for 20 minutes.

Stir in the rice and cook for about 20 minutes or until the rice is tender. Serve with more red pepper sauce.

MAKES 8 SERVINGS.

# King Cake

½ cup plus 1 tablespoon butter
⅔ cup evaporated milk
½ cup sugar
2 teaspoons salt
2 envelopes active dry yeast
⅓ cup warm water
4 eggs
6 cups all-purpose flour

½ cup firmly packed brown sugar
¾ cup sugar
1 tablespoon ground cinnamon
½ cup butter, melted and divided evenly

1 egg, beaten
⅓ cup yellow-colored sugar
⅓ cup purple-colored sugar
⅓ cup green-colored sugar

2 plastic babies (¾-inch) or 2 beans

*I*n a small sauce pan melt ½ cup of butter with the milk, ⅓ cup sugar, and salt over low heat, stirring occasionally. Then allow the mixture to cool to lukewarm. In a large mixing bowl combine 2 tablespoons of sugar, the yeast, and warm water. Let stand for about 5 to 10 minutes or until foaming. Beat the eggs into the foaming yeast, then add the cooled milk mixture. Stir in the flour, ½ cup at a time, reserving 1 cup of flour for the kneading surface. Turn the dough out onto the floured surface and knead for about 5 to 10 minutes until smooth,. Grease a large mixing bowl with 1 tablespoon of butter. Place the dough in the bowl and turn once to grease the top, cover, and let rise in a warm place for about 1 hour and 30 minutes to 2 hours until doubled. While the dough is rising, mix the filling.

In a small bowl mix the brown sugar, sugar, and cinnamon and set aside. When the dough is doubled, punch down and divide in half. On a floured surface roll one of the halves into a rectangle about 15 x 30 inches. Brush with half of the melted butter and spread the brown sugar mixture over the dough. Cut into 3 lengthwise strips. Fold each strip lengthwise toward the center to make a roll, sealing the seam. Braid the rolls and make a circle by joining the ends. Repeat with the other half of the dough. Place each cake on a baking sheet, cover with a damp cloth, and let rise again for 1 hour or until double.

Brush each cake with beaten egg and sprinkle the top with colored sugars, alternating the colors. Bake at 350° for 20 minutes. Remove the cakes and insert plastic babies from underneath the cake.

MAKES 8 TO 12 SERVINGS.

# Presidents' Day

Presidents' Day can be celebrated in a variety of ways. We can choose to emphasize the traditional observation and brush up on our biographies of Washington and Lincoln. Or we can choose a president whose administration made significant contributions in our opinion, and spend some time discussing those contributions. Another option is to focus on what sets a good leader apart from a great one. However you decide to celebrate, with this meal the vote will be unanimous for your appointment as Ambassador of the Cuisine!

---

HERB DIP WITH ASPARAGUS

CORNMEAL BISCUITS

AN HONEST MEAT LOAF

PARSLEY EGG NOODLES

ORANGE MINT PEAS

DRIED CHERRY CHOCOLATE BROWNIES

---

Lord God Almighty,

I ask not to be enrolled amongst the earthly great and rich, but to be numbered with the spiritually blessed.

Make it my present, supreme, persevering concern to obtain those blessings which are spiritual in their nature, eternal in their continuance, satisfying in their possession.

Preserve me from a false estimate of the whole or a part of my character;

May I pay regard to my principles as well as my conduct, my motives as well as my actions.

Help me never to mistake the excitement of my passions for the renewing of the Holy Spirit, never to judge my religion by occasional impressions and impulses, but by my constant and prevailing disposition.

May my heart be right with thee, and my life as becometh the gospel.

May I maintain a supreme regard to another and better world, and feel and confess myself a stranger and a pilgrim here.

Afford me all the direction, defence, support, and consolation my journey hence requires, and grant me a mind stayed on thee.

Give me a large abundance of the supply of the Spirit of Jesus, that I may be prepared for every duty, love thee in all my mercies, submit to thee in every trial, trust thee when walking in darkness, have peace in thee amidst life's changes.

Lord, I believe. Help thou my unbelief and uncertainties.

## Herb Dip with Asparagus

1 8-ounce package cream cheese, softened
⅓ cup sour cream, or more
3 green onions, chopped
2 tablespoons capers, drained
2 tablespoons finely chopped fresh parsley
1 tablespoon Dijon mustard
⅛ teaspoon dried tarragon
⅛ teaspoon dried basil
⅛ teaspoon dried marjoram
Salt and pepper to taste
1 teaspoon lemon pepper seasoning
2 pounds thin asparagus, blanched for dipping

In a food processor combine all of the ingredients except the asparagus and blend until smooth, using just enough sour cream to achieve a soft consistency. Cover and chill.

Serve with blanched asparagus for dipping.
MAKES 6 SERVINGS.

## Cornmeal Biscuits

2 cups all-purpose flour
¾ cup coarsely ground cornmeal
2 teaspoons dried parsley
1 tablespoon baking powder
1 teaspoon salt
½ teaspoon baking soda
½ cup butter or margarine
1 cup buttermilk

In a large bowl combine the flour, cornmeal, parsley, baking powder, salt, and baking soda, and stir well. Cut in the butter with a pastry blender until the mixture resembles coarse meal. Add the buttermilk, stirring until the dry ingredients are moistened. Turn the dough out onto a floured surface, and knead lightly 3 or 4 times.

Roll the dough to ½-inch thickness. Cut with a 2½-inch biscuit cutter. Place the biscuits on a lightly floured baking sheet. Bake at 450° for 10 to 12 minutes or until lightly browned.
MAKES ABOUT 2 DOZEN.

## An Honest Meat Loaf

3 pounds chopped sirloin
1 cup chopped celery
1 cup chopped onion
Salt and pepper to taste
1 egg, beaten
1 tablespoon Worcestershire sauce
1 cup breadcrumbs
½ cup sour cream
Dried basil and tarragon to taste
1 12-ounce bottle chili sauce
3 strips bacon

In a large bowl combine all of the ingredients except the chili sauce and bacon. Shape into a loaf and place in a loaf pan. Pour the chili sauce over the loaf, and top with slices of uncooked bacon. Bake at 400° for 1 hour.
MAKES 6 SERVINGS.

## Parsley Egg Noodles

1½ pounds fresh or dried wide egg noodles
4 tablespoons unsalted butter
3 to 4 tablespoons finely chopped fresh parsley
Salt and freshly ground black pepper to taste

In a large pot of salted boiling water cook the noodles until al dente. Drain well.

In the same pot melt the butter, add the noodles and toss well, coating completely. Add some parsley, season well with salt and pepper, and stir constantly until very hot. Serve garnished with the remaining parsley.
MAKES 6 SERVINGS.

# Orange Mint Peas

2 10-ounce packages frozen peas
⅓ cup fresh orange juice
2 tablespoons freshly grated orange peel
2 teaspoons lemon juice
2 teaspoons sugar
2 teaspoons dried mint (or 1 tablespoon
    crushed fresh)
2 tablespoons butter
Salt and white pepper to taste

Cook the peas according to the package directions, but do not overcook. Drain.

Add the orange juice, orange peel, lemon juice, sugar, and mint. Stir to blend. Add the butter. Season to taste with salt and pepper.

MAKES 6 SERVINGS.

# Dried Cherry Chocolate Brownies

¾ cup unsalted butter
6 1-ounce squares unsweetened chocolate,
    chopped
2½ cups sugar
4 eggs
1 egg yolk
1½ teaspoons vanilla extract
1 teaspoon almond extract
1 cup plus 2 tablespoons all-purpose flour
1 teaspoon ground cinnamon
1 cup dried cherries
1 cup semisweet chocolate chips
Confectioners' sugar

Butter a 9 x 13-inch glass baking dish. In a heavy large saucepan melt the butter and chocolate over low heat, stirring until smooth. Remove the pan from the heat, and mix in the sugar. Add the eggs one at a time, then the yolk. Add the vanilla, almond extract, flour, and cinnamon, and stir until blended. Stir in the cherries and chocolate chips. Spread the batter in the prepared baking dish. Bake at 350° for 30 to 35 minutes or until the brownies are firm around the edges and a wooden pick comes out with a few crumbs when inserted in the center. Sprinkle with confectioners' sugar while still warm.

MAKES 16 SQUARES.

# Anniversary Luncheon

*A little less attention to romantic fantasies and a little more to gratitude for everyday graces might be in order when celebrating this extraordinary day. We often take for granted the warm body sleeping beside us, the quiet, uneventful evening, or the too quickly passed cacophonous ones if we're in the season of life known as the child rearing years. Take time to celebrate the small things that make us fall in love, and stay in love, and weave us strongly together.*

STRAWBERRY-SPINACH SALAD

CHEESE-DILL SCONES

STUFFED CHICKEN BREASTS

RICE PILAF WITH PECANS

RASPBERRY TART

*Bless, O our God, the fire here laid,*
*As thou didst bless the Virgin Maid;*
*O God, the hearth and peats be blest,*
*As thou didst bless thy day of rest.*

*Bless, O our God, the household folk*
*according as Lord Jesus spoke;*
*Bless, O our God, the family,*
*As offered it should be to thee.*

*Bless, O our God, the house entire,*
*Bless, O our God, the warmth and fire,*
*Bless, O our God, the hearth alway;*
*Be thou thyself our strength and stay.*

*Bless us, O God Life-Being, well,*
*Blessing, O Christ of loving, tell*
*Blessing, O Holy Spirit spell*
*With each and every one to dwell,*
*With each and every one to dwell.*

# Strawberry-Spinach Salad

12 ounces fresh spinach
1 jicama, peeled and cut in julienne strips
1 basket strawberries, halved
3 cups bean sprouts

1 cup strawberries, halved
2 tablespoons red wine vinegar or raspberry
    vinegar
2 tablespoons sugar
¼ cup oil
Few drops sesame oil
Salt and pepper to taste

*I*n a large bowl combine the spinach, jicama, strawberries, and bean sprouts. In a food processor purée 1 cup of strawberries, the red wine vinegar, sugar, oil, sesame oil, and salt and pepper to taste. Toss the dressing with the salad ingredients just before serving.

MAKES 8 SERVINGS.

# Cheese-Dill Scones

2 large eggs
⅓ cup plus 1 tablespoon buttermilk
⅓ cup minced fresh dill
1 cup whole wheat flour
1 cup unbleached all purpose flour
1 cup yellow cornmeal
2 tablespoons sugar
2 teaspoons baking powder
¾ teaspoon salt
1 teaspoon pepper
½ cup plus 2 tablespoons chilled unsalted
    butter, cut into pieces
1¾ cups grated sharp Cheddar cheese

¾ cup unsalted butter, softened
¼ cup prepared honey mustard

*L*ightly butter a baking sheet. In a medium bowl beat the eggs, buttermilk, and minced fresh dill to blend. In a large bowl combine the flours, cornmeal, sugar, baking powder, salt, and pepper. Cut in the butter until the mixture resembles coarse meal. Add the egg mixture and grated Cheddar cheese. Stir to mix well. The dough will be stiff and crumbly. Knead gently until the dough just holds together. Turn the dough out onto a floured surface and pat to 1-inch thickness. Cut into rounds with a small biscuit cutter. Bake at 375° on the top rack of the oven for about 30 minutes. Transfer to a rack, and cool the scones slightly.

In a small bowl beat the butter with the honey mustard until blended. Serve the warm scones with the honey mustard butter.

MAKES ABOUT 2 DOZEN.

# Stuffed Chicken Breasts

½ pound fresh spinach, washed and chopped
½ to 1 cup chopped fresh basil
1 cup shredded mozzarella cheese
1 cup ricotta cheese
¾ teaspoon fresh thyme
1½ teaspoons fresh tarragon
4 whole chicken breasts, skinned, boned, and
    split
Salt and pepper to taste
3 tablespoons oil
Grape leaves

*I*n a large bowl combine the spinach, basil, mozzarella, ricotta, thyme, and tarragon.

Cut a pocket in the thick side of each chicken breast. Stuff with spinach mixture and close with a wooden pick. Sprinkle with salt and pepper. Place the stuffed chicken breasts in a baking pan. Bake at 350° for 1 hour. Serve hot or cold.

Cut the chicken breasts crosswise and arrange slices on a tray lined with grape leaves.

MAKES 8 SERVINGS.

# Rice Pilaf with Pecans

3 tablespoons olive oil
1 cup (1-inch) julienne-cut carrots
¾ cup finely chopped onion
5 cups low-salt chicken broth
1 cup orange juice
3 cups uncooked long grain rice
½ cup golden raisins
1 tablespoon sugar
¾ teaspoon salt
¼ teaspoon ground cinnamon
6 tablespoons finely chopped pecans

In a large Dutch oven heat the oil over medium-high heat and sauté the carrots and onion for 5 minutes. Add the broth and orange juice, and bring to a boil. Add the rice, raisins, sugar, salt, and cinnamon. Cover, reduce the heat, and simmer for 20 minutes or until the liquid is absorbed. Sprinkle with pecans.

MAKES 8 TO 10 SERVINGS.

# Raspberry Tart

1 cup all-purpose flour
2 tablespoons sugar
⅛ teaspoon salt
½ cup (1 stick) butter or margarine, cold
2 to 3 tablespoons cold water

¼ teaspoon ground cinnamon
⅔ cup sugar
¼ cup all-purpose flour
6 cups fresh raspberries, divided
Whipping cream

In a medium bowl combine 1 cup of flour, 2 tablespoons of sugar, and salt. Cut in the butter until crumbly. Sprinkle with the water, 1 tablespoon at a time, until the dough is just moist and holds together. Press the pastry into the bottom and 1-inch up the side of a 9-inch springform pan. Set aside.

In a small bowl combine the cinnamon, ⅔ cup of sugar, and ¼ cup of flour. Sprinkle half of the cinnamon mixture over the bottom of the pastry. Top with 4 cups of raspberries. Sprinkle the remaining cinnamon mixture over the raspberries. Bake at 400° on the lowest oven rack for 50 to 60 minutes or until golden and bubbly. Remove from the oven and cool on a wire rack.

Remove the side of the springform pan carefully after the tart has completely cooled. Top with the remaining 2 cups of raspberries. Cut into wedges. Pour 2 tablespoons of cream on each serving plate. Place a tart wedge on the cream.

MAKES 8 TO 10 SERVINGS.

# Dinner Before the Theater

*If all the world's a stage, then treat this dinner as such! Choose the cast of characters carefully to assure the proper mood is set for maximum enjoyment of the performance! The task of choosing the menu has been done for you. Now you can arrange the lighting, costume, music, and props to enhance the evening's theatrical mood.*

---

BOURSIN WITH FRENCH BREAD SLICES

TOMATO SALAD

FRESH HERB POPOVERS

THYME-MARINATED ROAST PORK

POPPY SEED ONIONS

GREEN BEANS WITH WALNUTS AND LEMON

DARK CHOCOLATE CRÈME BRÛLÉE

---

Lord get us up above the world. Come, Holy Spirit, heavenly Dove, and mount and bear us on Thy wings, far from these inferior sorrows and inferior joys, up where eternal ages roll. May we ascend in joyful contemplation, and may our spirit come back again, strong for all its service, armed for all its battles, armoured for all its dangers, and made ready to live heaven on earth, until bye-and-bye we shall live heaven in heaven. Great Father, be with Thy waiting people, and in great trouble do Thou greatly help; any that are despondant do Thou sweetly comfort and cheer; any that have erred, and are smarting under their own sin, do Thou bring them back and heal their wounds; any that this day are panting after holiness do Thou give them the desire of their hearts; any that are longing for usefulness do Thou lead them into ways of usefulness.

SELECTION FROM "THE WONDERS OF CALVARY" BY C. H. SPURGEON

## Boursin with French Bread Slices

1 clove garlic
2 8-ounce packages cream cheese, softened
1 cup butter or margarine, softened
1 teaspoon dried oregano
¼ teaspoon dried basil
¼ teaspoon dried dillweed
¼ teaspoon dried thyme
¼ teaspoon pepper

French bread slices

*I*n a food processor finely chop the garlic, stopping once to scrape down the sides of the bowl. Add the cream cheese and remaining ingredients, and process until smooth, stopping twice to scrape down the sides. Serve with slices of French bread.

Note: The Boursin mixture may be refrigerated up to 1 week or frozen up to 3 months.

MAKES ABOUT 3 CUPS.

## Tomato Salad

12 ripe tomatoes
9 tablespoons olive oil
1 tablespoon wine vinegar
1 tablespoon Dijon mustard
½ teaspoon salt
1 teaspoon pepper
4 shallots, peeled and slivered
3 tablespoons finely chopped parsley (or
   snipped chives)

*P*eel, slice, and seed the tomatoes, and arrange on a shallow dish. In a jar with a tight-fitting lid combine the oil, vinegar, mustard, salt, and pepper. Pour some of the vinaigrette over the tomatoes and store the remainder of the vinaigrette in the refrigerator. Sprinkle the shallots over tomatoes, then add the chopped herbs.

MAKES 6 SERVINGS.

## Fresh Herb Popovers

1 cup all-purpose flour
¼ teaspoon salt
2 large eggs
1 cup milk
½ teaspoon finely chopped fresh thyme
1 tablespoon unsalted butter, melted
2 tablespoons unsalted butter

*I*n a medium bowl combine the flour, salt, eggs, milk, thyme, and melted butter. Beat with a wood spoon until the mixture is the consistency of heavy cream. Divide the remaining 2 tablespoons of butter into 6 pieces and place 1 piece in each cup of a popover pan. Place the pan in a 450° oven for 1 minute until the butter is bubbly. Fill each cup half full of batter. Bake at 450° for 20 minutes. Reduce the heat to 350° and continue baking for an additional 15 to 20 minutes.

MAKES 6 POPOVERS.

# Thyme-Marinated Roast Pork

3 garlic cloves, peeled
¼ cup finely chopped fresh parsley
1 tablespoon dried thyme
1 tablespoon olive oil
Salt
1 cup dry white wine
1 5- to 7-pound boneless pork loin
Freshly ground black pepper to taste
1 small onion, finely chopped
2 garlic cloves, peeled and finely minced
1 cup homemade tomato sauce
1 tablespoon unsalted butter

In a food processor combine 3 cloves of garlic, the parsley, thyme, olive oil, 1 teaspoon of salt, and 1 tablespoon of the wine to a smooth paste.

With a sharp knife make small slits in the meat. Force generous quantities of the paste into the slits. Rub the remaining mixture all over the roast. Put the pork in a large roasting pan and pour on the remaining wine. Cover and marinate for several hours, or refrigerate overnight, turning the meat several times.

Drain off and reserve the wine. Sprinkle the top of the roast with salt and pepper and roast at 400° for 10 to 15 minutes. Reduce the oven temperature to 325° and cook for approximately 2 hours more or until a meat thermometer reads 185°, about 35 minutes per pound. Transfer the roast to a heated serving platter, remove the string, and keep the roast warm.

Pour off all but 2 tablespoons of fat from the roasting pan. Add the onion and minced garlic, and sauté gently over medium low for 2 to 3 minutes. Deglaze the pan with the reserved wine over high heat. Add the tomato sauce and cook until reduced to half. Remove the pan from the heat and swirl in the butter. Season with salt and pepper. Carve the roast into thin slices and serve with spoonfuls of the sauce.

MAKES 6 SERVINGS.

# Poppy Seed Onions

6 medium onions, thinly sliced
½ teaspoon salt
¼ teaspoon pepper
1 tablespoon poppy seed
1 3-ounce package cream cheese, softened
½ cup milk

Separate the sliced onions into rings and place in a 1-quart casserole. Sprinkle with salt, pepper, and poppy seeds. In a small bowl blend the cream cheese with the milk until smooth. Pour the mixture over the onions, and cover with foil. Bake at 350° for 1 hour.

MAKES 6 SERVINGS.

# Green Beans with Walnuts and Lemon

⅔ cup walnut halves
2 pounds green beans, cut on the diagonal into 2-inch pieces
6 tablespoons unsalted butter
2 tablespoons fresh lemon juice
2 teaspoons finely grated lemon peel
Salt and freshly ground pepper to taste

Toast the walnuts on a baking sheet at 450° for about 3 minutes until golden. Chop coarsely.

In a steamer bring 2 inches of water to a boil. Steam the beans for about 8 minutes until tender but still bright green. Drain well. Transfer the beans to a medium bowl, and add the butter, lemon juice, and lemon peel. Toss until the butter melts. Season to taste with salt and generous amounts of pepper and toss again. Transfer the beans to a serving dish, sprinkle the walnuts on top, and serve.

MAKES 6 SERVINGS.

# Dark Chocolate Crème Brûlée

2 cups whipping cream
2 cups half and half
8 ounces semisweet chocolate, finely chopped
8 large egg yolks
⅓ cup plus 8 tablespoons sugar

*I*n a large heavy saucepan bring the cream and half and half to a boil. Reduce the heat to low and add the chocolate. Whisk constantly until melted and smooth. Remove the pan from the heat. In a large bowl whisk the yolks and ⅓ cup of sugar to blend. Gradually whisk in the hot chocolate mixture. Strain.

Divide the custard among eight ¾-cup custard cups. Place the cups in a large baking pan. Add enough hot water to the pan to come halfway up the sides of the cups. Bake at 300° for about 50 minutes or until the custards are set. Remove the custards from the water and cool for 2 hours. Cover and refrigerate overnight.

Preheat the broiler. Sprinkle each custard with 1 tablespoon of sugar. Broil until the sugar turns golden, watching closely to avoid burning, about 3 minutes. Refrigerate until the custards are set, 1 to 2 hours.

MAKES 8 SERVINGS.

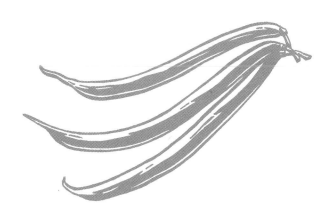

# Ash Wednesday Dinner

*The first day of Lent often brings to mind our own sacrifices. Better to remember the Sacrifice that is the focus of the Lenten season. It can be refreshing and draw us even closer to our inner circle to observe a somber time with others who wish to take time from their hectic schedules to think on serious things.*

CHEESE MUFFINS

COMPANY CHICKEN SUPREME

BROCCOLI AND CHERRY TOMATOES

STREUSEL-TOPPED PEAR PIE

*SELF-ACQUAINTANCE*

Dear Lord! Accept a sinful heart,
Which of itself complains,
And mourns, with much and frequent smart,
The evil it contains.

There fiery seeds of anger lurk,
Which often hurt my frame;
And wait but for the tempter's work
To fan them to a flame.

Legality holds out a bribe
To purchase life from Thee;
And discontent would fain prescribe
How Thou shalt deal with me.

While unbelief withstands Thy grace,
And puts the mercy by,
Presumption, with a brow of brass,
Says, "Give me, or I die!"

How eager are my thoughts to roam
In quest of what they love!
But ah! When duty calls them home,
How heavily they move!

Oh, cleanse me in a Saviour's blood,
Transform me by Thy power,
And make me Thy belov'd abode,
And let me roam no more.

# Cheese Muffins

2 cups all-purpose flour
1 tablespoon baking powder
¼ teaspoon pepper
2 tablespoons sugar
½ teaspoon garlic salt
1 cup grated Cheddar cheese
1 egg
1 cup milk
¼ cup melted butter

Grease 12 muffin cups. In a large bowl combine the dry ingredients. Add the liquid ingredients and stir until just moistened. Pour the batter into the prepared muffin cups. Bake at 400° for 20 minutes, or until lightly browned.

MAKES 12 MUFFINS.

# Company Chicken Supreme

12 chicken breast halves
2 cups sour cream
¼ cup lemon juice
3 teaspoons Worcestershire sauce
1 teaspoon celery salt
1 teaspoon paprika
2 cloves garlic, minced
½ teaspoon pepper
½ teaspoon salt
¾ cup dry breadcrumbs
¾ cup butter or margarine

In a large shallow baking dish arrange the chicken pieces in a single layer.

In a large bowl combine the sour cream, lemon juice, Worcestershire sauce, celery salt, paprika, garlic, pepper, and salt. Pour the mixture over the chicken, coating each piece well. Cover and refrigerate for several hours or overnight.

Remove the chicken from the cream mixture, coat each piece evenly with breadcrumbs. Place the chicken pieces in a large shallow pan. In a small saucepan melt the butter. Spoon half of the butter over the chicken. Bake at 350° for 45 minutes.

Drizzle the chicken with the remaining butter, and bake about 20 minutes longer or until the chicken is tender and brown.

MAKES 6 SERVINGS.

# Broccoli and Cherry Tomatoes

1 large bunch broccoli
¼ cup butter
3 tablespoons fresh lemon juice
½ teaspoon dried basil
½ pint cherry tomatoes, sliced in half
Salt and freshly ground pepper to taste

In a large pot steam the broccoli until tender-crisp. Rinse under cold water, pat dry, and cut into small florets. In a small saucepan melt the butter. Add the lemon juice and basil. Place the broccoli in a skillet over high heat and pour lemon butter over it. Cook for 1 or 2 minutes, stirring constantly. Add the cherry tomatoes, salt, and pepper, and toss briefly. Serve immediately.

MAKES 4 TO 6 SERVINGS.

# Streusel-Topped Pear Pie

4½ cups fresh pears, peeled, cored, and sliced
½ cup sugar
¼ cup all-purpose flour
2 tablespoons fresh lemon juice
¼ teaspoon salt
1 9-inch unbaked pie shell

1 cup all-purpose flour
½ teaspoon salt
½ cup unsalted butter
½ cup packed light brown sugar
1 teaspoon ground cinnamon
¼ teaspoon grated nutmeg
¼ teaspoon ground cloves
¼ cup butter
½ cup shredded Cheddar cheese

Vanilla ice cream

In a large bowl toss the pears with ½ cup of sugar, ¼ cup of flour, the lemon juice, and ¼ teaspoon of salt. Spoon the mixture into the unbaked pie shell.

In a small bowl combine 1 cup of flour, ½ teaspoon of salt, the butter, brown sugar, cinnamon, nutmeg, and cloves. Cut in the butter and cheese until crumbly. Spread the topping over the filling. Bake at 375° for 30 to 40 minutes. Cover with foil, and bake 10 to 20 minutes longer.

Serve with vanilla ice cream.

MAKES 8 TO 10 SERVINGS.

# *Purim*

How fascinating that the Book of Esther, a sublime story of faith and trust, is the only book contained in the Holy Scriptures which doesn't mention God's name! In late winter, Jewish families celebrate Purim, or the Feast of Lots, in remembrance of God's saving the Jewish people from certain destruction through the faith and wise actions of the beautiful Queen Esther. The proper way to observe Purim is to read aloud the Book of Esther with great gusto, booing the evil Haman, cheering his demise, and cooing over the good Queen Esther and her uncle Mordecai. It is a family celebration everyone can enjoy!

MUSHROOM AND BARLEY SOUP

REAL RYE BREAD

POT ROAST

CHOCOLATE-DIPPED FRUIT BALLS

HAMANTASCHEN

APPLESAUCE-GLAZED POPPY SEED CAKE

"*T*hen Esther told them to reply to Mordecai: "Go, gather all the Jews who are present in Shushan, and fast for me; neither eat nor drink for three days, night or day. My maids and I will fast likewise. And so I will go to the king, which is against the law; and if I perish, I perish!"

ESTHER 4:15–16

"So they called these days Purim, after the name Pur [Lot]. Therefore, because of all the words of this letter, what they had seen concerning this matter, and what had happened to them, the Jews established and imposed it upon themselves and their descendants and all who would join them, that without fail they should celebrate these two days every year, according to the written instructions and according to the prescribed time, that these days should be remembered and kept throughout every generation, every family, every province, and every city, that these days of Purim should not fail to be observed among the Jews, and that the memory of them should not perish among their descendants."

ESTHER 9:26–28

## Mushroom and Barley Soup

4 tablespoons butter
1 onion, chopped
1 stalk celery, diced
1 carrot, diced
8 cups beef stock
½ cup pearl barley, rinsed and picked over
Salt and freshly ground pepper to taste
1 pound button mushrooms, sliced
1 8-ounce container sour cream
Freshly chopped parsley to garnish

In a skillet melt 2 tablespoons of butter and sauté the onion, celery, and carrot until tender. Set aside. In a large heavy saucepan combine the beef stock, barley, sautéed vegetables, salt, and pepper, and bring to a boil. Reduce the heat, cover, and simmer for 1 hour or until the barley is tender. In a skillet melt the remaining 2 tablespoons of butter and sauté the mushrooms. Add the mushrooms to the soup and stir in the sour cream. Cook over low heat just until heated through. Adjust the seasoning. Spoon into soup bowls and garnish with parsley.

MAKES 6 SERVINGS.

## Real Rye Bread

2 teaspoons active dry yeast (not rapid rise)
3 tablespoons sugar
¼ cup lukewarm water (110°)
6½ cups bread flour (or as needed)
2½ cups water
2 cups rye flour
¼ cup caraway seeds
1 tablespoon salt
1 tablespoon oil
2 teaspoons cornmeal

In a small bowl combine the yeast, ½ teaspoon of sugar, and ¼ cup of lukewarm water. Set aside in a draft-free place for 10 to 20 minutes until bubbly.

In a large bowl combine the yeast mixture, 3 cups of flour, 2 tablespoons of the remaining sugar, and 2½ cups of water. Whisk until very smooth. Cover with plastic wrap, and set aside for 4 to 5 hours or refrigerate overnight.

In a medium bowl combine 2 cups of flour, the rye flour, the remaining 2½ teaspoons of sugar, caraway seeds, and salt. Stir the mixture into the sponge, add the oil, and mix just until smooth. Mix in flour until the dough is no longer sticky. Turn onto a floured board, and knead for 10 minutes, adding flour as necessary to keep the dough from sticking. The dough should be smooth and elastic. If necessary, divide the dough in half to knead until smooth, then knead the two portions together.

Shape the dough into a ball, and place in an oiled bowl. Turn to coat, cover with plastic wrap or a damp towel, and let the dough rise for 1 hour or until doubled in bulk.

Punch down the dough. Knead lightly, then set aside to rise until doubled in bulk.

Sprinkle a baking sheet with the cornmeal. Shape the dough into an 8-inch ball, and place it on the baking sheet. Cover with a large inverted bowl. Let the dough rise until doubled in bulk.

Make 2 parallel cuts across the top of the loaf, then make 2 parallel cross slashes. Transfer the dough to a heated baking sheet. Bake at 450° for 15 minutes. Reduce the oven temperature to 400° and continue to bake for 65 minutes or until the bread is golden brown and sounds hollow when tapped.

MAKES 12 SERVINGS.

## Pot Roast

½ ounce dried mushrooms, rinsed and broken
    up
¾ teaspoon mild curry powder
¾ teaspoon ground cumin
¾ teaspoon ground allspice
1 tablespoon unbleached all-purpose flour
1 2-pound center-cut slice top or bottom round
    beef, about 1½ inches thick

2 tablespoons olive oil

3 medium carrots, trimmed, peeled, and coarsely chopped

4 ribs celery, trimmed, coarse strings removed, and chopped

1 medium turnip, peeled, ends trimmed, and coarsely chopped

4 large cloves garlic, minced

2 tablespoons balsamic vinegar

Large dill sprigs

½ teaspoon dried thyme

1 bay leaf

1 28-ounce can Italian peeled tomatoes, drained, liquid reserved

1½ tablespoons dark brown sugar

⅓ cup dark seeded raisins

1½ tablespoons fresh lemon juice

¼ teaspoon each salt and black pepper

Minced fresh dill

*P*lace the mushrooms in a cup. Add enough water to barely cover, and soak for 15 minutes. In another cup combine and blend the curry powder, cumin, and allspice with the flour.

Dry the meat. Sprinkle and rub all over with the flour mixture, reserving any leftovers. In a large heavy Dutch oven heat 1 tablespoon of oil over medium high heat, and brown the meat on each side. Transfer to a plate. Add the remaining oil, and sauté the carrots, celery, and turnip until they begin to brown. Stir in the garlic, and cook for 1 minute. Blend in any remaining flour mixture. Pour the vinegar around the sides of the pot, scraping up any browned particles. Cook for 1 minute.

In a rinsed piece of cotton cheesecloth wrap the dill sprigs, thyme, and bay leaf, and tie with white cotton thread.

Purée or mash the tomatoes. Add the tomatoes to the Dutch oven with ½ cup of reserved tomato juices, the mushrooms and soaking liquid, sugar, raisins, and dill bundle. Bring to a boil. Return the browned meat to the pot, turning several times to coat. Reduce the heat, cover, and sim-

mer for about 3 hours or until tender, turning and basting every hour. Remove the bay leaf. Remove the pot from the heat and let stand, covered, for 15 minutes.

Transfer the meat to a carving board, and cover to keep warm. Return the Dutch oven to the heat. Add the lemon juice, salt, and pepper, and cook the sauce until the liquid is reduced by ⅓.

Cut the meat into ½-inch slices. Arrange on a serving platter. Drizzle with some of the sauce, and sprinkle with dill. Serve the remaining sauce separately.

MAKES 6 SERVINGS.

## *Chocolate-Dipped Fruit Balls*

2 pounds dried fruit (raisins, figs, apricots, or pitted prunes or dates)

1 cup walnuts

1 to 2 tablespoons fruit juice

Confectioners' sugar for dredging

4 ounces semisweet chocolate, chopped

*I*n a food processor finely chop the dried fruit and the walnuts. Mix in enough of the juice to hold the mixture together. Shape the mixture into 1-inch balls, roll the balls lightly in the sugar, and let them stand at room temperature, uncovered, for 24 hours. In the top of a double boiler set over barely simmering water melt the chocolate, stirring occasionally until smooth. Remove the pan from the heat. Coat half of each ball with the chocolate, letting the excess drip off and wiping the underside of the ball gently against the side of the double boiler. Chill the balls on a baking sheet lined with parchment paper until the chocolate has hardened.

Note: The fruit balls keep, chilled, in an airtight container for up to 2 weeks.

MAKES ABOUT 50 TO 60 FRUIT BALLS.

## Hamantaschen

¼ cup 1-minute quick oats
2⅓ cups unbleached flour (or as needed)
1 teaspoon baking powder
½ teaspoon baking soda
½ teaspoon salt
¼ teaspoon ground cinnamon
¼ teaspoon ground ginger
¼ teaspoon ground coriander
3 tablespoons each firmly packed light brown
    sugar
3 tablespoons honey
¼ cup sweet butter-margarine blend, melted
2 tablespoons olive oil
2 large eggs
¼ teaspoon vanilla extract
3 tablespoons ice water

½ pound dried apricots
2 8-ounce cans soft pitted prunes
2 cups unsweetened apple juice
2 tablespoons packed light brown sugar
1 teaspoon ground cinnamon
½ teaspoon ground coriander
1 teaspoon minced lemon peel
2 tablespoons flavorful honey
1 teaspoon vanilla extract
2 teaspoons confectioners' sugar

*I*n a food processor pulverize the oats. Add 2¼ cups of flour, the baking powder, baking soda, salt and spices. Combine in 2 on/off turns.

In a measuring cup combine the sugar, honey, melted butter, and olive oil, beating with a fork to blend. Beat the eggs, vanilla, and water into the mixture. With the machine running, drizzle the mixture through the feed tube, and process until the mixture forms 1 or 2 balls. If the mixture is too sticky, sprinkle with the remaining flour and process briefly. Gather up and shape into 2 balls. Place each ball on a sheet of waxed paper. Gently press each piece into a 6-inch circle. Fold up the paper around each circle, lay flat on a plate, and refrigerate for 2 hours or until firm.

To prepare the filling, place the apricots in a strainer. Rinse under cold running water, separating each piece. Transfer to a medium heavy saucepan. Add the prunes, apple juice, sugar, spices and lemon peel. Bring the mixture to a boil. Reduce the heat to simmering. Cover and cook for 20 minutes. Uncover. Raise the heat to a slow-boil and cook until the liquid is reduced by half, about 8 minutes, stirring often. Remove the pan from the heat. Cover and let stand until cooled. Purée through a food mill into a medium bowl. Stir in the honey and vanilla.

Preheat oven to 350°. On a lightly floured board roll out each circle of dough to ⅛-inch thickness. Cut into 3-inch rounds with a lattice-edged cookie cutter or wine goblet. Re-roll the scraps after briefly chilling. Place a teaspoonful of purée in the center of each circle. Fold up the edges by thirds, leaving an opening at the center and pinching the edges together where they meet. The finished shape should be triangular. Place on lightly greased cookie sheets about 1 inch apart. Bake at 350° in the center of the oven for 13 to 15 minutes until lightly browned.

Cool on a wire rack for 20 minutes. Sprinkle confectioners' sugar over the cookies. Serve slightly warm.

MAKES ABOUT 30 HAMANTASCHEN.

## Applesauce-Glazed Poppy Seed Cake

1½ cups buttermilk
½ cup poppy seeds
2 tablespoons unsweetened carob powder
2 tablespoons honey
2½ cups unbleached flour
2 teaspoons baking powder
1 teaspoon baking soda
1 teaspoon ground cinnamon
½ teaspoon ground allspice
5 tablespoons sweet butter-margarine blend
½ cup plus 2 tablespoons firmly packed dark
    brown sugar
3 tablespoons sugar
1 cup applesauce
1 teaspoon vanilla extract

3 eggs
⅛ teaspoon cream of tartar
¼ cup coarsely chopped walnuts

*L*ightly grease an 8-inch springform pan with sweet butter/margarine blend. In a small heavy saucepan combine the buttermilk, seeds, carob, and honey. Heat until warmed, stirring several times. Remove the pan from the heat and let stand.

In a medium bowl sift together the flour, baking powder, baking soda and spices. In a large bowl beat the sweet butter-margarine blend and the sugars with an electric mixer on high speed, scraping down the sides of the bowl once. On medium speed add ⅓ cup of applesauce and the vanilla to the batter. Separate the eggs, dropping 2 yolks into the batter and 3 whites into a separate bowl. Blend the yolks with the batter. On low speed, add the dry ingredients alternately with the buttermilk mixture.

Beat the egg whites with an electric mixer on medium speed until foamy. Sprinkle in the cream of tartar and beat on high speed until soft but cohesive peaks form. Fold the egg whites into the batter. Pour into the prepared pan. Bake at 350° in the center of the oven for 55 minutes. The cake may crack in several spots.

Spread the remaining applesauce over the cake. Sprinkle with nuts, pressing gently into the cake. Place under a broiler for 4 to 5 minutes to glaze. Remove the pan from the oven and cool on a rack for 10 minutes before removing the rim of the pan. Let the cake cool for 30 minutes before transferring to a serving plate. Serve warm or at room temperature.

MAKES 10 SERVINGS.

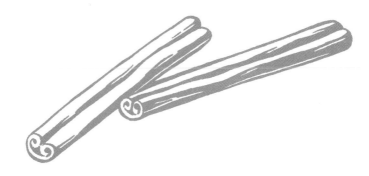

# Isabella Beeton's Birthday: A Blessing in Deed

*As a young bride in 19th century England, Isabella Beeton quickly assumed the role of partner in her husband's publishing business with her enormously succesful Mrs. Beeton's Book of Household Managment. The collectable first editions, far more interesting than their more recent counterparts, included sections not only on cookery, but also on the duties of the mistress of the household, table service, legal advice, medical information, and instructions for dealing with servants! As a matter of course for both her era and disposition, her book included recipes and instructions for the sickroom and an admonition to care for the poor.*

*Sir Arthur Conan Doyle, in his study of married life entitled, "A Duet, with an Occasional Chorus," makes his heroine say, "Mrs. Beeton must have been the finest housekeeper in the world. Therefore, Mr. Beeton must have been the happiest and most comfortable man." Her book of household management was never intended to be limited to use by any one of England's proverbial social classes. Rather, it was a celebration of the commonality and good intentions of every new bride to make her house a home.*

*As poor Mrs. Beeton died in her twenties leaving a husband and family behind, perhaps it would have pleased her to know we would choose her name for a menu planned around the needs of a sick or poor friend in need.*

---

STRAWBERRY AND TOMATO SALAD

WHOLE WHEAT-POTATO CLOVERLEAF ROLLS

ROAST PHEASANT WITH BREAD SAUCE

SPLIT PEAS WITH SAFFRON

CHOCOLATE ALMOND CAKE WITH MARMALADE CREAM

---

O God of earth and altar,
Bow down and hear our cry;
Our earthly rulers falter,
Our people drift and die;
The walls of gold entomb us,
The swords of scorn divide,
Take not thy thunder from us,
But take away our pride.

From all that terror teaches,
From lies of tongue and pen,
From all the easy speeches
That comfort cruel men,
From sale and profanation
Of honor and the sword,
From sleep and from damnation,
Deliver us, good Lord!

G. K. CHESTERTON (1874–1936)

[ 224 ]

## Strawberry and Tomato Salad

1 pound firm tomatoes, peeled
Salt and paprika to taste
1 tablespoon lemon juice
12 ounces firm strawberries, hulled and
    quartered
2 tablespoons oil
Whole strawberries and 1 cucumber, thinly
    sliced for garnish

*C*ut the tomatoes in half and remove the seeds and pulp, reserving these for another use. Cut the tomatoes into thin strips and place in a medium bowl. Sprinkle with salt and paprika to taste. Sprinkle with lemon juice. Add the strawberries. Transfer the mixture to a serving platter or salad bowl. Drizzle with oil and garnish with whole strawberries and cucumber slices.

MAKES 6 SERVINGS.

## Whole Wheat-Potato Cloverleaf Rolls

1½ cups whole wheat flour
1¼ to 1½ cups all-purpose flour
1½ teaspoons salt
1 tablespoon sugar
1 ¼-ounce package quick rising dry yeast
1 medium potato, boiled, peeled, and mashed
    with a fork
1 cup milk
¼ cup unsalted butter
1 large egg, lightly beaten
6 tablespoons unsalted butter, melted

*I*n a large bowl combine the whole wheat flour, 1 cup of flour, the salt, sugar, and yeast.

In a small saucepan heat the mashed potato with the milk and ¼ cup of butter, stirring constantly until the butter is melted. Add the potato mixture to the dry ingredients and stir until well blended. Whisk in the egg and add enough of the remaining flour to make a soft but workable dough. Turn onto a floured surface and knead for 8 to 10 minutes or until smooth and elastic.

Place the dough in a buttered bowl, cover, and let rise in a warm place for 20 to 40 minutes or until doubled in bulk.

Lightly butter 24 muffin cups. Punch the dough down. Shape the dough into 1-inch balls. Dip each ball into the melted butter and tuck three into each muffin cup. Let the rolls rise in a warm place for about 10 minutes, or until almost double in bulk.

Brush the rolls with the remaining butter. Bake at 400° for 15 to 20 minutes or until the rolls sound hollow when tapped. Carefully lift each onto a wire rack to cool slightly.

MAKES 24 ROLLS.

## Roast Pheasant with Bread Sauce

6 tablespoons butter
3 tablespoons all-purpose flour
1 brace pheasant
1 teaspoon dried sage
4 slices bacon
Bread Sauce (recipe follows)

*I*n a roasting pan melt 4 tablespoons of butter. Sprinkle 2 tablespoons of flour over the pheasants. In a large skillet gently brown them over medium heat for 2 or 3 minutes. Place half of the remaining butter and the sage inside each pheasant.

Place the pheasants breast-side up in a roasting pan and cover with the bacon slices. Roast at 400° for 35 minutes, basting occasionally. Be careful not to overcook the birds or they will become dry.

Transfer the pheasants to a warm serving dish. Let the birds rest for at least 10 minutes before serving.

Serve with Bread Sauce (recipe follows).

MAKES 4 TO 6 SERVINGS.

## Bread Sauce

1 small onion, peeled and studded with 3
    cloves
2 cups milk
2½ cups fresh white breadcrumbs
2 tablespoons butter
Pinch grated nutmeg
2 tablespoons sour cream
Salt and freshly ground pepper to taste

In the top of a double boiler over simmering water combine the onion and milk. Bring the milk to just below the boiling point. Remove the pan from the water, and set aside for 20 minutes to infuse the milk with the flavor of onions and cloves.

    Discard the onion, and add the breadcrumbs to the milk. Return the pan to the simmering water. Cook, stirring constantly, until the sauce thickens. Stir in the butter, nutmeg, and sour cream. Season with salt and pepper to taste.

    MAKES 2 CUPS.

## Split Peas with Saffron

1 pound dried split peas
½ teaspoon saffron
¼ cup butter
1 teaspoon salt
6 tablespoons sugar
1 tablespoon cider vinegar
Pepper to taste

In a large pot boil the split peas in lightly salted water for about 1 hour or until tender. About 20 minutes before the peas are done, add ¼ teaspoon of saffron.

    Drain the peas. In a large saucepan melt the butter with the remaining saffron over low heat. Add the salt, 4 tablespoons of sugar, vinegar, and pepper. Cook until the sugar has dissolved. Add

the peas and stir over low heat until well coated. Transfer to an ovenproof casserole or shallow pot and sprinkle with the remaining sugar. Place under the broiler for about 1 minute or until the surface is glazed with a crust of sugar.

    MAKES 6 SERVINGS.

## Chocolate Almond Cake with Marmalade Cream

½ cup plus 2 tablespoons ground almonds
6 ounces semisweet chocolate, broken into
    chunks
6 tablespoons unsalted butter
¼ cup sugar
3 large eggs, separated
¾ cup fine fresh breadcrumbs

¾ cup heavy cream
¾ cup marmalade

Butter an 8-inch square pan, and dust it with 2 tablespoons of the ground almonds.

    In a medium saucepan heat the chocolate and butter over low heat until melted. Remove the pan from the heat and stir in the sugar and egg yolks. Stir in ½ cup of the ground almonds and the bread crumbs.

    In a separate bowl beat the egg whites until stiff but not dry. Spoon about a quarter of the chocolate mixture into the egg whites, and fold gently together. Pour in the remaining chocolate mixture, and fold lightly but thoroughly. Pour the batter into the prepared pan. Bake at 375° in the center of the oven for 25 minutes, or until almost, but not quite, set in the middle. Cool in the pan on a wire rack.

    In a medium bowl whip the cream until stiff peaks form. Stir in the marmalade. Whip briefly to rethicken, and pipe the cream on top of the cake.

    MAKES 6 TO 8 SERVINGS.

# Saint Patrick's Day

*Are ye wearin' the green today? We've made sure ye'll be eatin' it, friend, along with your delighted guests on March seventeenth. St. Patrick brought the message of Christianity to the Green Isle. Contemporary writers argue persuasively that during and after the fall of Rome, isolated Irish monks and scribes are responsible for keeping the writings of the Christian faith as well as the Greek and Roman classics, extant for future civilizations. When you model Irish hospitality with this St. Patrick's Day party, you too, are graciously carrying on the tradition of the civilizing of your culture. Isn't that just what you had in mind, now?*

---

BOXTY BREAD

TRADITIONAL IRISH STEW

COLCANNON

POACHED SALMON WITH EMERALD SAUCE

APPLE CAKE

CREME DE MENTHE BROWNIES

---

*Christ, be with me, Christ before me, Christ behind me,*
*Christ in me, Christ beneath me, Christ above me,*
*Christ on my right, Christ on my left,*
*Christ where I live, Christ where I sit, Christ where I arise,*
*Christ in the heart of every one who thinks of me,*
*Christ in the mouth of everyone who speaks of me,*
*Christ in every eye that sees me,*
*Christ in every ear that hears me.*
*Salvation is of the Lord,*
*Salvation is of the Lord,*
*Salvation is of the Christ,*
*May your salvation, O Lord, be ever with us.*

ST. PATRICK (389–461)

# Boxty Bread

2 pounds large red-skinned potatoes
4 cups unbleached flour
Salt and pepper to taste
¼ cup unsalted butter, melted

Lightly grease a baking sheet. Wash the potatoes well and divide them into 2 portions. Boil one portion for about 25 minutes or until done. In a large bowl mash the cooked potatoes.

While half of the potatoes are boiling, peel the remaining potatoes and grate them coarsely. Place the grated potatoes in a clean tea towel and wring them over a bowl to collect the juices. Mashed the boiled potatoes. Mix the drained grated potatoes with the mashed potatoes. The potato juice should have a watery liquid on the top and white starch at the bottom. Pour off the water and add the starch to the potato mixture.

Sift the flour, salt, and pepper together over the potatoes 1 cup at a time, mixing well after each addition. Add the melted butter, then turn the dough onto a floured board and knead lightly. Shape the dough into 4 flat rounds about 1 inch thick. Place on the prepared baking sheet. Score each round into quarters, cutting only partway through so that each farl can be broken off after baking. Bake at 375° for 20 minutes. Reduce the heat to 350° and bake for an additional 45 minutes or until brown on the top and cooked inside.

Serve hot, splitting each farl off the round, and then further splitting each horizontally. Spread each half with butter.

MAKES 16 FARLS.

# Traditional Irish Stew

3 pounds boneless lamb shoulder, cut into
1-inch pieces
1 tablespoon minced fresh parsley leaves
1 teaspoon dried thyme, crumbled
Salt and freshly ground pepper to taste
6 cups chicken broth

3 pounds boiling potatoes
1 large onion, chopped fine
1 pound carrots, cut into ½-inch pieces
1 bunch celery, trimmed and ribs cut into ½-inch pieces
6 tablespoons all-purpose flour
¼ cup oil

In an 8-quart stockpot combine the lamb, parsley, thyme, salt, pepper, and 4 cups of chicken broth. Bring the mixture to a boil. Reduce the heat, cover, and simmer for 1 hour and 30 minutes.

Peel the potatoes and cut into 1-inch pieces. Add the potatoes, onion, carrots, celery, and remaining 2 cups of broth to the lamb mixture, cover, and simmer for 1 hour.

In a small bowl whisk together flour and oil until smooth, and stir into the simmering stew until well blended. Simmer the stew, uncovered, for 3 to 5 minutes until thickened. Season with salt and pepper.

MAKES 6 SERVINGS.

# Colcannon

½ cup butter
1 cup finely chopped onion (or leek)
½ cup milk
2 pounds potatoes, cooked and mashed
3 cups cooked cabbage

In a large skillet melt the butter and sauté the onion gently until softened. Add the milk and the mashed potatoes, and stir until heated through.

Mince the cabbage finely and beat into the mixture over a low heat until the mixture is pale green and fluffy.

MAKES 6 SERVINGS.

# Poached Salmon with Emerald Sauce

6 medium leeks
2 quarts water

¾ teaspoon salt
6 medium potatoes
2 cups water
½ cup cider vinegar
1 teaspoon salt
½ teaspoon ground allspice
6 salmon steaks (2 pounds)
2 tablespoons butter or margarine, melted
2 tablespoons chopped fresh parsley
Emerald Sauce (recipe follows)

Remove the roots, tough outer leaves, and tops from the leeks, leaving 2 inches of dark leaves. Wash the leeks well, and split in half lengthwise to within 1 inch of the bulb end. Rinse again.

In a large Dutch oven bring 2 quarts of water and ¾ teaspoon of salt to a boil. Add the leeks and potatoes. Reduce the heat, cover, and simmer for 10 to 15 minutes or until the leeks are tender. Remove the leeks, and keep warm. Cook the potatoes an additional 20 to 25 minutes or until tender. Drain and keep warm.

In a large skillet combine 2 cups of water, the vinegar, 1 teaspoon of salt, and allspice. Bring the mixture to a boil. Add the salmon. Reduce the heat, cover, and simmer for 8 to 10 minutes or until the fish flakes easily when tested with a fork.

Cut the potatoes into quarters; drizzle with butter, and sprinkle with parsley. Place the potatoes, leeks, and salmon on a serving platter. Pour Emerald Sauce over the salmon.

MAKES 6 SERVINGS.

## Emerald Sauce

2 tablespoons butter, melted
2 tablespoons all-purpose flour
1 cup milk
½ cup puréed fresh spinach
1 egg yolk
¼ cup half and half
½ teaspoon salt
¼ teaspoon white pepper

In a heavy saucepan melt the butter in over low heat and blend in the flour, stirring until smooth. Cook for 1 minute, stirring constantly. Gradually add the milk, and cook over medium heat until the mixture is thickened, stirring occasionally. Add the spinach, and cook for 1 minute, stirring constantly. Pour the mixture into the container of an electric blender and process until smooth. Return the mixture to the saucepan.

In a small bowl combine the egg yolk and half and half. Gradually stir about one-fourth of the hot mixture into the yolk mixture. Return the mixture to the saucepan, stirring constantly. Cook over medium heat for 1 minute, stirring constantly. Stir in the salt and pepper.

MAKES 1½ CUPS.

## Apple Cake

1 teaspoon ground cinnamon
1½ cups self-rising flour
¾ cup butter or margarine
¾ cup superfine sugar
3 eggs
2 tablespoons milk
2 to 3 tart apples, peeled, cored, and thinly sliced

In a medium bowl sift together the flour and cinnamon. In a large bowl cream the butter and sugar until light and soft. Beat in 1 egg, add 1 tablespoon of the flour, and beat in another egg. Repeat once more, then fold in ⅔ of the remaining flour. Stir in the milk, then fold in the last of the flour.

Grease an 8½ x 11-inch roasting pan. Spread half the batter in the bottom. Distribute the apple slices over the batter, and cover with the rest of the batter. Bake at 350° for 15 minutes. Reduce the heat to 325° and continue baking for 30 minutes, until golden brown and firm to the touch.

MAKES ABOUT 12 SERVINGS.

## Crème de Menthe Brownies

4 eggs
2 cups sugar
4 1-ounce squares unsweetened baking
    chocolate
1 cup margarine or butter
1 cup all-purpose flour
Dash salt
½ teaspoon peppermint extract
½ to 1 cup pecans, chopped

¼ cup margarine or butter, melted
2 tablespoons half and half
1½ teaspoons peppermint extract
2 cups confectioners' sugar
Few drops green food coloring

2 1-ounce squares unsweetened baking
    chocolate
2 tablespoons margarine or butter

In a large bowl beat the eggs and add the sugar. In a saucepan, melt 4 squares of chocolate and 1 cup of margarine. Add the chocolate mixture to the egg mixture and mix well. Add the flour, salt, ½ teaspoon of peppermint extract, and pecans. Pour into a greased 9 x 13-inch baking pan. Bake at 375° for 20 to 25 minutes. Allow to cool.

In a medium bowl combine ¼ cup of margarine, the half and half, 1½ teaspoons of peppermint extract, and confectioners' sugar, and blend well. Add the green food coloring and spread over the cooled brownies. Refrigerate for 15 to 20 minutes.

In a small saucepan melt 2 squares of chocolate and 2 tablespoons of margarine. Drizzle the chocolate over the brownies. Tilt the pan to cover. Cool in the refrigerator for at least 5 minutes, or refrigerate for 24 hours before serving.

MAKES ABOUT 12 SERVINGS.

# Index